CONCISE COURS

DAVIES ON CONTRACT

OTHER BOOKS IN THIS SERIES:

AUSTRALIA
The Law Book Company Ltd
Brisbane ■ Sydney ■ Melbourne ■ Perth

CANADA
The Carswell Company Ltd
Ottawa ■ Toronto ■ Calgary ■ Montreal ■ Vancouver

INDIA
N. M. Tripathi (Private) Ltd
Bombay
and
Eastern Law House (Private) Ltd
Calcutta
M.P.P. House
Bangalore
Universal Book Traders
Delhi
Aditya Books
Delhi

ISRAEL
Steimatzky's Agency Ltd
Tel Aviv

JAPAN
MacMillan Shuppan KK
Tokyo

PAKISTAN
Pakistan Law House
Karachi

CONCISE COURSE TEXTS

DAVIES ON CONTRACT

by

ROBERT UPEX, M.A., LL.M.

of the Middle Temple, Barrister
Professor of Law and Head of the School of Law at Kingston University,
a part-time Chairman of Industrial Tribunals
(England and Wales)

SEVENTH EDITION

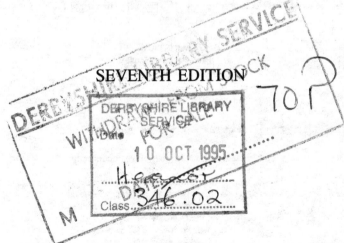
LONDON
SWEET & MAXWELL
1995

First Edition	1970
Second Impression	1972
Third Impression	1972
Second Edition	1973
Second Impression	1974
Third Impression	1975
Third Edition	1977
Second Impression	1978
Fourth Edition	1981
Second Impression	1983
Third Impression	1984
Fourth Impression	1985
Fifth Edition	1986
Sixth Edition	1991
Seventh Edition	1995

Published by
Sweet & Maxwell Limited
South Quay Plaza, 183 Marsh Wall,
London E14 9FT
Computerset by Wyvern Typesetting, Bristol
Printed in England by Clays Ltd, St Ives plc

No natural forests were destroyed to make this product; only farmed timber was used and replanted.

A CIP catalogue record
for this book is available
from the British Library

ISBN: 0421 522 801

Index prepared by *Jeanne Bradbury*

PREFACE TO THE SEVENTH EDITION

THE previous edition, the sixth, was the first I undertook after Ron Davies decided to bow out and hand over to me. That edition was published five years after its predecessor, but it did not seem to me that the seventh edition should wait so long before seeing the light of day. I am glad, therefore, of the opportunity to prepare a new edition of the book now and to follow the pattern set by earlier editions.

In writing this new edition, I have tried to follow the aims of the earlier editions of the book and to maintain the high standards set by them. I have also tried to ensure that it remains an up-to-date account of this area of the law. I have done some judicious pruning of the text where appropriate and have, for example, removed the text on restrictive trading agreements from Chapter 11, taking the view that it is not appropriate for a textbook of this sort to try to deal with such detailed and complex rules in a brief space. I have also updated some of the examples. In making these changes, however, I have tried to retain the clarity and elegance of language that characterised the editions written by Ron Davies.

In the four years that have elapsed since the sixth edition was published, there has been a steady flow of judicial authority, particularly from the Court of Appeal and the House of Lords, which has meant that most of the chapters have required attention. In the last edition, I included a commentary on the Law of Property (Miscellaneous Provisions) Act 1989, but it was too early for there to have been any judicial decisions on that Act. Sufficient time has now elapsed, however, for the courts to consider the Act and I have included a discussion of the decisions in *Record v. Bell* (1991), *Spiro v. Glencrown Properties Ltd* (1991) and *Total Clothing Ltd v. Guinea Properties Ltd* (1992). Over the years covered by the new edition, there has been a steady flow of decisions on the doctrine of undue influence, particularly in the sphere of the relationship between husband and wife. Three of the most recent decisions of the Court of Appeal—in *Massey v. Midland Bank plc, Banco Exterior Internacional v. Mann* and *TSB Bank plc v Camfield*—were all reported too late for me to include any discussion of them. The first two concern the question whether the bank was to be fixed with notice of the husband's undue influence, the third with whether a charge should be set aside in its entirety after a misrepresentation by the husband that the charge would be for a limited amount. More detailed consideration of these cases will have to await a new edition.

As with other areas of the law, the influence of European law is beginning to be felt. The Directive on Unfair Terms in Consumer Contracts was adopted by the Member States on April 5, 1993. The United Kingdom has brought in the Unfair Terms in Consumer Contracts Regulations 1994 in compliance. I have included a discussion of these provisions in Chapter 6. No doubt there will be cases to consider by the time of the next edition of this book.

I would like to express my continued gratitude to my colleague David Beety, who has again revised Chapter 15 for me.

I have endeavoured to state the law as at the beginning of April 1995.

April 1995   Robert Upex

PREFACE TO THE FIRST EDITION

THIS book tries to give a shorter and simpler account of the law of contract than is provided by the well-known textbooks.

The book has no footnotes. After each case mentioned in the text I give the date and where applicable, the initials "H.L.", "C.A." or "P.C.", standing for House of Lords, Court of Appeal or Privy Council. A reference for each case is given in the Table of Cases.

In my drive for simplicity I have tried to write a conversational style. I have even decided, after appropriately anxious consideration, to break with tradition to the extent of using the first person singular. I have ventured to say such things as "I think that *U v W* was wrongly decided", rather than "It is submitted . . .", or "In the view of the present writer . . .", or (more insidiously) "The better opinion is . . .".

I acknowledge with gratitude my debt to other books on contract, and to three in particular. When I was a student I fed (so to speak) on *Cheshire and Fifoot*, and when, after nearly 20 years' practising the law, I returned to academic life as a teacher, I was able to feast on that book—and on *Treitel* and on *Smith and Thomas's Casebook* as well.

I am extremely grateful to my friend and colleague, Dr Michael Goodman, who read the whole of the typescript of this book and made many valuable suggestions.

There is a widely held belief amongst non-lawyers that the law never changes. This is not correct, the law is constantly changing, and the pace of change is likely to quicken in the near future. I think that the two most important things that have happened in the law during my time are the founding of the Law Commission in 1965 and the statement by the Lord Chancellor in 1966 that the Lords of Appeal would henceforth feel free to depart from a previous decision of the House of Lords "when it appears right to do so". Between them, these two events have the potentiality to revolutionise the law—not least the law of contract.

In the meantime, I have tried to state the law as it stands today.

January 1, 1970   F.R.D.

CONTENTS

TABLE OF CASES

xi

TABLE OF CASES

TABLE OF CASES

TABLE OF CASES

TABLE OF CASES

TABLE OF STATUTES

xxii

INTRODUCTION

A CONTRACT is an agreement which binds the parties to it. Some agreements are not contracts; for example, an agreement to meet under the clock at Selfridges: what distinguishes contractual agreements from other agreements is the feature of binding legal obligation. Some legal obligations (for example, in the law of torts) arise without agreement: what distinguishes contractual obligations from other obligations is the feature of agreement.

Although agreement is a basic element of every contract, it should be noted that the agreement is not always of such a kind that it would be so called in popular speech.

First, the courts take an objective, rather than a subjective, view of agreement, and if a person has so conducted himself as to give the appearance that he has agreed, then he may be held to have agreed, even though, in his own mind, he has not.

Secondly, where one of the parties holds a monopoly position the other party has no real choice, and can hardly be said, in a popular sense, to agree. For example, if a householder wants to have electricity in his home he has to take it from an electricity company, and his "agreement" to their terms of supply is more notional than real. The same absence of real choice arises where, although there is no monopoly position, one of the parties belongs to a group who have agreed together to put forward identical terms. Many trade associations have drawn up "standard form contracts" upon which alone their members are willing to contract. The impact of these standard form contracts (sometimes called contracts of adhesion) is particularly felt where they contain exemption clauses (see Chap. 6).

Thirdly, the law sometimes imposes terms upon one or both of the parties. The courts have developed a doctrine of implied terms, holding that a term sometimes exists in a contract even though it has not been expressly stated by the parties. In theory an unexpressed term is only applied by the court where it arises from the presumed intention of the parties. If that is so, then the doctrine of the implied term does not at all conflict with the idea that contract is based on agreement. But there are cases in which the courts seem to be imposing terms rather than merely deriving them from the intention of the parties. And in some

1

areas of the law implied terms which have become well settled by judicial decisions are later set out in an Act of Parliament. An example of this process is to be found in the implied terms incorporated into a contract for the sale of goods by the Sale of Goods Act 1893. But that statute expressly reserved to the contracting parties the right to exclude those statutory terms if they so wished, so the principle of agreement was not really infringed. But by subsequent Acts, including the Sale of Goods Act 1979 (which repealed the Sale of Goods Act 1893), that position has been altered. Some implied terms cannot ever be excluded by the parties, and others cannot be excluded in a "consumer sale", and only in certain circumstances in a non-consumer sale. At this point one can truly say that the agreement of the parties is being limited by law. Moreover, there are many fields of activity in which, without there being any preceding history of judicially implied terms, statute law restricts the freedom of persons to agree their own contractual terms. The letting of residential property is such a field.

Subject to these qualifications, it is still broadly true to say that agreement is a necessary feature of a contract.

The other necessary feature of a contract is binding obligation. To restate the opening proposition, a contract is an agreement which binds the parties to it. This is sometimes put in slightly different words, namely, that "a contract is an agreement which is enforceable at law". That is a true statement, provided that the word "enforceable" is correctly understood. It might be thought that if a party can get his contract "enforced" that means that he can necessarily get from the court an order compelling the other party to perform his part of the contract. This is not so. Whilst the court will sometimes make such an order, called an order of specific performance, it will not always do so. Indeed, by far the most usual remedy for breach of contract is an order for damages. That means that the party in fault is not ordered to perform the contract, but is ordered to make a money payment to the plaintiff for not having performed it. In lawyers' language an order for damages is as much "enforcement" as is an order of specific performance.

A more fundamental point about lawyers' language is that the word "law" itself has several meanings. It can mean *a* law, or it can mean common law as distinct from equity, or it can mean the whole body of legal rules, including both common law and equity.

There are some topics in this book which can only be fully understood by reference to history, and the history reveals the different contributions which have been made by common law and equity. But it is important to understand that by a process beginning with the Supreme Court of Judicature Act 1873 the systems of common law and equity have been fused. Professor Ashburner, writing in 1902 and referring to the Judicature Act, said: "... the two streams of jurisdiction [law and equity], though they run in the same channel, run side by side and do not mingle their waters." In *United Scientific Holdings Ltd v. Burnley Borough Council* (1978, H.L.) Lord Diplock said: "... this metaphor has in my view become both mischievous and deceptive ... As at the confluence of the Rhône and Saône, it may be possible for a short distance to discern the source from which each part of the combined stream came, but there comes a point at which this ceases to be possible. If Professor Ashburner's fluvial metaphor is to be retained at all, the waters of the confluent streams of law and equity have surely mingled now."

In any discussion of the nature of a contract it is necessary to emphasise the feature of obligation. An agreement which does not bind the parties—an agreement, that is to say, which is not a legal obligation—is not a contract. A study of the law of contract is largely a study of actual cases which have been decided in the courts. The law is the cases, the cases are the law. But the student of contract law, though he must largely occupy himself with a study of litigation, should occasionally step back, as it were, and see the litigation in its true perspective. Contracts which give rise to litigation are a minute proportion of the vast numbers of contracts which are made every day. The overwhelming majority of contracts never give rise to any dispute whatever; where a dispute does arise, it is generally settled without recourse to the courts, or, indeed, without recourse to lawyers at all. The true importance of the law of contract is that its very existence *in the background*, with its principles and detailed rules, ensures that the activity of contracting runs smoothly on.

We all engage in the activity of contracting; in that sense we are all contractors. It would be a great mistake to think that it is only other people who make contracts. It would be a great mistake to think that a contract is necessarily an important and complicated transaction, such as an undertaking to build a power station. We all make contracts in the course of our everyday lives. Buying a packet of tea or a pint of bitter, renting a flat, buying a house, getting a job, even taking a bus—all these activities involve a contract. In all these activities, two (or more) persons agree and bind themselves.

3

So we come back to the opening proposition that a contract is an agreement which binds the parties to it.

This book examines the contractual bond.

PART ONE

TYING THE BOND

CHAPTER ONE

OFFER AND ACCEPTANCE

A contract is based on agreement, which arises from offer and acceptance. One person makes an offer; another person accepts that offer. When that has happened, and provided that the other necessary factors, consideration and intention to contract, are present, there is a contract. Consideration will be dealt with in Chapter 2; intention to contract in Chapter 3.

OFFER

An offer is a proposition put by one person (or persons) to another person (or persons) coupled with an indication that he is willing to be held to that proposition. The offeror (that is, the person who makes the offer) may make the offer to a particular person, or to a group of persons or to "the whole world". The offer may be in writing, or spoken, or by conduct. Thus the offer may take any form between an elaborate document with numerous clauses and sub-clauses and an ordinary everyday act of conduct, such as a bus driver pulling up at a bus stop. The indication that the offeror is willing to be bound need not be stated in words (written or spoken); it may be, and frequently is, inferred from the nature of the offeror's proposition or from the circumstances in which the proposition is made.

True Offer Distinguished from Invitation to Treat

It is necessary to distinguish a true offer from an "offer to chaffer" (as some of the old cases call it) or from an "invitation to treat" (to use a more modern phrase). The importance of the distinction is that, if a true offer is made and accepted, the offeror is bound; on the other hand, if what the offeror said or did is not a true offer, the other person cannot create a contract by saying "I accept"; in other words, he cannot bind the offeror by saying "I accept". The distinction is important, but it is not always easy to make it. For an example of this, see *Gibson v. Manchester City Council* (1979, H.L.), a case involving council house sales.

Tenders

In connection with tenders the distinction between an offer and an invitation to treat is reasonably clear. If A asks a number of suppliers to put in tenders for supplying particular goods or services, he is not making an offer. This means that he is not bound to accept the lowest, or any other, tender. The position is similar where A asks one supplier to put in an estimate for supplying particular goods or services. It is not A who makes the offer; the offer comes from the supplier in the form of the tender or estimate: see *Spencer v. Harding* (1870).

On the other hand, there may be cases where the person inviting tenders may bind himself to accept the highest bid. This is what happened in *Harvela Investments Ltd v. Royal Trust Co. of Canada (CI) Ltd* (1985, H.L.). The Royal Trust Co. invited two parties to make sealed competitive bids for a block of shares; the parties were the plaintiffs and the second defendant, Sir Leonard Outerbridge. In their invitation, the Royal Trust Co. made the statement, "we bind ourselves to accept the highest offer". The plaintiffs made a bid of $2,175,000; the second defendant made a bid of "$2,100,000 . . . or $101,000 in excess of any other offer . . . expressed as a fixed monetary amount, whichever is higher". This second bid was what is known as a "referential bid". The House of Lords held that this kind of bid was invalid. They said that the purpose of a sale by fixed bidding was to provoke the best price which the prospective purchasers were prepared to pay regardless of what rival bidders were prepared to pay. It was inconsistent with this purpose to allow a referential bid, whose meaning could only be ascertained by looking at another bid. See also *Blackpool and Fylde Aero Club Ltd v. Blackpool Borough Council* (1990, C.A.).

Display of goods for sale

The rule that asking for tenders is not the making of an offer accords with common sense. But common sense is not so clearly satisfied with the parallel rule that the displaying of goods for sale is not the making of an offer. Of course, it is convenient to have a definite rule one way or the other, but the actual content of the rule seems somewhat arbitrary. The rule is, however, now firmly established. In *Pharmaceutical Society of Great Britain v. Boots Cash Chemists (Southern) Ltd* (1953, C.A.), the Society brought an action against Boots alleging that Boots were breaking the law laid down in the Pharmacy and Poisons Act 1933 which requires the sale of any article containing any substance included in Part I of the Poisons List to be made under the supervision of a registered pharmacist. Boots had a self-service shop in Edgware. A customer went in and selected articles from the shelves, put them in a wire basket, went up to the cash-desk and paid for them. There was a registered pharmacist standing by the cash-desk but not by the shelves. If the sale took place when the customer picked up the article, then (subject to another point in the case) Boots were in breach of the law; if the sale took place at the cash-desk, then they were not. The Court of Appeal held that the sale took place at the cash-desk. The display of articles on the shelves was not an offer, only an invitation to treat. The offer was made by the customer taking the article to the cash-desk. That offer could be, but need not be, accepted by Boots at the cash-desk. If it were so accepted the contract of sale would arise at that point, and so would be under the supervision of the registered pharmacist. The courts have taken the same view of goods displayed in a shop window. Indeed in *Fisher v. Bell* (1961) Lord Parker considered the point to be beyond argument. He said: "It is perfectly clear that according to the ordinary law of contract the display of an article with a price on it in a shop window is merely an invitation to treat. It is in no sense an offer for sale, the acceptance of which constitutes a contract." (The law is the same if the article is displayed without a price on it.)

Advertisements

The same rule applies to an advertisement by, for example, a trader stating that he is willing to sell some goods. The advertisement is not an offer, merely an invitation to treat. This point is well illustrated by *Partridge v. Crittenden* (1968). Mr Partridge was charged with unlawfully *offering for sale* a wild live bird (a brambling), contrary to section 6(1) of the Protection of Birds Act 1954. He had put in a periodical called *Cage and Aviary Birds* an advertisement which read "Bramblefinch cocks, bramblefinch hens, 25s. each". A Mr Thompson, having seen the advertisement, wrote up for a hen and enclosed the money. Mr Partridge sent him a hen. On those facts he was charged. It was held by the Divisional Court that the advertisement was an invitation to treat, not an offer for sale, and that therefore the offence charged was not established. (He could

9

have been charged, under the same section, with selling, rather than offering for sale; in that case, he would presumably have been convicted.) There are situations, however, where an advertisement will be held to be an offer, not a mere invitation to treat. This is so, for example, where an advertisement offers a reward for the return of lost property. If the finder returns the property, knowing of the reward offer, he is entitled to the reward. It is not open to the owner to say: "I was not making an offer, I was only inviting offers." Such a situation is sometimes described as a unilateral contract. This type of contract is a one-sided contract, in the sense that one party binds himself by a conditional promise leaving the other party free to perform the condition or not, as he pleases. It is a rare form of contract; most contracts are bilateral or multilateral. Both these may be called synallagmatic contracts. In a unilateral contract the offeror will not know whether the contract is valid and effective until the other party has performed his part. Such a unilateral contract arose in *Carlill v. Carbolic Smoke Ball Co.* (1893, C.A.). The defendants were the makers of a medicinal item called "The Carbolic Smoke Ball". They issued an advertisement in which they promised to pay £100 to anyone who caught influenza after having sniffed at the smoke ball for a specified period in a prescribed manner. They stated that they had deposited £1,000 with their bankers "to show their sincerity". Mrs Carlill saw the advertisement, bought a smoke ball, sniffed at it in the prescribed manner and then caught 'flu. She sued for the £100 and succeeded. The defence argued that the advertisement was not a true offer, but the Court of Appeal held that it was.

Doubts have sometimes been expressed as to whether unilateral contracts really constitute a separate category of contracts, but the Court of Appeal has held that there is such a category. See *United Dominions Trust (Commercial) Ltd v. Eagle Aircraft Services Ltd* (1968, C.A.).

Auction sales

The analysis of auction sales in terms of offer and acceptance is not entirely easy. The bidder is the offeror; his bid (which may be by words or by conduct, such as waving a catalogue) is the offer. The auctioneer accepts the offer by striking the table with the hammer. It follows that the auctioneer can withdraw an item at any time provided he has not accepted a bid. Previous bids, it seems, lapse as offers as soon as a higher bid is made. In *Harris v. Nickerson* (1873) it was decided that the advertising of an auction sale to be held at a particular time and place is not an offer. But it seems that an advertisement that a sale will be held "without reserve" is a definite offer, *if the sale once starts*, that the auctioneer will accept the highest bid. According to *Warlow v. Harrison* (1859) the auctioneer in such circumstances makes a contract with each bidder that he will sell to the highest bidder.

Negotiations for sale of land

In sales of land there are so many points to be settled between the parties that the courts are inclined to treat as a mere step in the negotiations a communication which in other circumstances might be held to be a definite offer. A good example of this is to be found in *Harvey v. Facey* (1893, P.C.). The plaintiffs telegraphed to the defendants: "Will you sell us Bumper Hall Pen? Telegraph lowest cash price." The defendants replied by telegraph: "Lowest price for Bumper Hall Pen £900." The plaintiffs telegraphed: "We agree to buy Bumper Hall Pen for £900 asked by you. Please send us your title deed . . . ." It was held by the Privy Council that there was no contract. The second telegram was not an offer but merely an indication of the price the defendants would want if they eventually decided to sell. Another example is to be found in *Clifton v. Palumbo* (1944, C.A.). The plaintiff estate owner wrote to the defendant: "I . . . am prepared to offer you or your nominee my Lytham estate for £600,000 . . . I also agree that a reasonable and sufficient time shall be granted to you for the examination and consideration of all the data and details necessary for the preparation of the Schedule of Completion." It was held by the Court of Appeal that this letter was not a definite offer. Consequently, the defendant's "acceptance" was ineffective and there was no contract.

ACCEPTANCE

Acceptance is best discussed under two heads: first, the fact of acceptance; secondly, the communication of acceptance.

The Fact of Acceptance

Two questions have to be dealt with here: (1) how does one recognise that acceptance has occurred as a fact? and (2) what amounts to acceptance?

Negotiations

When parties carry on complicated negotiations it is sometimes difficult to say when (if at all) an offer has been accepted. As in the case of *Clifton v. Palumbo*, it is sometimes hard to determine whether or not an offer has been made. It is harder still sometimes to say whether an acceptance has been made. This is because it is necessary to find two things instead of only one; an acceptance as well as an offer. What is more, it is necessary to find an acceptance that exactly fits the offer: see below. As negotiations go on, each party may advance a new point or withdraw a former point, and in the end they may disagree as to whether they have ever agreed. The court must then look at the whole course of the negotiations and decide whether the parties ever did agree to the same terms.

An example of this type of problem is to be found in *Walford v. Miles* (1992, H.L.). The defendants owned a photographic business, which they were interested in selling. After negotiations with the plaintiffs, they agreed in principle to sell the business to them "subject to contract". Soon after, it was further agreed that if the plaintiffs provided a comfort letter from their bank, the defendants would terminate negotiations with any third party and would not deal further with any third party. The comfort letter was duly provided, but the defendants sold the business to a third party. The plaintiffs claimed that there was a binding "lock-out" agreement, under which they had been given an exclusive opportunity to try to come to terms with the defendants and which was collateral to the negotiations for the sale of the business. The House of Lords said that a lock-out agreement may be an enforceable agreement, but went on to say that an agreement to negotiate in good faith for an unspecified period is not enforceable. They therefore held that the agreement in question was unenforceable. On the other hand, in *Pitt v. PHH Management Ltd* (1993, C.A.), the Court of Appeal found that there was a lock-out agreement, in the context of negotiations for the sale of land, and that the defendants were in breach of it. This case is considered more fully below: see p. 25 ("Subject to Contract").

Acceptance by conduct

Just as an offer may be made by conduct so may an acceptance. This is clearly so in the case of a unilateral contract. Thus if A offers a reward for the return of his lost dog, Fido, then B, by taking Fido to A, both accepts the offer of the reward and performs the act necessary to gain it. It is more important to note that a bilateral contract can be made by means of an acceptance by conduct. In *Brogden v. Metropolitan Railway Co.* (1877, H.L.)

Brogden had for years supplied the railway company with coal without a formal agreement. The company wished to regularise the situation, and so they sent a draft form of agreement to Brogden. He inserted a new term into the draft and returned it, marked "approved". The company's agent put it in his desk and it lay there for two years. For two years Brogden sent, and the company paid for, deliveries of coal in accordance with the terms of the draft. Then a dispute arose, and Brogden denied that any binding contract existed. The House of Lords held that a contract had been created by conduct, and that it came into existence either when the company ordered its first load of coal upon the terms of the draft or at least when Brogden supplied it.

Acceptance must exactly fit the offer

A reply to an offer is only effective as an acceptance if it accepts all the terms of the offer without qualification or addition. Thus in *Brogden*'s case Brogden's returning the draft, marked "approved", did not amount to an acceptance because he had introduced a new term. In *Jones v. Daniel* (1894) Daniel made a written offer to purchase Jones's property for £1,450. In reply Jones's solicitors wrote "accepting" the offer, and adding: "We enclose contract for your signature." The enclosed draft contract contained special terms not referred to in the offer, including the payment of a deposit of 10 per cent by the purchaser, a stipulation fixing the date for completion, and a provision limiting the title to be shown by the vendor. Daniel returned the document unsigned. It was held that the letters did not constitute a contract; the solicitors' letter with its enclosure was not an acceptance but a counter-offer. Daniel was free to accept or reject this counter-offer; he chose to reject it, and so no contract came into existence. For a more recent example, see *Rimeco Riggelsen & Metal Co. v. Queensborough Rolling Mill Co.* (1994) which involved the question whether an arbitration clause was included in an agreement.

A "battle of forms"

In some cases there occurs what has come to be called a "battle of forms". A makes an offer on his own printed form containing certain terms, and B accepts on *his* printed form which contains conflicting terms. A contract may well come into existence by conduct, but on which terms? Often the answer is that the party who fires the last shot wins, but this is too simple a proposition to meet all the varied facts of commercial life. The whole matter is discussed in *Butler Machine Tool Co. Ltd v. Ex-Cell-O Corporation (England) Ltd* (1979, C.A.).

13

The Communication of Acceptance

The offeree may have decided, in his own mind, that he accepts the offer, but that decision in itself does not amount in law to acceptance. It is necessary that he should communicate his acceptance to the offeror. Thus, in *Brogden's* case, the fact that the agent of the railway company put the amended draft contract in his drawer did not amount to acceptance, even though in his own mind he did accept the amendments. It would still not have amounted to acceptance if the agent had written on the draft, before putting it in his drawer, "Amendments accepted".

However, the terms of an offer may be such that the requirement of communication of acceptance is waived by the offeror. This is commonly the case in unilateral contracts. In *Carlill v. Carbolic Smoke Ball Co.* the court rejected the argument that Mrs Carlill should have notified the defendants of her intention to put their medicament to the test. Bowen L.J. said: "If I advertise to the world that my dog is lost and that anybody who brings the dog to a particular place will be paid some money, are all the police or other persons whose business it is to find lost dogs to be expected to sit down and write me a note saying that they have accepted my proposal?" In such a case acceptance does not require communication in the ordinary sense. But, of course, there is a kind of communication; the bringing along of the lost dog is, in a sense, a communication.

In *Carlill's* case it did not matter when acceptance took place; it was sufficient for the court to decide that acceptance had at some time taken place. But in some unilateral contract situations it is of great importance to decide when acceptance takes place. A difficulty arises from the coming together in one situation of fact of two rules: (1) that an offer can be withdrawn at any time before acceptance, and (2) that acceptance need not be communicated. If A promises £10 to anyone who returns his precious Fido, can he withdraw his offer when he sees Fido being walked along on a lead by B towards A's house? To put the question in another way, at what point in time does B accept the offer of a reward? In *Daulia Ltd v. Four Millbank Nominees Ltd* (1978, C.A.), Goff L.J. answered this question in the following terms: "Whilst I think that the true view of a unilateral contract must in general be that the offeror is entitled to require full performance of the condition which he has imposed and short of that he is not bound, that must be subject to one important qualification, which stems from the fact that there must be an implied obligation on the part of the offeror not to prevent the condition becoming satisfied, which obligation . . . must arise as soon as the offeree starts to perform." An example of this is *Errington v. Errington* (1952, C.A.). A father allowed his son and daughter-in-law to live in a house which he had bought for £750, of which he borrowed £500 on mortgage from a building society. He told them that if they paid the mortgage instalments the house would be theirs when the mortgage was paid off. The couple did not bind themselves to continue paying the mortgage instalments, but they began to pay them and did not fail to pay any instalment that was due. At this point of time the father died and his personal representatives purported to withdraw his offer. It was held by the Court of Appeal that it was too late to withdraw the offer. Denning L.J. said: "The father's promise was a unilateral contract—a promise of the house in return for their act of paying the instalments. It could not be revoked by him once the couple entered on performance of the act, but it would cease to bind him if they left it incomplete and unperformed, which they have not done." In most unilateral contracts the same act is both the acceptance and the consideration. On this view, however, given proper facts, the two may be separated, in that partial performance can amount to acceptance, while complete performance remains necessary to constitute consideration. (This point will become clearer after a study of Chapter 2, on consideration.)

The offeror may waive the requirement for acceptance to be communicated, as was mentioned earlier. He may not waive the requirement of communication in the sense of stating that silence is to amount to acceptance. In *Felthouse v. Bindley* (1862) a man called Felthouse discussed with his nephew, John, the possibility of buying a horse belonging to John. A few days after the oral discussion, John wrote to his uncle that he gathered there had been a misunderstanding: the uncle apparently believed that he had bought the horse for £30; the nephew believed that he had sold it for 30 guineas. The uncle then wrote in reply to his nephew proposing to split the difference, adding: "If I hear no more about him, I consider the horse mine at £30 15s." John did not reply to that letter, the uncle did not pay any money, and the horse remained in John's possession. Eight weeks later, John held an auction sale of his farming stock. He told the auctioneer, Bindley, not to sell this particular horse, as it had already been sold. By mistake the auctioneer sold the horse. Uncle Felthouse sued Bindley in conversion; he could only succeed in conversion if the horse was his at the time. His action failed; the court held that the horse was not his at the time, there having been no effective acceptance of his offer.

15

The case shows that even where acceptance is by conduct, that conduct requires to be communicated; after all, it was clear from the nephew's conduct that he mentally accepted his uncle's offer, but that conduct was not revealed to the uncle.

An important application of the principle in *Felthouse v. Bindley* is that if a trader sends goods to a householder by post, without request, he cannot claim later that the householder has contracted to buy them because he has remained silent in the face of the implied offer to sell. This matter is now to some extent governed by statute: see the Unsolicited Goods and Services Acts 1971 and 1975.

The general rule that acceptance, to be effective, must be communicated, stems from the basic principle that contract is based on agreement. If acceptance is not communicated the circle of agreement is not, or is not seen to be, complete.

The question then arises as to what happens if a person does an act which in fact fulfils the terms of an offer, though the actor did not know that the offer had been made. On principle the answer should be that there is no contract, because there has been no agreement. The point is more likely to arise in reward cases: A offers a reward, *e.g.* for information; B gives the information not knowing that a reward has been offered. Is there a contract? In other jurisdictions the courts have answered "No". In England the point is not entirely clear. In some textbooks it is suggested that *Gibbons v. Proctor* (1891 64 L.T. 594) decided the contrary. But the report of that case (*sub nom. Gibson v. Proctor*) at 55 J.P. 616 states further facts and gives a version of the judgment which is consistent with the answer "No".

If a person does know of the offer of a reward, it does not matter that he does the act of acceptance for some motive other than gaining the reward. For example, in *Carlill v. Carbolic Smoke Ball Co.*, Mrs Carlill recovered the £100 although her motive in sniffing at the smoke ball was presumably to avoid catching 'flu rather than to get the reward by getting 'flu.

A similar point arises in connection with "cross-offers", that is, offers which cross with each other in the post. If A writes to B offering to sell his car for £1,300, and B, before he has received that letter, writes to A offering to buy the same car for £1,300, is there a contract? In form there is no acceptance; both letters are offers. Can it be said that in substance B is accepting A's offer, or A is accepting B's offer? Again, on principle the answer should be "No". But the principle is not so strong as in the case of B's doing an act which, unknown to him, has been the subject of

A's offer of a reward. In the case of cross-offers, although there is no acceptance, there is a kind of agreement; both A and B want to make an exchange of a car for £1,300. This point has never been decided in England, but it has been stated, *obiter*, in *Tinn v. Hoffman* (1873) that in such a situation there is no contract.

The general rule that acceptance, to be effective, must be communicated to the offeror is beyond doubt. It is probable that the communication must be made by the offeree himself or by his authorised agent. In *Powell v. Lee* (1908) the plaintiff applied for the headmastership of a school. The managers of the school decided, by a narrow majority, to appoint him. One of the majority, without being authorised to do so, sent a telegram to the plaintiff telling him that he had been appointed. At a later meeting the managers rescinded their former resolution and appointed someone else. The plaintiff sued for damages for breach of contract. The court rejected his claim. The case is not entirely satisfactory as an authority, because the judgment seems to run together two reasons: that acceptance must be communicated by the offeree or his authorised agent, and that the fact that the managers did not authorise anybody to notify the plaintiff showed that they were reserving their right to reconsider the matter. Nevertheless it is submitted that, on principle, the decision is correct. If communication is necessary to effect a binding acceptance, then it must follow that the acceptor is not bound until communication has taken place. It would be strange if the acceptor could be deprived of his freedom to change his mind by the act of an unauthorised person.

As a general rule, acceptance takes place when, and only when, it is actually brought to the notice of the offeror. In *Entores Ltd v. Miles Far East Corporation* (1955, C.A.) Lord Denning gave a number of graphic examples. Thus, if A shouts an offer to B across a river and A does not hear B's reply because of the noise of a passing aircraft, there is no effective acceptance; if C makes an offer to D by telephone, and D's favourable reply is lost because the line is so bad, there is no contract.

Acceptance by post

The general rule that acceptance takes effect only when it is brought to the notice of the offeror raises difficulties where the acceptance is sent by post. The acceptance may be delayed, or even permanently lost, in the post. Is it to be said that there has been no acceptance? If so, that may be very hard on the acceptor, who may have been expressly invited to make his reply by post. If, on the other hand, it is to be said that a postal

17

acceptance takes effect from the moment it is posted, that may be hard on the offeror. Hearing nothing from the offeree, the offeror may put it out of his power to perform his offer and find himself liable in damages for breach of contract. This raises an almost insoluble problem in justice, and the courts have been content to lay down a rule upon a basis of convenience.

The rule is that an acceptance by post takes effect as soon as it is posted. This special rule relating to the post was laid down in *Adams v. Lindsell* (1818). On September 2, 1817, the defendants wrote to the plaintiffs offering to sell some wool and requiring an answer "in course of post". The letter of offer had been wrongly addressed, and it did not reach the plaintiffs until the evening of September 5. That same day the plaintiffs posted a letter of acceptance, which reached the defendants on September 9. The evidence was that if the letter of offer had been correctly addressed, a reply could have been expected "in course of post" by September 7. On September 8 the defendants sold the wool to someone else. It was held that a contract came into existence on September 5, when the plaintiffs posted their letter of acceptance. It may well be that in reaching this conclusion the court was influenced in favour of the plaintiffs by the fact that it was the defendant's fault (in misdirecting their letter of offer) which led to the delayed acceptance. However that may be, the rule then laid down, that postal acceptance dates from posting, has been the rule ever since, though not without one or two attempts to overturn it by judges who felt that it was inconsistent with a true doctrine of agreement. There is no meeting of minds, no consensus, if merely posting a letter can clinch a contract. The rule is an example of the point made in the Introduction to this book, that the law takes an objective, not a subjective, view of agreement.

The rule for postal acceptance applies even where the letter of acceptance is delayed in the post, and even where it is totally lost. This was laid down in *Household Fire (etc.) Insurance Co. v. Grant* (1879, C.A.). In this kind of extreme case the rule may operate very hardly on the offeror.

One justification of the rule is that it is easier to prove posting than it is to prove receipt of a letter. A letter is posted when it is put into an official letter-box or into the hands of an employee of the Post Office who is authorised to receive letters. It is not posting to put a letter into the hands of a postman who is only authorised to deliver letters. See *Re London and Northern Bank, ex p. Jones* (1900).

A telegram is on the same footing as a letter; a telegram of acceptance takes effect when it is handed in at a post office; see, *e.g. Cowan v. O'Connor* (1888).

An acceptance by telex has been distinguished from an acceptance by telegram. In *Entores Ltd v. Miles Far East Corporation* (1955, C.A.), it was held by the Court of Appeal that an acceptance took effect where it was received, not where it was sent. The issue in that case was "where", rather than "when", but, of course, the two go together, so that the rule is established that a telex acceptance takes effect when and where received. The evidence was that dispatch and receipt were not completely instantaneous, but the court took the view that they were so nearly so that the situation should be equated with a conversation face to face or by telephone and should be distinguished from correspondence. Where receipt of a telex message is not at all instantaneous, *e.g.* because the message is sent out of office hours, the postal rule would apply: see *Brinkibon Ltd v. Stahag Stahl und Stahlwarenhandelsgesellschaft mbH* (1983, H.L.). The House of Lords said that in such cases the problem must be resolved by reference to the intention of the parties, sound business practice and (in some cases) a judgment where the risk should lie.

It must not be supposed that an offeree is always, in all circumstances, free to accept by letter and then claim that his acceptance took effect at the moment of posting. The principle is that this special rule only applies where postal acceptance is prescribed by the offeror, or is indicated by the manner or terms of the offer, or is the common-sense mode of acceptance in the circumstances. The overriding consideration is reasonableness. If the offer comes by post, it is reasonable to use the post for acceptance, unless, of course, the offer says otherwise. If the offer does not come by post it is a question of fact whether it is reasonable to accept by post. The principle is fully discussed in *Henthorn v. Fraser* (1892, C.A.).

The special rule is subject to reasonableness in another sense also: it does not apply if, having regard to all the circumstances, including the nature of the subject-matter, the negotiating parties cannot have intended that there should be a binding agreement until the acceptance was received. This point was established by *Holwell Securities Ltd v. Hughes* (1974, C.A.).

Where the rule for postal acceptance does apply it raises a problem that is not present in face-to-face encounters. If B, in the presence of A, accepts A's offer, B cannot withdraw his acceptance; the deed is done, and if B has made a bad bargain "it is his funeral". But if A and B are not in each other's presence, and B accepts A's offer by posting a letter to him, can he then withdraw his acceptance? It may well be physically possible for him to do so, but is it legally effective? B may post a letter of acceptance and then (*e.g.*) telephone a withdrawal which reaches the offeror before the letter of acceptance. There is no English decision on this point. There is a Scottish case, *Dunmore v. Alexander* (1830), which suggests that the offeree can withdraw his acceptance. There is a New Zealand case the other way: *Wenkheim v. Arndt* (1873). That case suggests that the effect of a letter of acceptance cannot be altered once it has been put into the post. For various reasons neither case is entirely satisfactory even as persuasive authority, and the English courts, if faced with the problem, would decide the matter on principle. In my view, principle requires that the offeree, having posted a letter of acceptance, should not be free to withdraw it. Acceptance takes effect from posting, thus binding the offeror; it should equally bind the offeree.

TERMINATION OF OFFER

There are five ways in which an offer may terminate without ripening into a contract.

1. Revocation

An offer can be revoked (that is, withdrawn) at any time before it is accepted. Revocation, to be effective, must be communicated to the offeree; the offeror cannot revoke his offer simply by a mental decision that he no longer wishes to proceed.

Unlike an acceptance, a revocation need not be communicated by the party himself. It is sufficient if the offeree learns from a third party that the offer has been revoked. Thus, in *Dickinson v. Dodds* (1876, C.A.), Dodds offered to sell a house to Dickinson for £800, the offer "to be left over until Friday, June 12, 9 a.m.". On Thursday, June 11, Dodds sold the house to one Allan, and that same evening Dickinson was told of the sale by a man called Berry. Before 9 a.m. on June 12, Dickinson handed to Dodds a letter of acceptance. The Court of Appeal held that there was no contract; Dodds' offer had been withdrawn before acceptance.

The revocation must be actually communicated to the offeree. This is so even though the post is used as the channel of communication. The rule that an acceptance by post takes effect from the moment of posting does not apply to a revocation of offer. This point is well illustrated by *Byrne v. Van Tienhoven* (1880). On October 1 the defendants posted a letter in Cardiff to the plaintiffs in New York, offering to sell 1,000 boxes of tinplates. On October 8 they posted a letter revoking the offer. On October 11 the plaintiffs received the offer letter and telegraphed their acceptance. On October 20 the letter of revocation reached the plaintiffs. It was held that the revocation took effect only on October 20, and that that was too late, as the plaintiffs had already accepted. This is a clear instance of how the law prefers an objective to a subjective view of agreement. Subjectively viewed, there was no agreement here; at the moment of acceptance, on October 11, the offeror was not willing to contract. But because the offeree did not know of this unwillingness he was held entitled to accept.

2. Refusal and Counter-offer

Refusal of an offer puts an end to the offer. If A offers to sell his guitar to B for £20, and B says: ''No thanks, I wouldn't take that if you paid me'', B's refusal puts an end to A's offer.

Similarly, A may offer to sell his guitar to C for £20, and C may say: ''I'll give you £15 for it.'' C's answer is a counter-offer, and that, like a refusal, puts an end to the offer. We saw earlier on that an acceptance must exactly fit the offer. It is now possible to take that point a stage further. If the response of the offeree shows an inclination to contract on terms different from those of the offer, that response is a counter-offer, and it destroys the offer. The point arose in a neat form in *Hyde v. Wrench* (1840). Wrench offered to sell his farm for £1,000. Hyde responded by saying that he would give £950 for it. Wrench wrote rejecting this proposal. Hyde then wrote to say that he would give £1,000 after all. Hyde sued Wrench, trying to enforce a sale at £1,000. He failed. It was held that no contract came into existence. Hyde's response (£950) was a counter-offer, which put an end to the offer (£1,000). The counter-offer was refused, and so did not lead to a contract. The subsequent ''acceptance'' by Hyde of the original offer was not an acceptance at all; it could not be because there was no offer in existence. It was itself another offer (by Hyde) which Wrench was quite entitled to refuse.

There are limits to this rule, however. It would be a mistake to think that every answer which does not exactly accept the offer is a counter-offer. It is quite possible for an offeree to respond to an offer by making an inquiry as to whether the offeror would be prepared to amend some term of his offer. Thus, in *Stevenson v. McLean* (1880) the defendants offered to sell some iron to the plaintiffs for cash. The plaintiffs asked whether they could have four months' credit. That inquiry was held not to be a counter-offer, but only a request for information, with the result that later acceptance of the original offer created a binding contract. Again, if the offeree makes his acceptance "subject to contract", the introduction of that phrase does not make his acceptance into a counter-offer: see further p. 25, below.

3. Lapse of Time

If an offer is stated to be open for a fixed time, then it cannot be accepted after that time. If no time is stated in the offer, then the offer lapses after a reasonable time. What is a reasonable time is a question of fact, depending on the means of the offer and the subject-matter of the offer. Thus, if an offer is sent by telegram, an acceptance by letter might well be held to be too late: see *Quenerduaine v. Cole* (1883). Similarly, an offer to sell perishable goods, or an offer to sell something (such as a block of shares) which fluctuates rapidly in market value, would lapse after quite a short time. It is not possible to lay down detailed rules; the whole circumstances of the offer must be looked at.

It is not entirely clear whether effluxion of time causes the offer to lapse in the sense that the offeror is deemed to withdraw the offer or in the sense that the offeree is deemed to refuse the offer. In *Manchester Diocesan Council of Education v. Commercial & General Investments Ltd* (1970) Buckley J. preferred the latter view.

4. Non-Occurrence of Condition

An offer which is expressly or impliedly made subject to some condition cannot be accepted if the condition fails. A very important practical

22

application of this principle is that an offer to buy goods (or to take goods on hire-purchase) is subject to an implied condition that they will continue, until acceptance, in substantially the same state as they were in at the time of offer. In *Financings Ltd v. Stimson* (1962, C.A.), where this principle was applied, Donovan L.J. said: "Who would offer to purchase a car on terms that if it were severely damaged before the offer was accepted, he, the offeror, would pay the bill? . . . The county court judge held that there must, therefore, be implied a term that until acceptance the goods would remain in substantially the same state as at the date of the offer; and I think this is both good sense and good law."

5. Death

The effect of death on an offer is a surprisingly difficult question. At first sight one would think that there is an implied term in every offer that it is conditional upon the continued existence of the offeror and the offeree. But this does not appear to be the law. It seems that, if the offeree does not know that the offeror has died, an acceptance will be valid if the nature of the contract is such that it can be performed by the offeror's personal representatives: see *Bradbury v. Morgan* (1862). There is no direct English authority on the converse situation, where the offeree dies. Probably the offer comes to an end, by operation of law, on the death of the offeree. A Canadian case, *Re Irvine* (1928), points that way.

It is important to note that the question whether death puts an end to an offer is quite separate from the question whether death puts an end (and with what effect) to a contract. The effect of death after acceptance will be dealt with in Chapters 14 and 18.

CERTAINTY

A contract may fail to come into existence, even though there is offer and acceptance, because of uncertainty as to what has been agreed. Thus in *Scammell v. Ouston* (1941, H.L.), the parties agreed that Ouston should acquire from Scammell a new motor-van "on hire-purchase terms". The House of Lords held that the agreement was too vague to be enforced, since hire-purchase terms were many and various, and it was impossible to decide on which hire-purchase terms the parties intended to contract. But in *Hillas v. Arcos* (1932, H.L.) the House of Lords upheld an agreement for the purchase of timber "of fair specification", holding that, in the light of the previous course of dealing between the parties, and in the light of "the legal implication in contracts of what is reasonable", the words used were sufficiently certain. The House of Lords emphasised in *Scammell v. Ouston* (which was later than *Hillas v. Arcos*) that the court will, if possible, implement and not defeat reasonable expectations; they will, if possible, follow the example of *Hillas v. Arcos*. This desire of the courts not to "incur the reproach of being the destroyer of bargains" (a phrase used by Lord Tomlin in *Hillas v. Arcos*) was well shown in *Nicolene Ltd v. Simmonds* (1953, C.A.). There was an agreement for the sale and purchase of a large quantity of steel bars. The terms were perfectly clear except for a statement that the transaction was to be subject to "the usual conditions of acceptance". The Court of Appeal held that, there being no "usual conditions of acceptance", the words were meaningless and must be ignored. Denning L.J. observed that if the court were to hold otherwise, "you would find defaulters all scanning their contracts to find some meaningless clause on which to ride free".

Problems of a similar sort may also arise where the contract provides for machinery to resolve disputes between the parties. In *Sudbrook Trading Estate Ltd v. Eggleton* (1983, H.L.), for example, a lease gave lessees (tenants) an option to purchase premises at a price to be agreed upon by two valuers; one valuer was to be nominated by the lessor, the other by the lessees. In default of agreement, an umpire was to be appointed by the valuers. The lessees tried to exercise the option, but the lessors refused to appoint a valuer and claimed that the option clause was void for uncertainty. The House of Lords said that the question in such a case was whether the machinery agreed upon by the parties was an essential factor in determining the price to be paid or whether it was simply a means of ensuring that a fair price was paid. Only where the machinery was essential and had not been implemented would the agreement be held to be incomplete and not binding. On the facts, the House of Lords held that the machinery was not essential and ordered an inquiry into the fair value of the premises. The lack of certainty was also probably an underlying reason for the House of Lords' refusal to uphold the "lock-out" agreement in *Walford v. Miles* (1992): see p. 12, above.

"SUBJECT TO CONTRACT"

It is common practice in negotiations for the sale and purchase of land ("land", in law, includes a building, *e.g.* a house) for the intending purchaser to make an offer which is expressed to be "subject to contract". In that event it is well settled that neither party is bound unless and until a definitive contract is made between the parties.

The phrase "subject to contract" has become a kind of magic formula, and the rule that neither party is bound is so well known that authority for it is sometimes lost sight of. If authority is wanted, it is to be found in *Chillingworth v. Esche* (1924, C.A.). The clear general rule is that the phrase is conditional, in that the condition to be fulfilled before a contract comes into existence is that there should be an exchange of contracts; before that event, either party can withdraw. The rule is not confined to agreements for the sale of land. In principle it could apply to any kind of agreement; it is only that in practice the phrase is most often used in agreements relating to land. Also, it is not always the purchaser who introduces the phrase "subject to contract". It may be introduced by the potential vendor. After all, it may be that the vendor is the offeror. But even the offeree, whether vendor or purchaser, may be the one who introduces the phrase. If the offeree does so, saying "I accept, subject to contract", that is not a true acceptance, and he is not bound. On the other hand, such a statement does not amount to a refusal or a counter-offer.

The general rule may be displaced in exceptional circumstances which persuade the court not to give the words their usual meaning; for an example, see *Alpenstow Ltd v. Regalian Properties plc* (1985). The general rule may also be displaced if the court finds that there was a collateral agreement, such as a lock-out agreement. This is what happened in *Pitt v. PHH Asset Management Ltd* (1993). The plaintiff and another would-be purchaser (B) were both trying to buy a property; both made an offer to buy for £200,000,but the plaintiff's was accepted subject to contract. B increased her offer to £210,000. When the selling agent told the plaintiff that the acceptance of his offer had been withdrawn, he threatened an injunction to prevent the sale. He and the selling agent then reached an oral agreement that the defendant would sell him the property for £200,000 and would not consider any other offers provided the plaintiff exchanged contracts within two weeks of exchange of a draft contract. The Court of Appeal held that this agreement was a lock-out agreement by which the defendant agreed not to consider any further offers for the sale of the property for a limited period. It was therefore capable of being a binding contract independently of the continuing negotiations and despite the fact that they were subject to contract.

Where some phrase other than the precise phrase "subject to contract" is used, it is often a difficult task for the courts to decide whether a provision in an agreement that some other normal document should subsequently be drawn up does or does not render the original agreement incomplete. An example of this difficulty is to be found in *Warrior Records v. Hayes* (1966, C.A.).

This matter of "subject to contract" is closely involved with the requirement of written evidence of a contract for sale of land. See p. 91, below.

THE LIMITS OF OFFER AND ACCEPTANCE

It is almost invariably possible to analyse agreement into offer and acceptance. But there are circumstances in which this analysis is impossible or highly artificial. A good example is to be found in *Clarke v. Dunraven* (1897, H.L.). The owners of two yachts entered them for the Mudhook Yacht Club Regatta. Each owner undertook, in a letter to the Club secretary, to obey all the rules of the Club. These rules included an obligation to pay "all damages" caused by fouling. While manoeuvring for the start, the Satanita fouled and sank the Valkyrie. The owner of the Valkyrie sued the owner of the Satanita for damages. By statute the liability of a colliding ship in such circumstances was limited to £8 per ton on the registered tonnage of that ship. The plaintiff argued that this general law was overridden by the defendant's contractual undertaking to pay "all damages". So the vital question was whether there was or was not a contract between the two owners. The difficulty was that their immediate relations were not with each other but with the Yacht Club. Despite this, it was held that a contract existed between them; it was created either when they entered their yachts for the race, or, at the latest, when they actually sailed. It is not always possible to point to an offer and an acceptance, but there may still be an agreement there. In the vast majority of situations, however, the bones of the agreement are plain to see—offer and acceptance.

NOTE ON MISTAKE

In this book "mistake" is dealt with in Chapter 10. It is right to point out, however, that some (but not all) kinds of mistake amount to a failure by the offeror and offeree to reach agreement. Those kinds of mistake, therefore, could have been discussed in this chapter on offer and acceptance. In my opinion, they are more conveniently dealt with at a later stage.

CHAPTER TWO

CONSIDERATION

AN agreement does not, by itself, have legal effect so as to bind the parties at law. Two further elements are required: consideration and the intention to contract. The purpose of this chapter is to explain the meaning of consideration; intention to contract will be looked at in Chapter 3.

The provisions of the Law of Property (Miscellaneous Provisions) Act 1989 have affected the legal requirements relating to seals in deeds. Before their enactment, it was sometimes said that a seal was an alternative to consideration and that a contract under seal did not need consideration. The present position is considered at the end of this chapter.

WHAT IS CONSIDERATION?

In *Currie v. Misa* (1875) consideration was defined as follows: "A valuable consideration, in the sense of the law, may consist either in some right, interest, profit, or benefit accruing to the one party, or some forbearance, detriment, loss, or responsibility given, suffered or undertaken by the other." That could be shortened into the statement that consideration is some benefit accruing to one party or some detriment suffered by the other. Often the benefit and the detriment are the same thing looked at from different points of view. In an action in contract the plaintiff will be suing in his capacity as promisee. He has been given a promise by the defendant which the defendant is not carrying out. That is why he is suing. To succeed he has to show that he gave consideration; he has to show that he gave some benefit to the defendant or that he himself suffered some detriment.

For example, suppose that a butcher, at a customer's request, delivers a piece of beef to the customer; the customer refuses to pay and the butcher is suing him for the agreed price. The butcher can show that he gave consideration; the delivery of the piece of beef was a benefit given to the customer and the giving up of the piece of beef was a detriment suffered by the butcher. This is a simple example. The situation may be more subtle than that, however, because consideration does not necessarily take the form of an act; it may take the form of a promise. The butcher may have promised to deliver a piece of beef on Saturday, and the customer promised to pay for it on delivery. The butcher does not deliver the beef. The customer can sue the butcher although he has not paid for the beef. When he sues the butcher the customer can point to his promise to pay as being the consideration for the butcher's promise to deliver the beef. The promise to pay is a detriment to the customer and a benefit to the butcher. The customer is relieved, in the events that have happened, from having to carry out his promise. It is enough that he was ready and willing to perform it at the due time.

Where, as in the last example, the consideration consists, on both sides, of a promise, each party is both promisor and promisee; he gives a promise and receives a promise. But if either party brings an action for breach of contract he will be suing as promisee.

The plaintiff, then, has to show that he gave something *in return for* the promise which was made to him, and that something, that *quid pro quo*, may be either an act or a promise.

Thus, consideration is one side of a bargain. The consideration given by the plaintiff and the consideration given by the defendant together make up a bargain. Neither party in a contract is making a free gift to the other; each is striking a bargain with the other.

The "doctrine of consideration" is that an agreement will only be enforceable as a contract if it contains consideration; that is, it will only be enforceable as a contract if it is a bargain. It need not be a good bargain; it may be a thoroughly bad bargain. This aspect of the doctrine is discussed below.

Consideration must be Sufficient but need not be Adequate

In ordinary speech the words "sufficient" and "adequate" mean much the same thing. In the law of contract "sufficient" consideration means such consideration as the law will recognise. "Adequate" consideration means a *quid pro quo* which is equal in value to that for which it is the return. In that sense consideration need not be adequate. As long as some value has been given, the courts will not ask whether adequate value has been given. If A promises to sell his car to B for £100, the £100 is a sufficient consideration. But it may not be an adequate consideration, unless the car is in a very dilapidated state. The courts will not concern themselves with that; they will not investigate the condition of the car to see whether £100 is a fair price for it.

The statement that consideration must be sufficient only means that consideration must be of such a kind as has been accepted by the courts as being valid consideration. It would take too long to examine all the kinds of consideration which have been held to be valid. The only practicable way to approach the matter is to look in turn at the kinds of consideration which have been held to be not valid or sufficient. These are: (1) consideration which does not move from the plaintiff; (2) past consideration; and (3) consideration which does not contribute to the bargain.

Consideration which does not move from the plaintiff

Consideration which does not move from the plaintiff is not sufficient consideration.

The plaintiff is normally the promisee in contract cases. He has been given a promise by the defendant, and he is now suing to enforce that promise. He will fail in his action if consideration did not move from him, *i.e.* if he did not provide consideration. There may have been a consideration but if it moved from or was provided by somebody else, it will not help the plaintiff. Thus, A may say to B: "I promise to put £10,000 into your fish-and-chip business if X does the same." X does provide £10,000, but A does not. B cannot successfully sue A. The consideration has not moved from B, but from X, and that is not sufficient. B is the promisee but he has not provided consideration.

Nor can B sue A if the promise of A has not been made to B but to X. In *Tweddle v. Atkinson* (1861) an agreement was made between William Guy and John Tweddle by which each promised the other that he would pay a sum of money to William Tweddle, who was the son of John Tweddle and the prospective son-in-law of William Guy. William Guy died without having paid, and William Tweddle sued his executors. He failed, on the ground that he was "a stranger to the consideration". In this case, of course, the plaintiff had not merely not provided consideration; he was not even the promisee (the person to whom the promise was given).

The fact that William Tweddle was not the promisee opens up another ground on which a plaintiff in his position would fail in his action. The doctrine of "privity of contract" says that a person who is not a party to

30

a contract cannot sue on it. This matter will be dealt with later, in Chapter 13. But it must be mentioned here, because the rule that consideration must move from the promisee should not be seen as being separate from the doctrine of privity. In fact, they may be treated as being two ways of looking at the same thing. This is because of the notion of contract as bargain. If a person gives no consideration for a promise he cannot sue on that promise, whether or not he is the person to whom the promise is made. If he is the promisee he is a party to the agreement, but since contract is bargain and he plays no part in the bargain, he is not a party to the contract.

While consideration must move from the promisee, it need not move to the promisor. Suppose that there is an agreement, as in *Tweddle v. Atkinson*, between X and A, that each will pay a sum of money to B, and that X pays up and A does not. X can sue A, just as John Tweddle could have sued William Guy (or his executors); it does not matter that the consideration moving from X does not move to A; it is a detriment to X, incurred at the request of A.

Past consideration

Past consideration is not sufficient consideration. If a person is suing to enforce a promise, and the only consideration which he has given is past consideration, he will fail in his action. If A promises B £5 because B cleaned A's car last Tuesday, B cannot sue on that promise because the consideration furnished by B is past consideration. When A's promise was made B's act was already in the past.

Past consideration must be distinguished from executed consideration. If A offers a reward to anyone who finds and returns his lost dog, Fido, and B finds Fido and returns him to A and claims the reward, B has already performed his consideration when he makes his claim. That is executed consideration and is perfectly valid. When B made his claim his act was in the past, but it was not in the past when A made his promise.

For the sake of completeness, a third form of consideration should be mentioned here—executory consideration. A promise is executory consideration; it is a promise that something will be executed (that is, done) in the future. Executory consideration is perfectly valid.

Past consideration can be identified by chronology. If a promise is made after the act in relation to which it is given, the act is past consideration. Thus a guarantee given after a sale is given for a past consideration and cannot be sued on. In *Roscorla v. Thomas* (1842) Thomas sold a horse

31

to Roscorla for £30. After the sale Thomas promised that it was sound and free from vice. It was not. Roscorla sued for damages for breach of warranty. He failed; the only consideration which he had given was the purchase price and clearly that was not given for the promise, since at the time of the promise that consideration was already past. Note the use of the word "promise" here. In ordinary speech "promise" always relates to the future; in the law of contract it usually does so, but sometimes it is used of a statement of present fact or even of past fact.

The question whether consideration is past or not is one of fact, and the wording of the contract is not decisive. In *Re McArdle* (1951, C.A.) a man left a house by will to his widow for life and then to his children. During the widow's life her daughter-in-law (who lived in the house) made various improvements to the house. After this work had been done all the children signed a document addressed to the daughter-in-law stating that "in consideration of your carrying out certain alterations and improvements to the property, ... we ... hereby agree that the executors ... shall repay to you from the ... estate, when ... distributed, the sum of £488 in settlement of the amount spent on such improvements". The Court of Appeal held that this was past consideration. On the other hand, in *Goldshede v. Swan* (1847) a promise was made "in consideration of your having today advanced ... £750". The plaintiff proved in evidence that the advance was made at the same time as the promise, and the court held that this was not a case of past consideration. Although the wording was in the past tense, the evidence showed that the consideration was not in fact past; in *Re McArdle*, although the wording was in the present tense, the evidence showed that in fact the consideration was past.

Goldshede v. Swan also illustrates the point that the chronological test is not to be pressed to an extreme; if the act and the promise take place at substantially the same time, the act is not past consideration.

The general rule is that a past act is past consideration. But a past act is outside this rule if two conditions are satisfied: (1) that the act was done at the request of the promisor; and (2) that the parties all along contemplated that payment would be made.

In *Lampleigh v. Brathwait* (1615) Brathwait had killed a man. He then asked Lampleigh to do all he could to get a pardon from the King. Lampleigh went to Royston and Newmarket, when the King was there, for this purpose at his own expense, and Brathwait then promised him £100. He broke his promise and Lampleigh sued him. The court gave judgment for the plaintiff: "... mere voluntary courtesy will not have a consideration to uphold an assumpsit. But if that courtesy were moved by a suit or request of the party that gives the assumpsit, it will bind, for the promise, though it follows, yet it is not naked, but couples itself with the suit before. . . .''

The judgment in *Lampleigh v. Brathwait* emphasises the point that the service was done at the request of the promisor. It does not expressly state that the parties all along contemplated that payment would be made; possibly this is implicit in the judgment. However that may be, it is clear now that such contemplation is essential if a past act is to be saved from invalidity. See, for example, *Kennedy v. Broun* (1863), *Re Casey's Patents, Stewart v. Casey* (1892, C.A.) and *Pao On v. Lau Yiu Long* (1980, P.C.).

Consideration which does not contribute to the bargain

Consideration which does not contribute to the bargain is not sufficient consideration. Of course, since consideration need not be adequate, the value of the consideration may be very small indeed. The benefit to the promisor or the detriment to the promisee may be very small indeed. The bargain made between the promisor and the promisee may be, from the promisor's point of view, a very bad bargain. But so long as there is a bargain at all, and so long as there is some contribution, however small, coming from the promisee, the promisor can be held to his promise.

It is important to distinguish a situation where a promise is made for a very small consideration from a situation where a promise of gift is made in a conditional form. Three propositions may be stated: (1) a promise by A to give his car to B is not binding, as it is the promise of a gift; (2) a promise by A to transfer his car to B for £1 is binding, as it is supported by consideration (albeit very small) moving from B; (3) a promise by A to transfer his car to B if B will collect it from A's garage is (except in exceptional circumstances) a conditional gift, which, being a gift, is not binding. Of the three situations there is only one in which there is a bargain, situation (2). It is only in situation (2) that there is a contractual bond.

There remain a number of situations where the question ''Does the consideration make any contribution?'' is difficult to answer. Those situations must now be examined in turn.

Trivial acts

A trivial act may make a contribution. In *Chappell & Co. Ltd v. Nestlé Co. Ltd* (1960, H.L.) the plaintiffs owned the copyright in a piece of music called "Rockin' Shoes". The defendants (Nestlé) arranged for another company to make records of "Rockin' Shoes". Nestlé then offered the records to the public for 1s. 6d. plus three wrappers from their sixpenny bars of chocolate. When the wrappers came in to Nestlé they were thrown away. Nestlé offered to pay Chappells a royalty at six-and-a-half per cent of 1s. 6d. per record. Chappells refused the offer. Section 8 of the Copyright Act 1956 (the relevant legislation at the time) permitted a person to make a record of a piece of music for retail sale if he gave notice to the copyright owner and paid him a royalty of six-and-a-half per cent "of the ordinary retail selling price". Chappells sued for breach of copyright. The issue was whether the ordinary retail selling price was 1s. 6d. or something more. The House of Lords (by a majority) held that it was something more, on the grounds that the three wrappers were part of the consideration. It would seem to follow that if three wrappers can be part of the consideration, they could, on appropriate facts, be the whole consideration.

Forbearance to sue

If A has a right of action against B, but promises not to sue B, that promise is valid consideration for a promise by B. Suppose B owes money to A and the money is now due. If A promises not to sue for the time being, and B promises to pay a higher rate of interest, A can enforce B's promise. A's forbearance to sue is consideration: it contributes to the bargain, the debtor gets extra time to pay and the creditor suffers the detriment of being kept out of his money. That is quite straightforward where the person who forbears has a clearly valid claim. What is the law where the claim which the promisee gives up is not a valid claim? It is a question of degree. If the claim is clearly invalid, and the promisee knows it is, giving it up is not consideration: *Wade v. Simeon* (1846). Thus a promise by a bookmaker not to sue his client for a lost bet is no consideration for some promise made in return by the client. The bookmaker would not be giving up anything of value, and so he would not be making any contribution to the bargain. This is because a bookmaker cannot sue his client for the amount of a lost bet: see Chapter 11. If the claim is not clearly valid, nor clearly invalid, but is doubtful, a promise to give it up is consideration provided that the person making that promise is behaving honestly and reasonably: *Cook v. Wright* (1861).

34

Performance of existing duty

If a person promises to do something which he is already under a duty to do, the question is whether that promise can be valid consideration for a promise made to him in return. If A promises B that he (A) will do something which he is already bound to do, can it be said that his promise makes any contribution to a bargain with B? The problem may arise in three situations: (1) A may make a promise to B that he will do something which he is already bound, by the general law, to do; (2) A may make a promise to B that he will do something which he is already bound, by a contract with B, to do; (3) A may make a promise to B that he will do something which he is already bound, by a contract with C, to do.

(1) Duty imposed by the general law. It is not clearly settled in law whether a person can or cannot rely, as consideration, on his promise to perform (or his performance of) a duty imposed by the general law. In *Collins v. Godefroy* (1831) Collins had attended on *subpoena* to give evidence for Godefroy in a case in which Godefroy was a litigant. Collins alleged that Godefroy promised to pay him six guineas for his loss of time. Collins failed in his action, on the ground that he was bound by the general law to attend the trial (because that is the effect of a *subpoena*). Consequently, in so attending he did not provide any consideration. There are other cases to the same effect, but they are based upon "public policy", and not upon lack of consideration. The point of "public policy" which arises in these cases is that it is contrary to the public interest that a person should be able to enforce payment for doing that which it is his public duty to do. ("Public policy" is dealt with in Chapter 11.)

It is settled that if a person does his public duty and exceeds it, that does amount to consideration. In *Glasbrook Bros Ltd v. Glamorgan C.C.* (1925, H.L.) a mine-owning company feared violence from strikers and asked for police protection for the mine. They asked for more protection than the police authority reasonably considered necessary, and they agreed to pay for it. The House of Lords held that the police were only under a general duty to provide reasonably necessary protection, and that as they had provided more than that, the police authority had given valid consideration and were entitled to payment for the extra protection provided.

In *Ward v. Byham* (1956, C.A.) the father of an illegitimate child promised the child's mother that he would pay her £1 a week allowance for the child "providing you can prove that she [the child] will be well looked

35

after and happy and also that she is allowed to decide for herself whether or not she wishes to come and live with you''. The Court of Appeal held that the mother could enforce the father's promise, although she was under a statutory duty to maintain the child. Morris and Parker L.JJ. based their decision on the view that the mother was undertaking to do more than her duty. Denning L.J. expressly reached his decision on the footing that the mother ''in looking after the child, is only doing what she is legally bound to do. Even so, I think that there was sufficient consideration to support the promise. I have always thought that a promise to perform an existing duty, or the performance of it, should be regarded as good consideration, because it is a benefit to the person to whom it is given''. In *Williams v. Williams* (1957, C.A.) Denning L.J. (as he then was) said: ''. . . a promise to perform an existing duty is, I think, sufficient consideration to support a promise, so long as there is nothing in the transaction which is contrary to the public interest.'' These statements by Lord Denning appear to be in conflict with *Collins v. Godefroy* (above), but it may well be that that case will now come to be regarded as right in its result (judgment for the defendant) but wrong in its reasoning (performance of existing duty not valid consideration). Its result could (at the time) have been reached on the ground of public policy.

(2) *Duty imposed by contract with promisor.* This is the situation where A is seeking to enforce a promise made to him by B, and is relying, as consideration, on his promise to do something (or his having done something) which he is already bound, by a contract with B, to do. In this situation A's promise is not valid consideration. A does not contribute anything to the new bargain with B. In *Stilk v. Myrick* (1809) the plaintiff, Stilk, was a seaman who had agreed to sail to the Baltic and back at £5 a month. There were 11 men in the crew. During the voyage two seamen deserted. The captain agreed to share the wages of the two deserters between the rest of the crew if they would work the ship back to London. When the ship reached London, Stilk asked for his share, and was refused. He sued. He failed, on the ground that he was already bound by contract to work the ship back to London. Lord Ellenborough expressly said that he was reaching his decision on the ground of lack of consideration and not on public policy.

The limits of the principle of *Stilk v. Myrick* are well shown in the later case of *Hartley v. Ponsonby* (1857). A ship left England with a crew of 36. At Port Philip many of the crew deserted, so that only 19 were left, of whom only five were able seamen. The captain promised the plaintiff (and others) an extra £40 to work the ship to Bombay. In due course the plaintiff received his regular wages, but the £40 was refused him. He sued for it, and he won. The court said that the ship was so short-handed that the voyage became a dangerous voyage. Consequently, the seamen were no longer bound to serve. Thus they were free of their original contract, and free also to make a new contract, in which their new promise to serve constituted valid consideration.

These issues have been examined more recently by the Court of Appeal in *Williams v. Roffey Bros & Nicholls (Contractors) Ltd* (1991). The plaintiff was sub-contracted to do carpentry work by the defendant building contractors on a block of flats they had contracted to refurbish. The plaintiff found himself in financial difficulties; the defendants were liable under a penalty clause in the main contract if it was not completed on time. So they agreed to pay him an extra £10,300 (£575 per flat) on completion to ensure that he continued with the work and completed on time. They paid him £1,500; he completed eight further flats. He then stopped work and brought an action against them. They denied that any part of the £10,300 could be claimed on the grounds that the agreement to pay was not supported by consideration. The Court of Appeal upheld the plaintiff's claim. They held that, where one party to a contract agrees to make a payment to the other over and above the contract price in order to secure the completion on time of the contract by that other, and by doing so obtains a benefit, such as the avoidance of a penalty payable to a third party, the obtaining of the benefit can amount to consideration for the payment of the additional sum. The agreement to pay the extra £10,300 was therefore supported by consideration. The Court of Appeal distinguished *Stilk v. Myrick*, but made it clear that they regarded the principle in that case as valid.

(3) Duty imposed by contract with third party. Where A makes a promise to B that he will do something which he is already bound, by a contract with C, to do, he can rely, as consideration, upon that promise (or upon his performance of that promise): see *Shadwell v. Shadwell* (1860), *Scotson v. Pegg* (1861) and *Chichester v. Cobb* (1866). *Scotson v. Pegg* has been expressly approved by the Privy Council in *New Zealand Shipping Co. Ltd v. A.M. Satterthwaite & Co. Ltd* (1975, P.C.); see also *Pao On v. Lau Yiu Long* (1980, P.C.) and p. 82, below.

In *Scotson v. Pegg* the plaintiffs had contracted to deliver a cargo of coal to X or "to the order of X" (*i.e.* "to anyone nominated by X"). X sold the cargo to the defendant and, exercising his right under the contract, ordered the plaintiffs to deliver it to the defendant. The defendant then promised the plaintiffs that he would unload the coal at a stated rate. The defendant did not unload the coal at the stated rate, and the plaintiffs sued him. They claimed that their delivery of the coal to the defendant was consideration for the defendant's promise. ("Delivery" in law simply means "making available.") The defendant (Pegg) argued that delivery of the coal was not consideration, because the plaintiffs were already bound by their contract with X to deliver it to him (Pegg). The court gave judgment for the plaintiffs, one judge saying that there was a benefit to the defendant, the other judge saying that there was a detriment to the plaintiffs.

Part payment of a debt

The common law position

If A pays, or promises to pay, *part* of a debt which he owes to B, and in return B promises to release A from the balance of the debt, the general rule is that B is not bound by such a promise; if B makes such a promise and then goes back on it and demands the balance of the debt, the law will see that he gets it. The reason is said to be that A has not given consideration for B's promise, and so B is not bound by his promise. A has not given consideration because he has only done, or promised to do, part of what he was already contractually bound to B to do. Logically this situation falls under the same principle as the situation considered above (*Stilk v. Myrick*, etc.), namely where A promises B that he will do something which he is already bound, by a contract with B, to do, and B in return promises extra remuneration. In that situation A will not be able to enforce B's promise, because he has not given consideration. In both situations A has not contributed anything to the new bargain. Although the underlying principle is the same in both situations, it is convenient to deal with the present situation separately. The earlier study of this principle showed that A could not succeed as plaintiff. Here the question is what will happen to A as defendant if he is sued by B for the balance of the debt.

A debt can only be discharged by "accord and satisfaction". Accord is agreement, and satisfaction is consideration. "Payment of a lesser sum on the day in satisfaction of a greater sum cannot be any satisfaction for the whole." This quotation from the report of the judgment in *Pinnel's* case (1602) is commonly called "the rule in *Pinnel's* case".

The rule in *Pinnel's* case was approved by the House of Lords in 1884 in the case of *Foakes v. Beer*. Mrs Beer had obtained a judgment against Dr Foakes for £2,090. Dr Foakes wanted time to pay, and the parties entered into a written agreement that if he would pay £2,090 by stated instalments Mrs Beer would not "take any proceedings whatever on the judgment". Every judgment debt carries interest, but the agreement between the parties made no mention of interest. In course of time Dr Foakes paid, by instalments, the whole sum of £2,090. Mrs Beer then claimed a further £360 as interest. Dr Foakes refused to pay, and Mrs Beer applied to the court for leave to proceed on the judgment. Dr Foakes relied on the agreement; Mrs Beer argued that Dr Foakes had given no consideration in the agreement. The House of Lords upheld Mrs Beer's claim, declining to upset the rule in *Pinnel's* case.

There are a number of qualifications to the rule at common law. Three qualifications appear in *Pinnel's* case itself. First, payment of a smaller sum before the due day, at the creditor's request, is valid consideration. Secondly, payment of a smaller sum at a different place, at the creditor's request, is valid consideration. Thirdly, payment of a smaller sum accompanied, at the creditor's request, by delivery of a chattel is valid consideration: ". . . the gift of a horse, hawk or robe, etc., in satisfaction is good." A fourth qualification has been added by later judicial decisions: that the rule does not apply where the creditor's claim is unliquidated or disputed. The reason is that in such a case the value of the creditor's claim is unknown; the sum offered by the debtor may not be any less—it may even be more—than the true value of the creditor's claim.

Until 1965 there was another qualification: payment of a smaller sum made by cheque or other negotiable instrument was treated as valid consideration for a promise to discharge the whole debt. The reasons for this qualification were tenuous, and in *D. & C. Builders Ltd v. Rees* (1966, C.A.) it was held by the Court of Appeal, overruling earlier cases, that payment of a lesser sum by cheque is no discharge of the balance. (For negotiable instruments, see Chapter 14.)

Two further qualifications to the rule in *Pinnel's* case still exist, which may be called the fifth and sixth qualifications. The fifth is where payment of part of a debt is made by a third party. If such payment is accepted by the creditor in full settlement, the payment is a good defence to a later action by the creditor against the debtor for the balance. In *Hirachand*

Punamchand v. Temple (1911, C.A.) the father of a young officer who was indebted to money-lenders sent them ''in full settlement'' a draft for a smaller amount. The money-lenders accepted the draft, and then sued the son. The Court of Appeal rejected their claim. It is not easy to find a convincing consideration in this situation, but the result is justifiable, since to allow the money-lenders' claim would have been a fraud on the father.

The sixth qualification arises in the case of agreements between debtors and their creditors. These are called ''individual voluntary arrangements'' comprising a composition with the creditors. A ''composition'' is an agreement between a debtor and all his creditors that he will pay them, and that they will accept, a ''dividend'' (a division of his assets, but less than his full debts) in full settlement of their claims. A creditor who has received a dividend under such an agreement will fail if he sues the debtor for the balance of his original claim; the consideration supporting the agreement by each creditor is the mutual agreement of the other creditors to accept part payment as a discharge of the whole debt: see, for example, *Good v. Cheesman* (1831) 2 B. & Ad. 328. In addition, under section 260(2) of the Insolvency Act 1986, a composition approved in accordance with the provisions of that Act is legally binding on all creditors.

Equity

Equity, which is founded on fairness, does not look with favour on a man who promises relief to another and then goes back on his promise. An example of this is *Hughes v. Metropolitan Railway Co.* (1877, H.L.). The facts of the case were that a landlord gave his tenant six months' notice to repair the premises. If the tenant failed to comply the lease could be forfeited. A month after the notice, the landlord started negotiations with the tenant for the purchase by the landlord of the residue of the lease. These negotiations were broken off two months later. During this time the defendant did nothing towards repairing the premises. When the notice had run for six months the landlord claimed to treat the lease as forfeited. The House of Lords held that he could not do so. The opening of negotiations amounted to a promise by the landlord that as long as they continued he would not enforce the notice. It was in reliance on this promise that the tenant had refrained from doing any repairs. The six months allowed for the repairs must run, therefore, only from the failure of the negotiations and the consequent withdrawal of the promise. The tenant was entitled in equity to relief from forfeiture. Lord Cairns said:

"... it is the first principle upon which all Courts of Equity proceed, that if parties who have entered into definite and distinct terms involving certain legal results-certain penalties or legal forfeiture-afterwards by their own act or with their own consent enter upon a course of negotiation which has the effect of leading one of the parties to suppose that the strict rights arising under the contract will not be enforced or will be kept in suspense or held in abeyance, the person who otherwise might have enforced those rights will not be allowed to enforce them where it would be inequitable, having regard to the dealings which have thus taken place between the parties."

This principle has been called "equitable estoppel", "quasi-estoppel" or "promissory estoppel". It is best to call it "promissory estoppel" because there is another kind of equitable estoppel, "proprietary estoppel", affecting owners of land (and, possibly, of other property). Promissory estoppel differs from estoppel strictly so-called because estoppel strictly so-called only operates to estop a person who has made a statement of present fact; it does not apply to a promise of future conduct. This view of strict estoppel was laid down by the House of Lords in *Jorden v. Money* (1854, H.L.). There, a lady, who had several times promised that she would not enforce a certain bond, was held not to be estopped from enforcing it.

The doctrine of promissory estoppel was given new life by Denning J. (as he then was) in 1947 in *Central London Property Trust Ltd v. High Trees House Ltd.* In September 1939 the plaintiffs had let a block of flats to the defendants. In January 1940 they agreed to accept half-rent, since many of the flats were unlet because of war conditions. In 1945 all the flats were let again and the plaintiffs claimed full rent for the last two quarters of 1945. Denning J. gave judgment for the plaintiffs on the grounds that the agreement of 1940 had, by the middle of 1945, ceased to operate by reason of change of circumstances. He said *obiter* that if the plaintiffs has sought to recover full rent for 1940 to 1945 they would have failed. The principle of *Hughes's* case would prevent them going back on their promise.

In *Combe v. Combe* (1951, C.A.) Lord Denning restated the doctrine in these words:

"The principle ... is that, where one party has, by his words or conduct, made to the other a promise or assurance which was

41

intended to affect the legal relations between them and to be acted on accordingly, then, once the other party has taken him at his word and acted on it, the one who gave the promise or assurance cannot afterwards be allowed to revert to the previous legal relations as if no such promise or assurance had been made by him, but he must accept their legal relations subject to the qualification which he himself has so introduced, even though it is not supported in point of law by any consideration but only by his word.''

But the promise must be clear and unequivocal.

In a later case, *Alan (W.J.) & Co. v. El Nasr Export & Import Co.* (1972, C.A.), Lord Denning said that, although it was essential to the doctrine of promissory estoppel that the debtor should have acted on the promise, it was not essential that he should have acted on it *to his detriment*. In *Brikom Investments Ltd v. Carr* (1979, C.A.) Lord Denning said that it was not necessary that a party should have acted on the promise in the sense of acting differently from the way he would have done if the promise had not been made to him; it was enough that he had *relied* on the promise in any way.

The doctrine only applies where it would be inequitable for the creditor to go back on his promise. This point is well illustrated by *D. & C. Builders Ltd v. Rees* (1966, C.A.). A firm of jobbing builders promised to accept £300 in full settlement of their claim for £482. Lord Denning said that because this promise had been extracted from the plaintiff creditors by intimidation on the part of the debtor, the debtor could not rely on the doctrine of promissory estoppel.

The present state of the law

How then, does the rule in *Pinnel's* case stand, after all this litigation? It is not entirely easy to reconcile *Hughes's* case on the one hand with *Jorden v. Money* and *Foakes v. Beer* on the other hand. They are all decisions of the House of Lords.

The following way of reconciling the cases is suggested. The rule in *Pinnel's* case still stands. Payment of a smaller sum does not discharge a larger debt (*Foakes v. Beer*). The creditor who makes a promise to forgo payment of the balance and then wishes to change his mind is not estopped in the strict sense (*Jorden v. Money*). But (*Hughes's* case) such a promise, albeit without any consideration given in return for it, is binding if the debtor has done something or not done something on the faith of the promise. It is only binding, however, to the extent of *suspending* the duty to pay: it is not binding for ever; the debt is not finally discharged. The duty to pay will revive if the creditor gives notice to the debtor that the suspension is at an end, or if the state of affairs which led to the promise comes to an end. Where the debtor's duty is to make periodic payments (as in the case of rent), to say that the doctrine is suspensory is ambiguous. It can either mean that after suspension has ended the debtor must make future payments in full but need not make up past lower payments to the full amount, or it can mean that he must do both. The latter view is preferable, because otherwise the periodic payer would be in a better position than the lump sum payer. (Events may happen, after the promise, which make the suspension permanent. But that does not invalidate the proposition that the doctrine itself is only suspensory.) See *Birmingham & District Land Co. v. L. & N.W. Railway* (1888, C.A.) and *Durham Fancy Goods Ltd v. Michael Jackson (Fancy Goods) Ltd* (1968).

It must be said, however, that Lord Denning clearly regarded the doctrine of promissory estoppel as being extinctive and not merely suspensory. He said in the *High Trees* case (1947): "The logical consequence, no doubt, is that a promise to accept a smaller sum in discharge of a larger sum, if acted upon, is binding notwithstanding the absence of consideration: and if the fusion of law and equity leads to this result, so much the better." In the later case of *D. & C. Builders Ltd v. Rees* (1966, C.A.) he said: "It is worth noticing that the principle may be applied, not only so as to suspend strict legal rights but also so as to preclude the enforcement of them." That view cannot be reconciled with *Foakes v. Beer*.

There was perhaps a hint in his judgment in *Alan v. El Nasr* (1972, C.A.) that Lord Denning was there modifying his earlier view. He said that the creditor's "strict rights are at any rate suspended . . . . He may on occasion be able to revert to his strict legal rights for the future by giving notice . . . . But there are cases where no withdrawal is possible. It may be too late to withdraw; or it cannot be done without injustice to the other party".

Even if the view comes to be generally accepted that promissory estoppel is extinctive and not merely suspensory, it may be that the doctrine of promissory estoppel will still not have so great an effect as a contractual promise supported by consideration. It was said in *Combe v. Combe* (1951, C.A.) that the doctrine is "a shield, not a sword", meaning that it can be a defence but not a cause of action. Promissory estoppel would give effect to a promise to waive payment of a debt, but it would not give effect to a promise to pay more for services already contracted for. To put it in another way, the rule in *Pinnel's* case would go, but the rule in *Stilk v. Myrick* would stand.

Consideration Attacked and Defended

The doctrine of consideration has not received universal applause. In the eighteenth century Lord Mansfield, Chief Justice of the King's Bench, tried, unsuccessfully, to root it out of the law. In the nineteenth century Jessel M.R. made this pungent criticism: "According to English Common Law a creditor may accept anything in satisfaction of his debt except a less amount of money. He might take a horse, or a canary or a tomtit if he chose, and that was accord and satisfaction; but by a most extraordinary peculiarity of the English Common Law, he could not take 19s. 6d. in the pound; that was *nudum pactum* . . . ": see *Couldery v. Bartrum* (1881, C.A.).

In 1937 the Law Revision Committee made a number of recommendations for amending the doctrine of consideration: see Sixth Interim Report, 1937, Cmd. 5449. None of these recommendations has so far been implemented. One of their recommendations was that a promise to keep an offer open should be binding, even where there is no consideration. The present law does certainly seem to work some hardship. In *Dickinson v. Dodds* (1876, C.A.) (see p. 20, above) it was held that an offer to sell land, "to be left until Friday" could be revoked on Thursday. The reason is that a promise to keep an offer open can only be enforced if it is supported by consideration. If Dickinson, or any person in a similar situation, wants to have an effective "option" he must pay for it. If Dickinson had given Dodds five pence for the option it would have been effective. Perhaps that instance does make the doctrine of consideration look rather silly.

But it is only silly at the edges. There is nothing silly about consideration in the vast majority of cases. The doctrine of consideration has been forcefully defended by Professor Hamson: "So far from being an accidental and unnecessary mystery, an accidental tomtit in an otherwise rational theory of contract, consideration in its essential nature is an aspect merely of the fundamental notion of bargain, other aspects of which, no less but no more important, are offer and acceptance. Consideration, offer and acceptance are an indivisible trinity, facets of one identical notion which is that of bargain'': see (1938) 54 L.Q.R. 233 at p. 234. Compare, however, the cooler assessment by a Law Lord in 1975. In *New Zealand Shipping Co. Ltd v. A.M. Satterthwaite & Co. Ltd* (1975, P.C.) Lord Wilberforce said: '' . . . English law, having committed itself to a rather technical and schematic doctrine of contract, in application takes a practical approach, often at the cost of forcing the facts to fit uneasily into the marked slots of offer, acceptance and consideration.''

In the most recent case to look at consideration, *Williams v. Roffey Bros & Nicholls (Contractors) Ltd* (1991), the Court of Appeal made clear its view that consideration remains a fundamental requirement for a valid contract. Russell L.J. said: ''Consideration there must still be but, in my judgment, the courts nowadays should be more ready to find its existence so as to reflect the intention of the parties to the contract where the bargaining powers are not unequal and where the finding of consideration reflects the true intention of the parties.''

CONSIDERATION AND DEEDS

Before the enactment of the Law of Property (Miscellaneous Provisions) Act 1989, a seal was sometimes said to be an alternative to consideration. A contract might be made ''under seal'' or ''by deed''. The seal was said to give a contract ''form'', and a contract under seal might be called a ''formal contract''. A contract not under seal was called a ''simple contract''. Before the 1989 Act, the rule was that a person might make a promise under seal which was enforceable even though there was no consideration. The 1989 Act has now abolished the requirement that a seal is necessary for the valid execution of an instrument as a deed by an individual: see section 1(1)(b). For an instrument to be a deed, it must make clear on its face that it is intended to be a deed and must be validly executed. Valid execution is a simplified procedure requiring the signature of the person making the deed, the attestation of the signature and delivery of the deed: see section 1(2) and (3).

The effect of this change in the law is that validly executed deeds are enforceable without the need for a seal and without the need for consideration as explained in this chapter.

CHAPTER THREE

INTENTION TO CONTRACT

Two elements necessary for a valid contract have been looked at: offer and acceptance and consideration. The third requirement—intention to contract—will be looked at in this chapter.

Some writers have argued that there is no separate requirement of intention to contract, and that if there is agreement and consideration—in other words, if there is a bargain—legal enforceability must follow. But the cases do not fit this theory. If A and B agree to lunch together, A promising to pay for the food and B promising to pay for the drink, there is a bargain (agreement plus consideration) but no legal obligations are created. The reason why no legal obligations are created is that none are intended.

So it can be said that intention to contract is a necessary element in the contractual bond. "Intention to contract" is not the same thing as the "willingness to be bound" which is that element in an offer which distinguishes it from an invitation to treat. "Willingness to be bound" means the offeror's readiness to perform his promise if the other party accepts it; "intention to contract" means the readiness of each party to accept the legal consequences if they do not perform their contract.

In this chapter agreements are classified into social and domestic agreements on the one hand and commercial agreements on the other.

SOCIAL AND DOMESTIC AGREEMENTS

Within the class of social and domestic agreements those between husband and wife are the most likely to be held to be not contractual.

In *Balfour v. Balfour* (1919, C.A.) the defendant was a civil servant stationed in Ceylon. He and his wife (the plaintiff) came to England on leave. When his leave was over he went back to Ceylon alone, and his wife stayed in England on her doctor's advice. The husband promised to pay her £30 a month. He did not keep this promise and his wife sued him. She succeeded at first instance, but the Court of Appeal allowed the husband's appeal. Atkin L.J. said: "... one of the most usual forms of agreement which does not constitute a contract appears to me to be the arrangements which are made between husband and wife ... and they are not contracts because the parties did not intend that they should be attended by legal consequences."

But even in arrangements between husband and wife the circumstances may be such as to lead a court to hold that legal relations are intended. In *Merritt v. Merritt* (1970, C.A.) the husband left the wife and went to live with another woman. The wife pressed the husband to make arrangements for the future, and they met and talked the matter over. The husband made certain oral promises and then, on the wife's insistence, he wrote and signed and dated this note: "In consideration of the fact that you will pay all charges in connection with the house ... until such time as the mortgage repayment has been completed, when the mortgage has been completed I will agree to transfer the property into your sole ownership." The wife paid off the mortgage, but the husband refused to transfer the house to the wife. She sued for a declaration, and the Court of Appeal made a declaration that the wife was now the sole beneficial owner of the matrimonial home, on the grounds that the principle of *Balfour v. Balfour* does not apply to a husband and wife who are not living in amity.

The principle of *Balfour v. Balfour* has been applied to an agreement between mother and daughter. In *Jones v. Padavatton* (1969, C.A.) a mother agreed with her daughter, a secretary in the United States, that if she would give up her job and read for the Bar in England the mother would provide maintenance for her. The daughter came to England and began to read for the Bar. Later the agreement was varied, the mother agreeing to provide a house for the daughter. On the mother's claim for possession of the house the Court of Appeal held that the arrangement was not intended to be legally binding and that the mother was entitled to possession.

In *Parker v. Clark* (1960) the plaintiffs were Commander and Mrs Parker; the defendants were Mr and Mrs Clark. Mrs Parker was the niece of Mrs Clark. The elderly couple (the Clarks) invited the Parkers to share their house. This involved the younger couple (the Parkers) in selling their own house. The arrangement was held to be legally binding. Devlin J.

said: ". . . The question [whether or not there is a binding contract] must, of course, depend on the intention of the parties, to be inferred from the language they use and from the circumstances in which they use it."

The same question may arise in respect of social, rather than domestic, arrangements and between parties who are not relatives. In *Coward v. Motor Insurers' Bureau* (1963, C.A.), Mr Coward was taken to work on the pillion of Mr Cole's motorcycle, in return for which service he paid a weekly sum. The question arose, in an insurance context, whether Mr Coward was a person carried "for hire or reward". It was held by the Court of Appeal that he was not, because neither party intended to enter into a legal contract. But the authority of *Coward's* case has been weakened by the more recent case of *Connell v. Motor Insurers' Bureau* (1969, C.A.). The facts were similar to those in *Coward's* case, yet the Court of Appeal said (*obiter*) that there was a contract.

COMMERCIAL AGREEMENTS

In commercial agreements there is a presumption that the parties do intend to make a legally enforceable contract. Thus it is not necessary, in the ordinary run of commercial transactions, for the plaintiff to give affirmative evidence that there was such an intention. But the defendant may defeat the presumption by reference to the words used by the parties and/or the circumstances in which they used them. The point is discussed by the House of Lords in *Esso Petroleum Co. Ltd v. Commissioners of Customs and Excise* (1976, H.L.). See also *Kleinwort Benson Ltd v. Malaysia Mining Corp. Bhd* (1989, C.A.).

"Honour Clauses"

If the parties have expressly declared that a transaction is not to be binding in law the courts will give effect to that declaration. Many football pools coupons contain the words "Binding in honour only", and it has been held that a dissatisfied punter (or "investor") cannot sue on a coupon containing those words. See, for example, *Appleson v. Littlewood* (1939, C.A.).

There is one reported case where a similar form of words was inserted into what was otherwise an ordinary agreement for the sale of goods: see

Rose and Frank Co. v. Crompton (1925, H.L.). The agreement contained the following clause: "This arrangement is not entered into . . . as a formal or legal agreement, and shall not be subject to legal jurisdiction in the Law Courts . . . but it is only a definite expression and record of the purpose and intention of the . . . parties concerned, to which they each honourably pledge themselves." It was held by the House of Lords that the agreement could not be sued upon.

But if there is any ambiguity in such a clause the courts will not shut themselves out from adjudicating. In *Edwards v. Skyways* (1964) an employee was dismissed as redundant. His employers promised to make him an *ex gratia* payment of a specified amount. It was held that the words *"ex gratia"* did not negative contractual intention; they simply meant that the employers did not admit any *pre-existing* liability on their part.

Although it is permissible for parties to agree that their agreement is not to have any legal effect at all (as in *Rose and Frank Co. v. Crompton*), an agreement which ousts the jurisdiction of the courts in favour of some other tribunal is treated by the courts as void as being contrary to public policy: see Chapter 11.

Collective Agreements

Collective agreements are agreements entered into by trade unions and employers and govern the rates of pay and conditions of work of their members. If the terms of such agreements are then incorporated (as they frequently are) into the individual employment contract of each employee those terms are legally binding on the parties, *i.e.* the employee and the employer. But that still leaves the question whether the collective bargain itself is an enforceable contract as between the parties to it, the trade union and the employer. There was very little authority on this point, but there was a general belief amongst trade unionists, industrialists and lawyers that collective bargains were not enforceable at common law. That belief was given judicial backing in *Ford Motor Company v. Amalgamated Union of Engineering and Foundry Workers* (1969). In that case it was held that a collective agreement is not intended to be legally enforceable, and accordingly the court will grant no relief for breach of such an agreement. This is an instance where an intention to contract is negatived, not by any actual words used by the parties, but by the circumstances surrounding their agreement.

49

The common law position has been affirmed by statute. Section 179 of the Trade Union and Labour Relations (Consolidation) Act 1992 states that a collective agreement is conclusively presumed not to have been intended by the parties to be a legally enforceable contract unless it is in writing and expressly provides that it is so intended.

Part Two

WHAT IS WITHIN THE BOND

Chapter Four

EXPRESS TERMS

TERMS AND REPRESENTATIONS

A contract contains a number of terms; the terms are, in effect, the obligations of the contract. So an employer may offer an employee a job at £10,000 a year, which the employee accepts. One of the *terms* of the contract is that the employer will pay the employee £10,000 a year.

Before they enter into the contract, the parties are likely to be involved in negotiations, particularly if it is a complex commercial contract. During the course of the negotiations, the parties may say or write all kinds of things, but it does not follow that all they have said or written are terms of the contract. There is a distinction between *terms*—which do become part of the contract—and *representations* (*i.e.* statements of fact or opinion)—which do not. This distinction becomes important where a statement which has been made turns out to be untrue. In that case, the judge has to decide which statements are contractual terms and which are non-contractual representations, inducing the contract but forming no part of it.

It may help here to consider an example. A discusses with B selling him his television. During the course of the discussion, B asks A all about it—its age, how much A has used it, whether it has teletext and so on. At the end of these negotiations, A agrees to sell him the television for £100. Clearly, the contract has more to it than the price. But not all A's answers will be classified as terms of the contract—some may be, some may be treated as representations.

The importance of the distinction between terms and representations arises where a statement is untrue, that is, where there is a misrepresentation. If a statement is a term of the contract, its untruth is a breach of contract, for which the injured party may claim, amongst other remedies, damages. He is entitled to damages even though the misstatement was made entirely innocently; that is, without fraud or negligence. If a statement is not a term of the contract, the injured party will only be entitled to damages if the misrepresentor has acted fraudulently or negligently; if the misrepresentor has acted wholly innocently the injured party will be entitled only to rescission, though the court has a discretion to order damages instead. These matters are dealt with fully in Chapter 8 on misrepresentation.

It will thus be seen that it is important to be able to decide whether a statement is a contractual term or not. The decision, though important, is difficult. The basic principle seems to be that it is a question of intention: did the maker of the statement intend it to be a term of the contract? But the test of intention is objective: would a reasonable person have taken the statement to be meant as a contractual term? That, of course, depends upon what exactly was said (or written) and upon the circumstances surrounding the transaction. Three guidelines emerge from the decided cases.

1. Strength of the Statement

If the person making the statement suggests that the other party should check it, the statement will not be treated as a term of the contract. In *Ecay v. Godfrey* (1947) the seller of a boat stated that it was sound, but advised the buyer to have it surveyed. This advice showed that the seller did not intend that his statement should be taken as a term of the contract. This principle may apply, even though the representor does not qualify his statement, if the circumstances are such that the other party would normally verify the statement. Thus statements about the condition of buildings to be sold or let are rarely treated as contractual terms, because the buyer or tenant normally has the property surveyed.

Conversely, if a statement is made in a dogmatic way, so that the other party is dissuaded from checking it, the statement will probably be held to be a contractual term. In *Schawel v. Reade* (1913, H.L.) the plaintiff was examining a horse with a view to buying it for stud purposes. The defendant said: "You need not look for anything: the horse is perfectly sound. If there was anything the matter with the horse I would tell you." The buyer in reliance on this statement bought the horse, which proved to be totally unfit for stud purposes. In the House of Lords the issue turned on the judge's direction to the jury and the jury's finding, but the important point is that all their Lordships said that the seller's statement was a contractual term.

2. Importance to the Representee

If the representee has made it known that he attaches great importance to a certain fact, and the other party then states that that fact is true, the statement will probably be treated as a contractual term. In *Bannerman v. White* (1861) an intending buyer of hops asked whether sulphur had been used in their treatment. He added that if it had, he would not even trouble to ask the price. It was held that the seller's (untrue) assurance that sulphur had not been used was a term of the contract.

3. Relative Degrees of Knowledge

If the maker of the statement has some special knowledge or skill compared with the other party, the statement may well be held to be a contractual term; if their degrees of knowledge are equal, or, *a fortiori*, if the recipient of the statement has the greater knowledge, the statement may well be held to be a non-contractual representation. In *Oscar Chess Ltd v. Williams* (1957, C.A.) the defendant traded in to the plaintiffs (car dealers) a Morris car which he honestly described as a 1948 model. He received an allowance for it of £290. It turned out to be a 1939 model, worth £175. The statement that the car was a 1948 model was held not to be a term of the contract. The seller was a private individual, who had taken his information from the registration book, which only later turned out to be forged. The buyers were car dealers and so were in at least as good a position as the seller to know the true age of the car.

In *Dick Bentley Productions Ltd v. Harold Smith (Motors) Ltd* (1965, C.A.) the defendant, who was a dealer, sold a Bentley, stating that it had only done 20,000 miles since a replacement engine had been fitted. In fact it had done nearly 100,000 miles since then. The Court of Appeal held that the defendant's statement was a term of the contract and that the plaintiffs were entitled to damages.

In the *Dick Bentley* case Lord Denning proposed what appears to be a new approach, that an inducing statement should be presumed to be a term of the contract, but that the presumption can be rebutted if the representor has not acted negligently or fraudulently. This test has the merit of containing an element of justice, but it also contains an element of irony. This is because where the maker of the statement has been negligent or fraudulent, the other party will have a remedy in damages even if the statement is held not to be a term of the contract; it is only important to the plaintiff that a statement should be held to be a contractual term where the defendant has been wholly innocent.

THE NATURE OF CONTRACTUAL TERMS

A contract may be made by words or conduct or partly by words and partly by conduct. The words may be written or spoken or partly written and partly spoken. The words, whether written or spoken, which the parties use in formulating their agreement are the express terms of the contract. But those express terms do not always constitute the whole contract; there may be other terms which fall to be implied into it. Implied terms will be examined in Chapter 5.

Where the contract is wholly in spoken words, the main task of the judge is to decide exactly what words were used. Where the contract is wholly in writing other problems may arise. The terms of a contract may be contained in more than one document. If the one document expressly refers to another, then that other document, so far as the reference extends, is incorporated into the contract. Thus, in a contract for the sale of land, there may be a clause stating: "The sale is subject to clause [X] of the National Conditions of Sale."

If one contractual document does not expressly refer to another, it may yet be held by the courts that that other document forms part of the contract. Thus in *Edwards v. Aberayron Mutual Ship Insurance Society Ltd* (1876) it was held that a policy of insurance could be read together with the rules of the mutual insurance society which had issued it, although the policy did not expressly refer to the rules.

Where written words have been used and also some spoken words, it is sometimes difficult to decide whether the written words constitute the whole of the contract. At this point, the parol evidence rule needs to be considered.

THE PAROL EVIDENCE RULE

There is a general rule that parol evidence cannot be admitted to add to, vary or contradict a deed or other written instrument. The word "parol" in this context means any extrinsic evidence. A clear instance of the working of the rule is furnished by the case of *Henderson v. Arthur* (1907, C.A.). A covenant in a lease under seal provided for payment of rent in advance. The lessee was not permitted to give evidence of a previous oral agreement that payment should be made by a bill of exchange maturing in three months' time. The two statements were contradictory; it is only common sense to prefer the later, and written, expression of intention.

If the parol evidence rule were applied over a broad front it would lead to injustice in many cases, but over the years it has been made subject to many exceptions so that its scope is quite limited. We proceed to consider the exceptions.

Rectification

In litigation concerning a contract two issues are often raised: construction and rectification. The plaintiff argues on the construction point that the meaning of the contract is "X". He further argues, in case the court decides against him on construction, that "X" was the subject of an antecedent expressed accord between the parties before the contract was reduced to writing and that, if the contract as written does not mean "X", its wording should be rectified to bring it into line with "X". On the construction point the parol evidence rule applies, shutting out extrinsic evidence. On the rectification point the parol evidence rule does not apply; indeed the point depends entirely on extrinsic evidence of a pre-contract accord between the parties. See *Joscelyne v. Nissen* (1970, C.A.) and *Prenn v. Simmonds* (1971, H.L.). See also p. 130, below.

It is important to bear in mind that rectification is an equitable remedy, which is available only at the discretion of the court. The rules governing the granting of equitable remedies thus come into play here; so, for example, rectification will not be granted in favour of a plaintiff who is guilty of excessive delay in seeking the remedy, since "delay defeats Equity".

Invalidity

The rule excludes extrinsic evidence of the contents of a contract, but not extrinsic evidence relating to its validity. Evidence of matters outside the writing can be given to show some invalidating cause, such as misrepresentation, mistake, incapacity, or absence of consideration.

Non-operation

Again, the rule does not prevent extrinsic evidence being given to prove that the contract does not yet operate or has ceased to operate. (See also p. 61, below.) In *Pym v. Campbell* (1856) the parties entered into a written agreement for the sale of an invention. When the plaintiff sued for a breach of this agreement the defendants were permitted to give evidence of an oral agreement that the written agreement was not to operate until a third party had approved the invention and that the third party never had approved it.

Custom

The parol evidence rule does not forbid extrinsic evidence of custom. In *Hutton v. Warren* (1836) a plaintiff tenant, who had been given notice to quit a farm, was permitted to give evidence of a local custom entitling him to a fair allowance for seeds and labour.

Incompleteness

The most important limitation on the parol evidence rule is that it does not apply where the written agreement is not the whole agreement. There is a puzzle here: if this sub-rule were universally applied it would knock out the parol evidence rule altogether. If the written agreement really was the whole agreement neither party would be seeking to introduce extrinsic evidence; conversely, if some non-written terms were intended to be part of the contract, the parol evidence rule would never exclude them. But the way the parol evidence rule works in practice is this: where one party is reasonably entitled to assume that the writing does contain all the terms of the contract, the other party will not be allowed to give evidence that it does not.

Two contrasting cases illustrate the point. In *Malpas v. L. & S.W. Rail. Co.* (1866) Malpas orally contracted with the defendants to carry his cattle from Guildford to King's Cross. He signed (without noticing its contents) a consignment note by which the cattle were "to be sent to Nine Elms Station" (an intermediate station). The cattle were delayed at Nine Elms and suffered injury. The plaintiff was allowed to give evidence that the full contract was for conveyance to King's Cross via Nine Elms. In *Hutton v. Watling* (1948, C.A.) there was a document headed "To sale of business". The document set out a number of terms, and contained a receipt for the price of the goodwill, and it was signed over a 6d. stamp. The purchaser sued to enforce one of the written terms; the vendor argued that the document was only a memorandum and sought to give evidence that there was an antecedent oral agreement different in its terms. This evidence was held inadmissible. Lord Greene M.R. said: "If the other party to the alleged contract, interpreting it as a reasonably intelligent person would do in the light of the relevant circumstances, takes it to be of a contractual nature, that concludes the matter and it is not possible to call oral evidence that it was a mere memorandum." (See also p. 219, below.)

COLLATERAL CONTRACTS

Over the past hundred years or so, the courts have been developing a doctrine—or device—relating to what are commonly called "collateral contracts". By means of this device the courts sometimes hold that a statement which is not a term of the main contract is nevertheless not a "mere" representation, because it is a term of another contract, standing side by side with the main contract. A good example of the working of this doctrine is to be found in the case of *De Lassalle v. Guildford* (1901, C.A.). The defendant was negotiating to let his house to the plaintiff. The plaintiff declined to hand over the counterpart of the lease until he was assured that the drains were in order. The defendant gave such an assurance, and the plaintiff then delivered the counterpart. The drains were not in order. The plaintiff sued for damages and succeeded in the Court of Appeal, on the grounds that there had been a breach, not of the tenancy contract (the lease did not refer to the condition of the drains) but of the collateral (drains) contract.

In such a case as this the collateral contract doctrine not only bypasses the "mere" representation argument; it also bypasses the parol evidence rule. It is able to bypass the parol evidence rule because although the collateral contract may add to the total obligations of the promisor it does not add to the main contract. But what happens if the collateral contract varies or contradicts the main contract? It would seem from such a case as *Henderson v. Arthur* (see p. 57, above) that a collateral contract cannot in such circumstances be set up. But if the case of *City & Westminster Properties (1934) Ltd v. Mudd* (1959) is rightly decided, even a contradictory collateral contract may be used, at least as a shield, though perhaps not as a sword. A tenant was presented with a lease which contained a covenant to use the premises for business purposes only. He had in fact been living at the premises for some time. When he queried the covenant he was given an oral assurance that he would be allowed to continue living at the premises. So he signed the lease. The lessors then brought an action for forfeiture of the lease for breach of covenant. It was held that the tenant could defend by relying on the oral assurance "as a clear contract".

It is not open to the courts to find a collateral contract unless all the necessary elements of a valid contract are indeed present. There must be agreement, consideration and an intention to be legally bound. Agreement and intention to contract do not require further exposition here. Consideration deserves some discussion. The consideration must of course be separate from the consideration in the main contract. In *De Lassalle v. Guildford* one could not say that the rent in the main contract was the consideration for the promise about the drains in the collateral contract. The consideration for the drains promise was the (implied) promise to enter into the main contract. It can be paraphrased thus: "If you will promise that the drains are in order I will execute the lease."

In *De Lassalle's* case, of course, the main contract and the collateral contract had the same parties. But such is the strength of the doctrine that it can happen that the collateral contract is between A and B though the main contract is between A and C. This was so in *Shanklin Pier Ltd v. Detel Products Ltd* (1951). The plaintiff owners of the pier (B) had engaged a firm, C, to paint the pier. B had the right to specify the materials to be used. The defendants, A, induced B to specify a particular paint (manufactured by A) by assuring B that it would last seven or 10 years. So C bought the paint from A. In fact it lasted about three months. B sued A and won. B was suing on the collateral (A–B) contract. The consideration given by B was that they caused C to enter into the A–C contract (the contract for purchase of the paint, the main contract).

The doctrine of the collateral contract is important and has a part to play in five other contexts. First, it may enable a person to side-step an exemption clause (see Chap. 6); secondly, it may enable a person to side-step the requirement of written evidence, in, *e.g.* a contract for the sale of land (see Chap. 7); thirdly, it may enable a person to side-step the invalidity which attaches to an illegal contract (see Chap. 11); fourthly, it may enable a person to avoid the question of the rule of privity of contract (see Chap. 13); and fifthly, it may enable a third party to sue a so-called "agent" (see Chap. 15).

CONDITIONS AND WARRANTIES

If a contract contains more than one term, which, except in the very simplest transactions, it will, it may well happen that the terms are not all of equal importance. The courts recognise this inequality, and since the end of the nineteenth century there has grown up a more or less uniform terminology to distinguish two degrees of importance. The more important terms are referred to as "conditions"; the less important as "warranties". Breach of condition gives the victim the right to treat the contract as repudiated, as it would be unjust to force him to accept something which differed in an important way from that which he contracted for. The victim is not bound to treat the contract as repudiated; he may instead affirm the contract. In either event he may claim damages. Breach of warranty, on the other hand, does not entitle the victim to treat the contract as repudiated, but only to claim damages. That is just, because a minor breach can be adequately remedied by a money payment. Looked at from the point of view of the party at fault, if his breach is a breach of condition he cannot enforce the contract if the other party has elected to treat it as repudiated; if his breach is only a breach of warranty he can enforce the contract, though he must pay damages for his breach.

These words, "condition" and "warranty", were used in the way just described in the Sale of Goods Act 1893 (now the Sale of Goods Act 1979) and they came to be widely used also in contracts other than for the sale of goods. Before 1893 there was no fixed usage. In particular the word "warranty" tended to be used (and still is, on occasion) as meaning any contractual term, as distinct from a "mere" representation. The word "condition" is perhaps not very happily chosen, because it ought logically to mean, and sometimes does mean, not a term of a contract, but an external fact upon which the existence or continuance of the contract depends. Thus in *Pym v. Campbell* (1856) a contract for the sale of an invention was conditional on the approval of the invention by a third party.

(See p. 58, above.) But there is some justification for using the word "condition" for a term in a contract which is more basic than a warranty; after all, the contract is conditional on such a term, in the sense that if the term is broken the contract may be put an end to.

This approach to contractual terms has been challenged in recent years. The starting point is the decision of the Court of Appeal in *Hong Kong Fir Shipping Co. Ltd v. Kawasaki Kisen Kaisha Ltd* (1962, C.A.). The plaintiffs chartered a ship to the defendants for a period of 24 months. The engine-room staff were incompetent and the machinery was ancient. As a result, 20 weeks were lost. The defendants claimed to treat the contract as at an end. The plaintiffs sued for wrongful repudiation. There had been a very sharp fall in freight rates, which made the defendant charterers keen to get out of the contract and the plaintiff shipowners keen to keep the contract in being. The plaintiffs admitted that they were in breach of a term in the contract which required them to provide a ship which was "in every way fitted for ordinary cargo service", and they admitted that the ship was unseaworthy. But the plaintiffs argued that their breach did not entitle the defendants to put an end to the contract, only to claim damages. The plaintiffs won. Diplock L.J. (as he then was) said: "the problem in this case is, in my view, neither solved nor soluble by debating whether the shipowner's express or implied undertaking to tender a seaworthy ship is a 'condition' or a 'warranty'." The solution was to be found by looking at the events which had occurred as the result of the breach and deciding whether those events deprived the charterers of "substantially the whole benefit which it was the intention of the parties they should obtain ... under the charterparty".

Thus far, the judgments of the Court of Appeal could be accommodated with the conventional system of conditions and warranties. One could simply add a rider to say that some contractual terms (which some writers have called "innominate terms") cannot be classified as either conditions or warranties. But in my view the effect of the *Hong Kong Fir* case is more radical than that. This is because the Court of Appeal insist that one must look at the results of the breach as from the point in time at which the charterers purported to terminate the contract. Thus one can no longer say (as one could have said under the conventional system) before ever there has been a breach at all: "Any breach of clause [X] will entitle the other party to terminate the contract, *because clause [X] is a condition.*" Of course, the parties can expressly state in the contract, if they so wish, what the legal consequences are to be in the event of a breach of any particular term. But if they do not so state, then until a breach has occurred, and the practical results of it have been assessed, one cannot say what the legal rights of the other party will be. Then, and then only, one can say what his rights are, by applying the test as to whether he has been deprived of substantially his whole intended benefit under the contract.

The *Hong Kong Fir* approach leaves the parties in a state of uncertainty, and a differently constituted Court of Appeal in *The Mihalis Angelos* (1971, C.A.) were clearly anxious to limit its application. They held that the "expected readiness to load" clause (a very common clause in a charterparty) was not innominate, but was a condition.

A third Court of Appeal decision has done much to resolve the potential conflict between the *Hong Kong Fir* case and *The Mihalis Angelos*: see *Cehave N.V. v. Bremer Handelsgesellschaft mbH; The Hansa Nord* (1976, C.A.). This case was concerned with a contract for the sale of 12,000 tons of citrus pulp pellets, to be used as an ingredient in cattle food. There were two main issues in the case: the one relevant here was whether a clause in the contract of sale that the pellets were to be shipped "in good condition" was a condition, a warranty or an intermediate term. The phrase "intermediate term" has the same meaning as "innominate term". It was held that the clause was an intermediate term, that its breach did not deprive the buyers of substantially the whole intended benefit under the contract, and that the buyers were not entitled to reject the whole cargo (*i.e.* treat the contract as at an end) but were only entitled to claim damages.

The effect of the *Cehave* case may be summarised in this way. When a breach occurs, the question may arise whether the innocent party is entitled to treat the contract as at an end. The answer to that question depends on the answers to a series of other questions. (1) Does the contract expressly provide that breach of a particular term will entitle the innocent party to put an end to the contract? If the answer is Yes, then that concludes the matter. If the answer is No, then the next question arises. (2) Does the contract impliedly so provide? If the term is described in the contract as a "condition", that points towards the answer "Yes". (See, for example, *Lombard North Central plc v. Butterworth* (1987, C.A.).) But it is not conclusive, as may be seen from the House of Lords case *L. Schuler AG v. Wickman Machine Tool Sales Ltd* (1974, H.L.). If the term is described as a "warranty", that is not conclusive of the answer No. If the answer is Yes, that concludes the matter. If the answer is No, then a third question arises. (3) Although the contract does not expressly or impliedly create a right to treat the contract as terminated, does some rule of law create that right? The answer may be Yes because of (a) a statute or (b) a judicial decision. An example of (a) is the group of *implied* terms laid down by sections 12(1), 13, 14 and 15 of the Sale of Goods Act 1979. (Notice, however, that the *Cehave* case expressly holds that an *express* term in a contract of sale of goods may be neither a condition nor a warranty but an innominate term.) An example of (b) is the decision in *The Mihalis Angelos* which said that the "expected readiness to load" clause in a charterparty is a condition entitling the innocent party to treat the contract as terminated. (See also *Cie Commerciale Sucres et Denrées v. C. Czarnikow Ltd* (1990, H.L.).) If the answer to question (3) is Yes, that concludes the matter. If the answer is No (*i.e.* neither 3(a) nor 3(b) applies) then a final question arises. (4) Has the innocent party been deprived substantially of what it was intended that he should get under the contract? If the answer is Yes, then he is entitled to treat the contract as terminated. If the answer is No, then he can only claim damages. One might call question (4) "the *Hong Kong Fir* question".

So far the discussion has concerned conditions, warranties and innominate (or intermediate) terms. Another phrase is sometimes used, namely "fundamental terms". It is probably wise to avoid use of this phrase because it is by no means settled what it means. Some judges and writers use it to mean the same as a condition. Other judges and writers use it to mean a term which underlies the whole contract so that if it is breached the performance becomes totally different from that which was contemplated by the contract. Where "fundamental term" is used in this latter sense, it approximates to the concept of total failure to perform the contract. This concept is at least as old as 1838. In that year, in the case of *Chanter v. Hopkins*, Lord Abinger C.B. said: "If a man offers to buy peas of another, and he sends him beans, he does not perform his contract; but that is not a warranty; there is no warranty that he should sell him peas; the contract is to sell peas, and if he sends them anything else in their stead, it is a non-performance of it." (Lord Abinger was using the word "warranty" in the pre-1893 sense, meaning any contractual term.) It follows, in my view, that "fundamental term" is not a satisfactory phrase to use for this concept.

A similar but distinct phrase found in the cases is "fundamental breach". This phrase too has not had a uniform meaning attached to it, but the way is now clear to give it one. In *Photo Productions Ltd v.*

Securicor Transport Ltd (1980, H.L.) Lord Diplock said that this phrase (if it is to be used at all) should, in the interests of clarity, be used to mean a breach which has the effect of depriving the innocent party of substantially the whole benefit that it was intended that he should get under the contract. In other words, "fundamental breach" is the equivalent, for breach of an intermediate term, of "breach of condition".

A useful phrase to have in mind is "repudiatory breach", which covers every kind of breach which entitles the victim to treat the contract as terminated by reason of its having been repudiated by the defaulting party.

This discussion of conditions and warranties has spoken of the innocent party ending the contract or terminating the contract or treating the contract as at an end or as terminated. This is because they are phrases which were used in numerous cases before the *Photo Productions* case (above). But in the *Photo Productions* case the House of Lords emphasised that the phrases are shorthand expressions and not strictly accurate because it is not really the contract itself which is ended; what is ended is the obligation of the innocent party to perform any further his contractual duties. This and related matters are discussed more fully at pp. 234–238, below.

CHAPTER FIVE

IMPLIED TERMS

THE express terms do not always make up the whole contract. There may be other terms which fall to be implied into it. For example, if A contracts to sell goods to B there will doubtless be express terms as to what goods are to be sold, and so forth. But there may not be (though there usually is) an express term as to the price. If that is so, there is an implied term that the buyer must pay a reasonable price.

TERMS IMPLIED BY THE COURTS

The basic principle of implied terms is that a term will be implied where it is necessary in order to bring the contract into line with the intention of the parties. The intention of the parties, in relation to implied terms, is sought, as in other contexts, from an objective rather than a subjective standpoint. What is being sought is the *presumed* intention of the parties, and the presumption must be made from a study of the whole circumstances of the transaction. An unexpressed term, then, is implied by the court to give effect to the presumed intention of the parties in the particular transaction which is before the court.

When an implied term has become well settled by a series of judicial decisions in similar circumstances it tends to harden, as it were, into a substantive rule of law. For example, in a contract of employment many matters which were originally implied terms, and are still called so, have become duties imposed by law. Thus, the employer has a duty to provide safe plant and machinery, a safe system of work, and reasonably competent fellow-employees. In recent years, implied terms have played an important part in the development of the law governing the employment relationship. An example is the implication of a term in an employee's contract that the employer will not conduct himself in a manner calculated or likely to destroy or seriously damage the relationship of confidence and trust between employer and employee: see *Courtaulds Northern Textiles Ltd v. Andrew* (1979). In some areas of law this hardening process has gone a stage further: implied terms have been written into a statute.

A useful starting point in considering implied terms is the case of *The Moorcock* (1889, C.A.). The defendants were wharfingers who had contracted to allow the plaintiff to discharge his ship at their jetty. Both parties realised that the ship would ground at low water. When the tide ebbed the ship settled on a ridge of hard ground beneath the mud and suffered damage. Although there was no express term that the berth would be safe, the plaintiff won his case. It was held by the Court of Appeal that there must be implied into the contract an undertaking by the wharfingers that the river bottom was, so far as reasonable care could make it, in such a condition as not to endanger the ship. Bowen L.J. said this:

> "... [T]he law is raising an implication from the presumed intention of the parties, with the object of giving to the transaction such efficacy as both parties must have intended that at all events it should have. In business transactions such as this, what the law desires to effect by the implication is to give such business efficacy to the transaction as must have been intended at all events by both parties who are businessmen."

Although this process of implication is a convenient way of repairing oversights or omissions, there is the risk of overworking it. Judges have regularly warned against treating Bowen L.J.'s words as a principle of law.

For the courts to imply a term it is not enough that the term should be reasonable; it must be both obvious and necessary: see *Liverpool City Council v. Irwin* (1977, H.L.). In *Shirlaw v. Southern Foundries (1926) Ltd* (1939, C.A.), MacKinnon L.J. said: "Prima facie that which in any contract is left to be implied and need not be expressed is something so obvious that it goes without saying; so that, if, while the parties were making their bargain, an officious bystander were to suggest some express provision for it in their agreement, they would testily suppress him with a common 'Oh, of course!'"

It follows from this test that a term will not be implied if one of the parties is ignorant of the matter to be implied. In *Sethia (1944) Ltd v. Partabmull Rameshwar* (1950, C.A., and affirmed by H.L.) the buyers of Indian jute sued the sellers for non-delivery. The sellers had been unable to deliver because they failed to obtain a quota for export to Genoa. The sellers argued that a term should be implied that the contract was "subject to quota". The Court of Appeal refused to imply the term. The buyers knew of the quota system, but they did not know that the sellers had no quota for Italy. Similarly, in *Walford v. Miles* (1992), the House of Lords refused to imply a term into a lock-out agreement that the vendor would not negotiate with anyone except the other party for an unspecified period, on the grounds that such a term would be uncertain.

Nevertheless, the process of implying terms is an important instrument in regulating the relationship between the parties to a contract. Two examples from recent cases show this. In *Scally v. Southern Health and Social Services Board* (1992), the House of Lords said that in cases where a contract (in this case, a contract of employment) gives a valuable benefit, the court may imply a term obliging the other party to it to take reasonable steps to bring to the attention of that person a term in the contract, so that he may enjoy its benefit. In *Johnstone v. Bloomsbury Health Authority* (1992) the Court of Appeal said that the exercise of an express term in a contract may be cut down by an implied term obliging the party relying on it to act reasonably. This last case arose in the context of hospital doctors' hours of work, under a clause in their contracts which stipulated a standard working week of 40 hours and an additional requirement to be available on call up to an average of 48 hours a week over a specified period.

A fruitful source of implied terms is custom. We saw at p. 58, above, an example of a custom being imported into a contract as an implied term in *Hutton v. Warren* (1836). The court held that the lease made between the parties must be read as including a certain agricultural custom. And there are many, many cases where a commercial custom has been similarly treated as part of a contract.

TERMS IMPLIED BY STATUTE

As has been pointed out already, some implied terms develop from being terms implied by the courts to being terms implied by statute. Thus, many of the implied terms set out in the Sale of Goods Act 1893 had been habitually implied by the courts in the years before 1893, and so the statute was simply declaring the existing common law. Two of the more important terms implied by the Sale of Goods Act 1979 are an implied condition that the goods shall be of merchantable quality and an implied condition that the goods shall be reasonably fit for the purpose for which they are being bought. (Both are subject to some qualifications.) Both these implied terms could, originally, be excluded by the parties if they so wished. Now, by virtue of the Unfair Contract Terms Act 1977, the terms cannot be excluded in a "consumer sale" and only in certain circumstances in a non-consumer sale.

Just as statutory implied terms commonly (though not always) derive from earlier common law implied terms, so in their turn statutory implied terms are sometimes adopted, by analogy, in the courts. For example, in *Samuels v. Davis* (1943, C.A.) the plaintiff dentist contracted to make a set of dentures. The defendant refused to pay for them on the ground that they were so unsatisfactory that they could not be used. There was argument whether the contract was a contract for sale of goods or a contract for work and materials. The Court of Appeal held that the question was irrelevant. If it was a contract for the sale of goods, the Sale of Goods Act imported a term that they should be reasonably fit for their purpose; if it was a contract for work and materials, the court would imply a term to the same effect.

Terms of reasonable fitness have been implied into all manner of contracts, including contracts of hire and contracts for repair. In the Sale of Goods Act the implied term of reasonable fitness is absolute, in the sense that the seller is liable for breach even if he has not been at all negligent. When the courts have applied a similar term to contracts other than for sale of goods they have usually implied the term in this absolute form. The contractor is said to be under "strict liability". In other contracts, where the implied term has grown up independently of the Sale of Goods Act, the undertaking is usually in a qualified form; thus, for example, a carrier of passengers is not absolutely liable, he has only "negligence liability".

The Supply of Goods and Services Act 1982 greatly extended the field of statutory implied terms. The Act introduced statutory implied terms for (1) contracts for the supply of goods, being (a) contracts for the transfer of property in goods (other than contracts, such as contracts of sale of goods and contracts of hire-purchase, already covered by statutes) and (b) contracts for the hire of goods; and (2) contracts for the supply of services. (Group (1)(a) includes contracts for work and materials.) It is noteworthy that in contracts for the supply of goods (both (1)(a) and (1)(b) above) the implied terms regarding quality and fitness impose strict liability,

69

whereas in contracts for the supply of services ((2) above) the implied terms regarding quality and fitness impose only negligence liability. An example of this last implied term is to be found in *Wilson v. Best Travel Ltd* (1993), a case in which a tourist suffered serious injuries whilst staying in a hotel on a holiday booked through the defendant tour operators. The court said that the duty of care owed by a tour operator to its customers under the Act was a duty to exercise reasonable care to exclude from the accommodation offered any hotel whose characteristics were such that guests could not spend a holiday there in reasonable safety.

CHAPTER SIX

EXEMPTION CLAUSES

AN exemption clause is a term in a contract which tries to exempt one of the parties from liability in certain events. The principles involved also apply to limitation clauses, which are clauses which seek to limit (rather than wholly exclude) a party's liability, and clauses which provide that complaints must be made within a certain period of time.

An exemption clause may be a perfectly legitimate device in contracts between parties of equal bargaining power. But where the parties are unequal, such a clause may work injustice. This is particularly so in what are called Standard Form Contracts. They usually arise where there is a monopoly or near monopoly, or where there is a strong trade association. Fields in which standard exemption clauses operate include travel by air, carriage of goods and insurance. In these and other fields, the contracts are sometimes called "contracts of adhesion".

A party wishing to rely on an exemption clause must show that it was a term of the contract, and that, properly construed, it covers the loss or damage which has occurred. Even if he can show both these things, the clause may still fail for one or more of several possible reasons. These matters will be examined in turn: term of the contract; construction; possible causes of failure.

It should be borne in mind that in very many (but not all) contracts, exemption clauses may fail because of the effect of the Unfair Contract Terms Act 1977 (see below, pp. 83), which is considered more fully later in the chapter. At that point, the relevant European legislation will be looked at: the Council Directive on Unfair Terms in Consumer Contracts (93/13 [1993] O.J. L95/29).

TERM OF THE CONTRACT

An exemption clause may become a term of the contract by signature or by notice.

Signature

If a person signs a contractual document he is bound by its terms, including any exemption clause it may contain, even if he does not read the document. In *L'Estrange v. Graucob* (1934) the plaintiff, who was a cafe proprietress, bought a cigarette vending machine. She signed, without reading, a "sales agreement" which contained a number of clauses "in regrettably small print but quite legible". The machine did not work properly. The defendants were held to be protected by a clause which excluded their liability.

Notice

If the contractual document is not signed, the question of notice arises. The exemption clause may be printed on a document which is handed to one party by the other or is posted up in the shop or booking hall or other place where the contract is made. In such a case the clause will only be incorporated into the contract, so as to become a term of it, if (a) the party affected knows of the clause or (b) reasonable steps are taken to bring it to his notice.

It is worth pointing out at this stage that there is no special magic relating to exemption clauses in this respect. An express clause of any kind will only be effective if it is incorporated into the contract. All the points considered below as to how it may become incorporated apply to any kind of clause: Was the clause contained in a signed contract? If not, was it contained in a document which was clearly meant to have contractual force? Was reasonably sufficient notice of it given? Was it given in time?

What kind of document?

The exemption clause will only be effective if it is contained in a document which is part of the contract. If the person concerned knew that the document was intended to form part of the contract, he is bound; if he did not know, then the test is whether a reasonable person would have taken the document to be a contractual document, as distinct from (for example) a mere receipt. In *Chapelton v. Barry U.D.C.* (1940, C.A.) the plaintiff hired a deck-chair at the seaside, and he was handed a ticket for which he paid 2d. On the back of the ticket it was stated that the Council were not to be liable in the event of "any accident or damage arising from the hire of the chair". When he sat on the chair, it collapsed and he was injured. The exemption was held not to protect the Council; the ticket was a mere receipt. On the other hand, a prominently displayed notice is capable of being a contractual document.

What degree of notice?

There is a large number of decided cases on this topic, often referred to as "the ticket cases". The guiding principle, however, can be deduced from one case, *Parker v. South Eastern Railway* (1877, C.A.). The plaintiff left a bag in a railway cloakroom. He paid 2d. for a ticket. On the front of the ticket were a number, a date, the opening times of the office, and the words "see back". On the back of the ticket was a clause (amongst others) stating: "The company will not be responsible for any package exceeding the value of £10." The plaintiff, later that day, presented his ticket, but the bag could not be found. He claimed £24 10s. as the value of the bag. The company pleaded the exemption clause. The jury were asked two questions: (1) Did the plaintiff read the clause? and (2) Was he under any obligation to read it? The jury answered "No" to both questions. The Court of Appeal ordered a new trial; the jury had been asked the wrong question; the correct second question (assuming the plaintiff had not read the clause) was: Did the railway company do what was reasonably sufficient to give the plaintiff notice of the clause? This case was applied by the Court of Appeal in *Interfoto Picture Library Ltd v. Stiletto Visual Programmes Ltd* (1988), where in fact an exclusion clause was not involved. The court made it clear that, where a condition in a contract is particularly onerous or unusual and would not generally be known to the other party, the person wishing to enforce the condition must show that it was fairly and reasonably brought to the other party's attention. It is clear that the restrictive approach to incorporation take in *Parker's* case, above, is still followed.

Most of the cases turn on such matters as what was said and done when the contract was entered into, what was on the front of the ticket, what was on the back of the ticket, whether the ticket was folded, whether the clause was obliterated by a date stamp, and whether the clause was buried in a mass of advertisements. But sometimes the decisive point lies in earlier dealing between the parties. In *Kendall v. Lillico* (1969, H.L.) the sellers sold some goods to the buyers under an oral contract and the next day sent them a "sold note" containing an exemption clause. As this "sold note" came after the contract had been made, it was too late to be of any effect. (On this, see below.) But there had been a consistent course of dealing between the parties over the previous three years, involving some 100 similar contracts, during which the sellers had, after each oral contract, sent the buyers a "sold note" containing the same clause. The House of Lords held that, before the instant contract, reasonable notice of the exemption clause had been given. The same result may be reached even where there have been no previous dealings between the parties, provided that the parties are in the same line of business and know that similar clauses are in common use in the business: see *British Crane Hire Corporation Ltd v. Ipswich Plant Hire Ltd* (1975, C.A.).

When was the notice given?

An exemption clause becomes a term of the contract only if notice of it is given before, or at the time of, contracting. In *Olley v. Marlborough Court Ltd* (1949, C.A.) a guest booked in at the reception desk of an hotel and paid for a week's stay. She then went up to the bedroom. On its wall was a notice stating that the hotel would not be liable for articles lost or stolen unless handed in for safe custody. She left her furs in the bedroom, closed the self-locking door and hung the key on a board in the reception office. The furs were stolen. The exemption clause did not help the defendants, because the contract was made at the reception desk and the plaintiff did not see, and could not have seen, the exemption clause until later. That subsequent notice could not affect her rights; it was simply not part of the contract.

In relation to exemption clauses, it may be very important to determine when the contract was made. The cases show that where a ticket (for example, a railway ticket) is bought at a booking office, the request of the passenger is thought of as an invitation to treat, the clerk's handing out of the ticket as an offer, and the passenger's paying the fare as an acceptance. In *Thornton v. Shoe Lane Parking* (1971, C.A.) the Court of Appeal had to deal with a case where the ticket was dispensed by an unattended machine. Lord Denning said that in such a case the offer lay in the sign "Parking" on the outside of the garage, and the acceptance lay in the customer's placing his car on the spot which caused the machine to operate. Conditions printed on the ticket which was then given out to the customer by the machine came too late.

74

CONSTRUCTION OF EXEMPTION CLAUSES

To construe means to interpret; construction means interpretation. This is a task which faces a court when dealing with any written contractual term. It is not possible here to go into all the rules of construction. Two rules are of particular importance in construing exemption clauses: (1) the *contra proferentem* rule and (2) the main purpose rule. At one time some judges tended to construe exemption clauses in isolation. In *Photo Productions Ltd v. Securicor Transport Ltd* (1980, H.L.) that idea was exploded; what has to be construed is the whole contract including any exemption clause.

Contra Proferentem Rule

This rule is to the effect that any ambiguity, or other doubt, in an exemption clause must be resolved against the person who is seeking to rely on it; that is, against the person who is proffering it. In *Baldry v. Marshall* (1925, C.A.) the plaintiff asked the defendants, who were motor dealers, for a car "suitable for touring purposes". The defendants suggested that a Bugatti car would be appropriate. After delivery it was found to be remarkably unsuitable for touring purposes, and the plaintiff sued to get his money back. The written contract included a guarantee for 12 months against mechanical defects, but expressly excluded "any other guarantee or warranty, statutory or otherwise". The Court of Appeal held that the stipulation for suitability for touring purposes was a condition, not a warranty, and that therefore the exemption clause did not apply.

In *Andrews v. Singer* (1934, C.A.) the plaintiffs contracted to buy some "new Singer cars" from the defendants. By a clause in the written contract "all conditions, warranties and liabilities, implied by statute, common law or otherwise" were excluded. One of the cars, when delivered, turned out to be a used car. The plaintiffs sued for damages and won. The Court of Appeal held that though the term "new Singer car" was a condition, it was not an implied, but an express, condition, and therefore the exemption clause did not apply to it, since it was expressed only to protect the sellers from liability for breach of implied conditions.

In *L'Estrange v. Graucob* (above, p. 72), however, the seller defeated even the ingenuity of the Court of Appeal. The clause there in issue stated that "any express or implied condition, statement or warranty, statutory or otherwise, is hereby excluded". That comprehensive clause successfully protected the defendant seller. The *contra proferentem* rule could not help the buyer.

Liability for negligence

A very important aspect of the *contra proferentem* rule is that very clear words must be used before a party will be held to be exempt from liability for negligence.

We saw at the end of Chapter 5, that, by an implied term, a contractor is sometimes held to have a strict liability and is sometimes held to have only negligence liability. If there is any doubt whether the words of an exemption clause exclude liability for negligence, they will be held to do so only if that is the only liability that the party has. In *Alderslade v. Hendon Laundry* (1945, C.A.) the defendants contracted to launder the plaintiff's handkerchiefs. The contract limited their liability for lost or damaged articles to 20 times the laundering charge. (This is a good example of a limitation clause, as distinct from a complete exemption clause.) The handkerchiefs were lost through the defendants' negligence. The Court of Appeal held that the limitation clause must apply, because if it did not apply to negligence liability it would "lack subject-matter"; there was no other liability it could apply to, since the launderers did not have strict liability. On the other hand, a contractor may be under a strict liability, as in *White v. John Warwick & Co. Ltd* (1953, C.A.) where the plaintiff hired a tradesman's cycle from the defendants. The written agreement stated that "nothing in this agreement shall render the owners liable for any personal injuries". While the plaintiff was riding the cycle, the saddle tilted forward and he was injured. The Court of Appeal held that the clause did not protect the owners. They were under strict liability as well as negligence liability. The somewhat vague wording of the clause was sufficient to exclude their strict liability but not their negligence liability.

But it must be remembered that this is only a rule of construction. If the words are clear enough, an exemption clause can exclude negligence liability as well as strict liability. On the other hand, if the words used are very unclear, they will not protect the contractor against negligence liability even where negligence is the only possible ground of liability. See

Hollier v. Rambler Motors (1972, C.A.). The decision of the House of Lords in *Scottish Special Housing Association v. Wimpey Construction UK Ltd* (1986) suggests a move away from the rather technical rules set out above. In that case, the relevant exclusion clause made no mention of the word "negligence". Despite that omission, the House of Lords held that, on its true construction, the clause excluded liability for negligence.

In this field there is a kind of borderland between contract and tort. The negligence liability in a contract overlaps with negligence as a tort. A party to a contract cannot defeat an exemption clause by threatening to sue in tort. If an exemption clause does protect a defendant from liability for contractual negligence, it equally protects him from liability for tortious negligence.

Where the Unfair Contract Terms Act 1977 applies, that Act lays additional restrictions on a party's ability to protect himself from liability for negligence whether contractual or tortious: see p. 83, below.

Main Purpose Rule

In *Glynn v. Margetson* (1893, H.L.) Lord Halsbury said: "Looking at the whole of the instrument, and seeing what one must regard . . . as its main purpose, one must reject words, indeed whole provisions, if they are inconsistent with what one assumes to be the main purpose of the contract." In that case oranges were to be carried by ship from Malaga to Liverpool. The bill of lading contained a clause permitting the ship to call at almost any port in Europe or Africa. The ship went east from Malaga, then back again, and only then to Liverpool. When it docked, the oranges were found to have deteriorated because of the delay. The carrier was held liable in spite of the permissive clause. The wide words of the clause must be cut down so as not to defeat the main object and intent of the contract, the carriage of oranges from Malaga to Liverpool. The clause only justified the carrier in calling at ports on the route between those places.

The "main purpose rule", then, is that in construing an exemption clause there is a presumption that it was not intended to defeat the main purpose of the contract. The rule was endorsed by the House of Lords in *Suisse Atlantique Societe d'Armement Maritime S.A. v. N.V. Rotterdamsche Kolen Centrale* (1967, H.L.). There is no doubt that the main purpose rule is a powerful instrument for limiting the effect of exemption clauses.

Section 3 of the Unfair Contract Terms Act 1977 (where it applies) gives statutory support to the "main purpose rule".

Fundamental Breach

In the years before 1967 there grew up what appeared to be a substantive rule of law that if a party committed a fundamental breach of his contract he was not entitled to rely on any exemption clause in the contract. In that year the *Suisse Atlantique* case (1967, H.L.) was decided by the House of Lords. Their Lordships "decided" (though, strictly, what they said on this point was *obiter*) that there is no rule of law that an exemption clause can never apply where there has been a fundamental breach; it is simply a question of construction whether an exemption clause applies in the events that have happened.

In *Photo Productions Ltd v. Securicor Transport Ltd* (1980, H.L.) the House of Lords reaffirmed the law as stated in *Suisse Atlantique*. In the *Photo Productions* case the plaintiffs were a company which owned a factory. They entered into a contract with the defendants, a security company, whereby the defendants were to provide a visiting patrol at night and at weekends. One Sunday night the duty patrol, one Musgrove, lit a small fire inside the factory; the fire got out of control, and the factory and its stock, worth together £615,000, were completely destroyed. The plaintiffs sued the defendants. The defendants relied on an exemption clause in the contract which provided: "Under no circumstances shall [Securicor] be responsible for any injurious act or default by any employee of [Securicor] unless such act or default could have been foreseen and avoided by the exercise of due diligence on the part of [Securicor] as his employer. . . ." The plaintiffs did not allege that Securicor were negligent in employing Musgrove. The House of Lords held that, although Securicor were in breach of their obligation to operate their service with due and proper regard to the safety and security of Photo Production's premises, all that the court had to do was to construe and apply the exemption clause; it was clear and unambiguous and it protected Securicor from liability. There was no question of Securicor being disqualified, because of their breach, from relying on the clause.

The *Photo Productions* case confirms that the question is simply one of construction: does the exemption clause cover the events which happened? On the whole, we can say that the more serious the breach (or the con-

78

sequences of the breach), the less likely is the court to interpret the exemption clause as applying to the breach. But it remains possible for a party to a contract to exclude liability for breach of a fundamental term or a breach which has serious consequences—*provided* that he uses clear words to cover the events which occur.

The contract in the *Photo Productions* case was made before the coming into force of the Unfair Contract Terms Act 1977 and so the Act did not apply, but it is interesting to note that the decision of the House of Lords is entirely in line with section 9(1) of the Act: see below.

POSSIBLE CAUSES OF FAILURE OF AN EXEMPTION CLAUSE

Even where an exemption clause is undoubtedly a term of the contract, and even where, on its true construction, it covers the loss or damage which has occurred, it may yet fail. Five possible causes of failure will be discussed here.

1. Misrepresentation

In *L'Estrange v. Graucob* (above) Scrutton L.J. said: "When a document containing contractual terms is signed, then in the absence of fraud, or . . . misrepresentation, the party signing it is bound, and it is wholly immaterial whether he has read the document or not." In *Curtis v. Chemical Cleaning and Dyeing Co.* (1951, C.A.) the plaintiff took to the defendants' shop a white satin wedding dress to have it cleaned. The dress was trimmed with beads and sequins. The shop assistant gave her a form to sign. The plaintiff asked what it was all about. The assistant replied that it exempted the company from the risk of damage to the beads and sequins. The plaintiff then signed the form, which in fact contained a clause stating that the company was not to be liable for any damage, however caused. When the dress was returned it was found to be stained. The plaintiff sued for damages and the defendants sought to rely on the clause. Following the observation of Scrutton L.J. in *L'Estrange v. Graucob*, the Court of Appeal held that the defendants could not rely on the clause, because the assistant had misrepresented its effect. There was no suggestion of fraud. Of course, if there were fraud, then the clause would certainly fail.

2. Overriding Oral Undertaking

Evans (J.) & Son (Portsmouth) Ltd v. Andrea Merzario Ltd (1976, C.A.) illustrates this point. The plaintiffs were importers of machines from Italy. The defendants were forwarding contractors. The course of dealing between the parties was on the standard conditions of the forwarding trade. Until 1967 the defendants had arranged for transportation of the plaintiff's goods in crates under deck, because the machines were liable to rust if carried on deck. In 1967 the defendants proposed to change over to transportation in containers. The defendants gave the plaintiffs an oral assurance that machines subsequently transported in containers would be shipped under deck. On the faith of that oral assurance, the plaintiffs agreed to the change-over to container transport, and gave the defendants an order for the carriage of a machine in a container. Because of an error on the part of the defendants, the container was shipped at Rotterdam on deck. The container fell off the deck and was lost overboard. The printed standard conditions of the forwarding trade which were incorporated into the contract gave the defendants complete freedom in respect of the means and procedure to be followed in the transportation of the goods, and contained exemption and limitation clauses. The plaintiffs sued for breach of contract and the defendants relied on the printed conditions. The Court of Appeal held unanimously that the oral undertaking overrode such of the clauses of the printed conditions as were repugnant to it. The majority of the court reached this decision on the ground that the oral undertaking constituted a term of the main contract. Lord Denning, though reaching the same decision, did so on the ground that the oral undertaking formed part of a collateral contract. (See below.)

3. Collateral Contract

The collateral contract device (see pp. 59–61 *et seq.*) may, on occasion, neutralise an exemption clause. In *Webster v. Higgin* (1948, C.A.) the plaintiff was a garage proprietor. His agent said to the defendant: "If you buy the Hillman 10 we will guarantee that it is in good condition." The defendant then entered into a hire-purchase contract with the plaintiff, and the contract contained an exemption clause. When the car was delivered it was not in a very good state; it was, in Lord Greene's words "nothing but a mass of second-hand and dilapidated ironmongery''. Not unnaturally, the defendant did not pay the instalments. The plaintiff sued for the return of the car and for the instalments due. The Court of Appeal held that the exemption clause in the main (H.P.) contract did not affect the "guarantee" in the previous (collateral) contract. The effect of the judgment was that the defendant could return the car and get back his deposit money.

In *Wester v. Higgin* the main contract and the collateral contract were both between the same parties. But the same principle can work where this is not so. In *Andrews v. Hopkinson* (1957) the plaintiff wanted a second-hand car. The defendant car dealer recommended one, using these words: "It's a good little bus. I would stake my life on it." The plaintiff agreed to take it on hire-purchase. The normal arrangements were made: the dealer sold the car to a finance company and the finance company let it on hire-purchase terms to the customer, the plaintiff. When the finance company delivered the car, the plaintiff signed a delivery note stating that he was "satisfied as to its condition". A week later the car suddenly swerved into a lorry; the car was wrecked and the plaintiff was seriously injured. It was established that the car had a long-standing fault in the steering. The terms of the delivery note might well have prevented the plaintiff from suing the finance company, but he sued the dealer for breach of the collateral contract, the "good little bus" contract, and obtained damages.

The collateral contract device does not, strictly speaking, cause the exemption clause to fail. The exemption clause does not itself fail, but it fails to prevent the plaintiff from getting a remedy.

4. Third Parties

A "third party" is a person who is not a party to a contract. Chapter 13 deals with the doctrine of privity of contract at greater length. Stated shortly, the doctrine is that a person who is not a party to a contract cannot benefit from the contract or suffer from it. This applies as much to an exemption clause as to any other kind of clause. The leading authority on the application of the doctrine to exemption clauses is *Scruttons Ltd v. Midland Silicones Ltd* (1962, H.L.). A drum of chemicals belonging to Midland Silicones was shipped from the United States to England. The contract of carriage limited the liability of the carrier to $500 per packet. (So it was a limitation clause, not an exemption clause, but the principles are the same.) The drum was damaged to the extent of £593, through the negligence of a company of stevedores (Scruttons), whom the carriers had employed to unload the ship. It was held by the House of Lords that the stevedores could not rely on the limitation clause in the contract of carriage, because they were not parties to that contract. It was also said that the stevedores could not rely on a similar limitation clause contained in the contract between the stevedores and the carrier. It should be noted that there were two contracts. The case decides that C cannot take the benefit of an exemption clause contained in a contract between A and B; and it assumes that C cannot impose on A the burden of an exemption clause contained in a contract between C and B.

An important point to grasp is that an employee is a third party in this context so that, even if his employer has a perfectly good exemption clause, the employee cannot benefit from it. In *Cosgrove v. Horsfall* (1945, C.A.) a person was travelling on a bus under a free pass which contained a term that neither the London Passenger Transport Board nor its servants would be liable to him for injury, however caused. The passenger was injured through the negligence of the bus driver. The passenger could not, or at any rate did not, sue the L.P.T.B., because of the exemption clause. But he successfully sued the driver. The driver was not a party to the licence or contract, and so could not rely on its exemption clause. This was so, even though the clause had expressly mentioned the Board's "servants".

A way round *Scruttons Ltd v. Midland Silicones Ltd* has been opened up by a decision of the Privy Council on appeal from New Zealand, *New Zealand Shipping Co. Ltd v. A.M. Satterthwaite & Co. Ltd (The Eurymedon)* (1975, P.C.). In that case the Privy Council, by a majority of three to two, held that the benefit of an exemption clause in a contract of carriage can be claimed by a stevedore provided that four conditions are satisfied: (1) the contract of carriage makes it clear that the stevedore is intended to be protected; (2) the contract of carriage makes it clear that the carrier is contracting not only on his own behalf but also as agent for the stevedore; (3) the carrier has authority from the stevedore so to contract; and (4) there is some consideration moving from the stevedore. In the instant case the consideration was held to be the performance of the unloading services by the stevedore. It did not matter that the stevedore was already under a contractual obligation to the carrier to perform unloading services. The case of *Scotson v. Pegg* (see p. 37, above) was expressly approved.

82

5. Legislation

Before the Unfair Contract Terms Act 1977, the legislature intervened in a modest way to control exemption clauses in some specific fields. That Act, however, was a massive intervention over a very wide field.

Examples of previous statutory intervention are to be found in section 149 of the Road Traffic Act 1988 (as it now is), which dealt with an agreement or undertaking between the user of a motor vehicle and a passenger seeking to restrict any liability of the user towards the passenger; section 29 of the Public Passenger Vehicles Act 1981, which makes void any provision in a contract which seeks to exclude or limit liability for death or personal injury of a passenger in a public service vehicle; and the Carriage of Goods by Sea Act 1971 (as amended), which makes it impossible for a sea carrier of goods to exclude liability for negligence under a contract to which the Act applies. Section 3 of the Misrepresentation Act 1967 stated that a provision in an agreement which sought to exclude or restrict liability for misrepresentation was to have effect only to the extent that a court thought fair and reasonable. The wording was slightly altered by the Unfair Contract Terms Act 1977. Misrepresentation will be looked at in Chapter 8.

Unfair Contract Terms Act 1977

The Unfair Contract Terms Act 1977 came into force on February 1, 1978, and does not apply to contracts made before that date. Despite its title, it deals with unfair exemption clauses, not all unfair contract terms.

In order to understand the Act it is first necessary to study two definitions, "business liability" and "deals as consumer". This is because most of the provisions in the Act apply only to business liability and because a consumer has a specially favoured status under the Act. "Business liability" is liability arising from things done by a person in the course of a business or from the occupation of business premises: see section 1(3). A person "deals as consumer" (see s. 12) if he does not make (or hold himself out as making) the contract in the course of a business and the other party does make the contract in the course of a business. If the contract is for the supply of goods, there is an additional point, that the goods must be of a type ordinarily supplied for private use or consumption. One effect of this definition is that where a non-business person contracts with another non-business person (*e.g.* in selling a second-hand car) neither party "deals as consumer".

83

The main provisions of the Act are as follows:

(1) Liability (that is, business liability) for death or personal injury resulting from negligence cannot be excluded or restricted by any contract term or notice: section 2(1).

(2) In the case of other loss or damage a person cannot so exclude or restrict his (business) liability for negligence except in so far as the term or notice satisfies the requirement of reasonableness: section 2(2). The requirement of reasonableness "is that the term shall have been a fair and reasonable one to be included having regard to the circumstances which were, or ought reasonably to have been, known to or in the contemplation of the parties when the contract was made": see section 11(1). Guidelines for the application of the reasonableness test are laid down in section 11(4) and (so far as concerns the supply of goods) in Schedule 2.

An example of the application of these provisions is the case of *Phillips Products Ltd v. Hyland and Hamstead Plant Hire Co. Ltd* (1987, C.A.), where the second defendants, Hamstead Hire, hired an excavator plus driver (the first defendant) to the plaintiffs. Condition 8 of the contract of hire provided that the driver was to be regarded as the employee of the hirers; they were to be responsible for all claims arising in connection with the operation of the excavator by the driver. An accident occurred as a result of the driver's negligence; the plaintiff's factory suffered considerable damage. So they sued the driver and the hire company, which relied on condition 8. The plaintiff argued that the condition did not cover the driver's negligence; alternatively, if it did, it was caught by section 2(2) of the Act and failed to satisfy the requirement of reasonableness. The hire company argued that the condition did not exclude or restrict liability; rather, it transferred liability to the hirers. The Court of Appeal rejected this argument and held the defendants liable. They said that the court must look at the substance and effect of the term rather than its form. Here, the effect of condition 8 was to negative a common law duty in tort which would otherwise have fallen on the hire company. This meant that the condition had the effect of excluding liability and so fell within section 2(2).

This case may be contrasted with the later case of *Thompson v. T. Lohan (Plant Hire) Ltd and J. W. Hurdiss Ltd* (1987, C.A.), which was decided by a different division of the Court of Appeal. The facts were similar to those of the preceding case; the condition in question was a new version of condition 8, but the variations are not significant for the purposes of the decision. The accident in this case occurred as a result of the driver's negligence, which caused the death of a fellow employee, the plaintiff.

The first defendants were the driver's general employers; the second defendants were the hirers. The plaintiff's widow sued the first defendants successfully; they then claimed that they should be indemnified by the second defendants (in other words, they wanted the second defendants to meet their liability to the plaintiff). The second defendants argued that condition 8 was contrary to section 2(1) of the Act. The Court of Appeal said that it was not. They said that section 2(1) was intended to prevent the restriction or exclusion of liability in relation to the victim of negligence and was not concerned with arrangements made by a wrongdoer with others for sharing or transferring the burden of compensating the victim. Condition 8 was therefore effective to transfer the liability for the driver's negligence to the second defendants.

The important distinction between the two cases is that in the *Phillips Products* case there was an attempt to exclude liability towards the victim, whereas in *Thompson's* case there was no such attempt.

(3) When one party deals as consumer or on the other party's written standard terms of business, that other party cannot (a) when himself in breach of contract, exclude or restrict his (business) liability in respect of the breach, or (b) claim to be entitled to render a contractual performance substantially different from that which was reasonably expected of him, or (c) claim to be entitled to render no performance at all, except (in all these cases) subject to the requirement of reasonableness: see section 3. This section applies to strict liability as well as liability for negligence.

(4) In contracts for the sale and hire-purchase of goods, implied terms as to title cannot be excluded at all; implied terms as to conformity of goods with description or sample or as to their quality or fitness for a particular purpose cannot be excluded as against a person dealing as consumer, and, as against non-consumers, can only be excluded subject to the requirement of reasonableness (section 6). This section is not confined to business liability.

(5) For other contracts under which possession or ownership of goods passes (*e.g.* hire) there are similar (but not identical) rules in section 7.

(6) Where the requirement of reasonableness applies, a term which satisfied the requirement remains effective even though the contract has been terminated by breach or by a party electing to treat it as repudiated: section 9(1).

(7) Where on a breach the contract is nevertheless affirmed by a party entitled to treat it as repudiated, this does not of itself exclude the requirement of reasonableness: section 9(2).

The Act does not set up a generalised prohibition of exemption clauses or a generalised requirement of reasonableness. There are many contracts to which it does not apply or does not fully apply, such as contracts of insurance and contracts relating to the transfer of land. Thus, in *Electricity Supply Nominees Ltd v. IAF Group plc* (1993), the dispute was between a landlord and a tenant and concerned the terms of a covenant in a lease. The judge held that the lease was outside the provisions of the Act: see also section 1(2) and Schedule 1.

The Act leaves some uncertainty as to what clauses are caught as being exemption clauses. This is a difficult problem. Compare two contracts. Contract A provides: "I undertake to deliver the goods by November 30. If delivery is delayed by strikes I shall not be liable." Contract B provides: "I undertake (subject to strikes) to deliver the goods by November 30." In Contract A there is clearly an exemption clause, that is to say, a clause restricting the contractor's *liability*. In Contract B the same result is achieved by restricting the contractor's *duty*. Is that restriction controlled by the Act? Section 13 deals with the matter. It seems from that section that the restriction of duty in Contract B is subjected to many of the provisions of the Act but not to (the very important) section 3 (see point (3) above). See *Smith v. Eric S. Bush (a firm)* (1990); *Harris v. Wyre Forest District Council* (1989, H.L.) and *Stewart Gill Ltd v. Horatio Myer & Co. Ltd* (1992), where section 13 is considered.

A recent example of the problems of deciding whether a particular clause is an exemption clause or not is *St Albans City and District Council v. International Computers Ltd* (1994). The defendants, a computer company, had a contract with standard terms and conditions, one of which limited their liability for loss to £100,000. The company supplied software containing an error to the Council; as a consequence, the Council set its community charge too low. It suffered a loss of more than £1 million. The company tried to rely on the limitation of liability clause, but the judge said that this was an exclusion clause which was affected by section 3 of the Act, since the Council had dealt on the company's standard terms of business. He went on to hold that the term was not fair and reasonable. A particular factor he considered was that the company was able to insure itself against this type of loss, whereas if the loss fell on the Council it would ultimately be borne by the local population. He said that it was not unreasonable that the person who made the profit should also carry the risk. The practical consequences counted in the Council's favour.

As was mentioned earlier, the short title of the Act is misleading. The Act does not only apply to contract terms nor only to contractual liability; it applies also to non-contractual notices and to tortious liability. The Act does not affect at all the principles upon which a court is to decide whether a particular exemption clause is or is not a term of the contract. The Act does affect very considerably the construction of exemption clauses—if it applies. A court dealing with the matter will have to decide whether the Act knocks out a particular clause entirely or makes it subject to the test of reasonableness or leaves it untouched. The Act adopts the *contra proferentem* rule in regard to the requirement of reasonableness: section 11(5) declares: "It is for those claiming that a contract term or notice satisfies the requirement of reasonableness to show that it does." The main purpose rule is given statutory support by section 3(2)(b). Where it applies, section 9(1) of the Act (see point (6) above) reaches the same result as the House of Lords reached (without the aid of the Act) in the *Photo Productions* case (see p. 78 above), that breach (whether fundamental or not) does not put an end to an otherwise valid exemption clause; it simply remains to be construed. Section 9(2) of the Act (see point (7) above) is presumably designed to knock out any possibility of a kind of converse argument, namely an argument that, where a party who is entitled to treat a contract as repudiated chooses instead to affirm the contract, the other party is freed from an otherwise applicable requirement of reasonableness. In that case, it remains a question of construction as to whether the requirement of reasonableness is or is not fulfilled.

Council Directive on Unfair Terms in Consumer Contracts

The directive was adopted by the Member States of the E.U. on April 5, 1993. Under its terms, they are obliged to bring in laws complying with it by December 31, 1994. The United Kingdom has brought in the Unfair Terms in Consumer Contracts Regulations 1994 in compliance. The relevant provisions of the directive are considered briefly here.

The directive applies to unfair terms in non-negotiated contracts between a seller or supplier and a consumer and to both written and oral contracts. An "unfair term" is defined in Article 3 as a "contractual term which has not been individually negotiated" and which "contrary to the requirement of good faith, . . . causes a significant imbalance in the parties' rights and obligations under the contract, to the detriment of the consumer". Article 3(2) amplifies what is meant by a term being "not individually negotiated". The annex to the directive contains an indicative list of terms which may be regarded as unfair and includes terms such as a term which requires any consumer who fails to fulfil his obligation to pay a disproportionately high sum in compensation and a term obliging the consumer to fulfil all his obligations where the seller or supplier does not perform his.

The unfairness of a term must be assessed by taking into account the nature of the goods or services covered by the contract and the circumstances at the time the contract was concluded: Article 4. The terms must be drafted in plain, intelligible language: Article 5. Adequate and effective means must be ensured so as to prevent the continued use of unfair terms, including provisions by which consumer organisations may take action for decisions that contractual terms are unfair.

The directive has been implemented by the Unfair Terms in Consumer Contracts Regulations 1994 (S.I. 1994 No. 3159), which came into effect on July 1, 1995.

PART THREE

DEFECTS IN THE BOND

In this Part of the book we shall be considering various factors which may make a contract to some extent defective. There are different degrees of defectiveness, represented by the words "unenforceable", "voidable", "void" and "illegal". In reading the chapters which follow the reader is advised to have these words well in mind.

CHAPTER SEVEN

ABSENCE OF REQUIRED FORMALITY

IN general, contracts can be made quite informally and writing is not usually necessary; a spoken word will do. But a few contracts require certain formalities. These are considered here.

DEEDS

A seal is no longer necessary for the valid execution of an instrument as a deed, as was seen in Chapter 2. The rule was abolished by section 1(1)(b) of the Law of Property (Miscellaneous Provisions) Act 1989. For a discussion of the relevant provisions, see p. 45.

CONTRACTS WHICH MUST BE IN WRITING

There are a few contracts which are required by statute to be in writing. Amongst these are share transfers, bills of exchange, promissory notes and certain consumer credit agreements, including regulated hire-purchase agreements. The most important contracts in this category are contracts relating to land.

Contracts relating to land are now governed by section 2 of the Law of Property (Miscellaneous Provisions) Act 1989, which came into effect on September 27, 1989. Section 2(1) stipulates that a contract for the sale (or other disposition) of an interest in land may only be made in writing; all the terms which the parties have expressly agreed must be incorporated in one document, or, where contracts are exchanged, in each document. It is possible for the terms of the agreement to be incorporated in the document by reference to some other document: see section 2(2). Further, the document incorporating the terms must be signed by or on behalf of each party to the contract: section 2(3). Where contracts are exchanged, the same document need not bear the signatures of both parties, who may sign separately.

The provisions of section 2(2) were considered in *Record v. Bell* (1991), a case which involved a letter of variation containing additional terms. The judge said that the letter could only be incorporated into the contract if the contract referred to or identified it. It could not be done by the letter referring to the contract. In this case, the letter of variation was attached to one of the contracts but not the other. The judge suggested that, had it been attached to both, section 2 would have been satisfied. He went on to hold, however, that there was a collateral contract. This was on the basis that the letter of variation was an offer of a warranty by the vendor's solicitor to the purchaser's solicitor as to the state of the title to induce him to exchange and that the offer was accepted by the exchange of contracts.

In *Tootal Clothing Ltd v. Guinea Properties Ltd* (1992), the landlord agreed, during negotiations for a lease of premises, to contribute to the cost of shop-fitting works. The lease did not mention that the landlord would contribute to the shop-fitting works. However, a second agreement was entered into on the same day as the lease agreement. This stated that it was supplemental to the lease agreement and that the landlord would contribute to the cost of the shop-fitting. The agreement was duly signed by both parties. When the work had been completed, the tenant asked for payment of the landlord's contribution , but the landlord refused on the grounds that section 2 barred recovery. The Court of Appeal held that section 2 only applies to executory land contracts and that, once the land contract had been executed by completion, the section had no further relevance to the enforceability of the supplemental agreement. Scott L.J. said that there was nothing to prevent the enforceability of such an agreement if parties chose to hive off part of the terms of their agreement into a separate contract distinct from the written land contract. This decision appears to be contrary to the intention, as expressed in section 2(1), that the terms of a land contract should be incorporated in that contract.

The grant of an option to purchase land falls within the scope of section 2; the exercise of the option, however, does not and so does not need to be signed by both parties: see *Spiro v. Glencrown Properties Ltd* (1991). The Act does not apply to lock-out agreements: see *Pitt v. PHH Asset Management Ltd* (1993); see also p. 25.

Certain types of contract are excluded from the operation of section 2 and need not be in writing: (1) contracts to grant a lease for a term of less than three years; (2) contracts made in the course of a public auction;

and (3) contracts regulated under the Financial Services Act 1986. See section 2(5).

Section 2(6) defines "interest in land" as meaning "any estate, interest or charge in or over land or in or over the proceeds of sale of land". This is a wide definition which embraces contracts to create an interest in land (*e.g.* a right of way), options and commercial contracts which affect land.

Non-compliance with the requirements of section 2 of the 1989 Act will mean that the contract will be completely invalid; in effect there will be no contract. It may be that incomplete compliance with section 2 will make an agreement enforceable in equity. But this will only be possible if what has happened will persuade a court that the situation should be treated as giving rise to an implied, resulting or constructive trust. The creation and operation of such trusts is expressly preserved by section 2(5) of the Act. This is not the place to consider the complex rules relating to such trusts, which should be pursued in a book on trusts.

CONTRACTS WHICH MUST BE EVIDENCED IN WRITING

There is a distinction between a requirement that a contract must be in writing and a requirement that a contract must be evidenced in writing. The first requirement can only be met by the making of a complete contract in writing; the second requirement can be met by something much less formal, as will be discussed below.

The Statute of Frauds

The Statute of Frauds 1677 required six classes of contracts to be evidenced in writing. The object of the Statute was to prevent frauds. The idea was that if a plaintiff was required to produce written evidence of the promise on which he was suing, that would shut out fraudulent claims based on perjured oral evidence. But the Statute tended in practice to produce as many frauds as it prevented. After all, though the requirement of written evidence made life difficult for fraudulent plaintiffs, it made it easy for fraudulent defendants. Consequently, judges tried to find ways of holding that the Statute did not apply; in 1954 the legislature passed the Law Reform (Enforcement of Contracts) Act, which reduced from six to two the classes of contract affected: contracts of guarantee, and contracts relating to land. This latter class is now further affected by the Law of Property (Miscellaneous Provisions) Act 1989 and is considered above.

Guarantees

Section 4 of the Statute of Frauds states: "No action shall be brought whereby to charge ... the defendant upon any special promise to answer for the debt, default or miscarriages of another person; ... unless the agreement upon which such action shall be brought, or some memorandum or note thereof, shall be in writing and signed by the party to be charged therewith or some other person thereunto by him lawfully authorised." It is not necessary that the agreement should itself be in writing; it is sufficient if there is a signed note or memorandum in writing, containing all the material terms. In the case of a note or memorandum of the agreement, the intention or capacity of the person signing the memorandum is irrelevant: see *Elpis Maritime Co. Ltd v. Marti Chartering Co. Inc., The Maria D* (1992, H.L.).

So the class of contract involved is that in which there is a promise "to answer for the debt, default or miscarriages of another person", that is the *liabilities* of that other person. Such a promise is a guarantee. A typical example is the guarantee of a bank overdraft, a loan from a bank to a customer. If A's father (B) undertakes to A's bank (C) that he, B, will hold himself responsible if A does not pay off his overdraft when requested, B is guaranteeing A's overdraft. There are three parties, A, B and C: the primary debtor is A; B will be liable only if A does not pay; C is the creditor. It should be noted that B makes his promise to C, the creditor. If B makes his promise to A, the debtor, that is not a guarantee within the Statute of Frauds. Also notice the form of B's promise: he promises that A will pay. If A does not pay, B becomes liable. If B promises C to pay off A's overdraft on request, that is not a guarantee but an indemnity, and is not within the Statute. That is because such a promise is not a promise to answer for the debt of another; it is a promise to pay a debt which the promisor is adopting as his own. For the same reason a guarantee (so-called) given by, for example, the manufacturer of a washing machine, is not within the Statute.

The next point to notice is that a guarantee is caught by the Statute only if it stands alone. Thus, if a guarantee is given as part of a larger transaction, the Statute does not apply. An example is to be found in what is called *del credere* agency. Suppose an agent is employed to sell goods on behalf of a principal; he may promise, for an extra commission, that if any particular buyer should fail to pay for goods, he (the agent) will make up the loss to the principal. Such an agent is a *del credere* agent. It is true that he enters into a contract of guarantee with his principal, but it has been held that, because that contract is only a part of the larger contract of agency, it is not within the Statute. See, for example, *Couturier v. Hastie* (1852).

Another aspect of the same principle is that, where an owner of property gives a guarantee in order to protect that property, the Statute does not apply. Thus in *Fitzgerald v. Dressler* (1859) C sold goods to A; A resold them to B at a higher price. C held a lien on the goods (that is, he was entitled to keep them until he was paid by A). B wanted to get possession of the goods, so he made an (oral) promise to C that, in return for C handing over the goods, he (B) would pay A's debt if A did not pay. It was held that the Statute did not apply, and that B was bound by his promise though it was not evidenced in writing. (C failed on another point, but that is not relevant here.)

The vast majority of guarantees are given in respect of contractual liabilities, but it has been held that the word "miscarriages" in the Statute is apt to include tortious liabilities. In *Kirkham v. Marter* (1819) A rode the plaintiff's horse without permission and killed it. The plaintiff threatened to sue A in tort. B, A's father, promised the plaintiff to pay him the agreed value of the horse if the plaintiff would drop his action. It was held that B's promise, which was oral, was not enforceable because of the Statute.

If the Statute of Frauds is not complied with the contract is unenforceable at law. In early days the contract was treated as void, but it has been settled law for over 100 years now that it is merely unenforceable. Thus, such a contract cannot found an action at law for damages, but it can be relied on as a defence.

It may seem odd to speak of an "unenforceable contract". It is almost a contradiction in terms, since the essence of a contract is that it is an agreement enforceable at law. But the phrase "unenforceable contract" is, in this context, hallowed by usage.

It is worth pointing out that the Statute of Frauds has had an enormous effect on the development of contract law in general. For example, it has been closely intertwined with the development of the parol evidence rule and the doctrine of collateral contracts.

CHAPTER EIGHT

MISREPRESENTATION

IN the negotiations leading up to a contract, many statements may be made. Some of those statements will be incorporated into the final contract, thus becoming contractual terms. Other statements, though not incorporated into the main contract, may be held to constitute a collateral contract. Other statements may not be incorporated into any contract at all. If a statement becomes a term in a main contract or in a collateral contract and then turns out to be untrue, its untruth amounts to a breach of contract. The party who suffers by the untruth has a right of action for breach of contract. His exact rights will depend on how important the statement was (a "condition" or a "warranty" in traditional language) or how serious are the effects of the breach.

Some statements do not become terms of any contract at all— main or collateral. Such statements have sometimes been called "mere representations", but are better called non-contractual representations. If such a statement turns out to be untrue its untruth is not a breach of contract, but the innocent party does have some remedies, as will be seen.

A non-contractual representation which is untrue is a misrepresentation. There are three kinds of misrepresentation: fraudulent, negligent and innocent misrepresentations. The remedies for misrepresentation vary, depending on the state of mind of the representor. That is not the case with contractual misstatements; there the remedy is not affected at all by the innocence or otherwise of the defendant. A misrepresentation is an untrue statement made by one party to the other which induces him to enter into the contract.

This chapter will look first at the nature of the statement involved and then at the nature of the inducement. After that fraudulent, negligent and innocent misrepresentations, and their effects, will be examined.

Statement of Fact

A misstatement amounts to a misrepresentation only if it is a statement of fact.

Fact, not opinion

If the statement is a statement of opinion and not of fact that is not a misrepresentation. In *Bisset v. Wilkinson* (1927, P.C.), for example, Bisset was selling a holding in New Zealand to Wilkinson. The holding had not previously been used as a sheep farm, and Wilkinson knew this. Bisset said that the land would support 2,000 sheep. This was held to be a statement of opinion and not of fact. But a statement of opinion may involve a statement of fact by implication. This point is well illustrated by *Smith v. Land and House Property Corporation* (1884, C.A.). The vendor of an hotel described it as "let to Mr. Frederick Fleck (a most desirable tenant)". The tenant was in fact in arrears with his rent. It was held that the statement was not a mere expression of opinion because the vendor was impliedly stating "that he knows facts which justify his opinion". See also *Esso Petroleum Ltd v. Mardon* (1976, C.A.).

Fact, not intention

If the statement is a statement of intention and not of fact that is not a misrepresentation. But a statement of intention may involve a statement of fact. In *Edgington v. Fitzmaurice* (1885, C.A.) the directors of a company invited a loan from the public and stated that the money would be used to improve the company's buildings and to extend the business. The real intention of the directors was to use the money to pay off the company's existing debts. Their statement of intention was held to be also a statement of fact. Bowen L.J. said: "There must be a misstatement of an existing fact: but the state of a man's mind is as much a fact as the state of his digestion." The directors had made a misstatement of their present intention as to their future conduct. Similarly, in *Goff v. Gauthier* (1991), the defendants exchanged contracts when they were told by the plaintiff's solicitor that the sale would be called off if they did not do so and a contract for sale would be sent to another purchaser. There was in fact no

97

such purchaser. This was held to amount to a misstatement of fact as to the vendor's intention.

Fact, not law

If the statement is a statement of law and not of fact it is not a misrepresentation. That is an easy thing to say but extremely hard to apply. At first sight one would think that the statement "John and Mary are married" is a statement of fact. But it may be that John has been married before and that there is some doubt as to whether his previous marriage has been legally terminated. In view of that doubt, the statement that John and Mary are married begins to look like a statement of law. Probably a bald assertion that they are married, without mention of the doubt, is a statement of fact.

Silence as Misrepresentation

The general rule is that mere silence is not misrepresentation. For example, in *Fletcher v. Krell* (1873) a woman applied for a post of governess without revealing that she was a divorcee. It was held that that did not amount to misrepresentation.

There are situations, however, where a failure to speak does amount to misrepresentation.

Change of circumstances

In *With v. O'Flanagan* (1936, C.A.) the defendant wanted to sell his medical practice. Negotiations for the sale to the plaintiff began in January. The defendant said that the practice was worth £2,000 a year, which at that time it was. The defendant then fell ill, and by May 1, when the contract of sale was signed, the practice had become virtually worthless. It was held that the defendant's silence in the face of this development was a misrepresentation.

The truth but not the whole truth

In *Nottingham Patent Brick and Tile Co. v. Butler* (1886, C.A.) the purchaser of some land asked the vendor's solicitor whether the land was subject to restrictive covenants. The solicitor replied that he was not aware of any. He did not go on to explain why he was not aware of any; namely, that he had not bothered to read the relevant documents. It was held that the solicitor's statement, though literally true, amounted to a misrepresentation.

Contracts of the utmost good faith

There are some contracts, called contracts *uberrimae fidei*, in which there is a duty to disclose material facts. The reason for the rule is that they are contracts in which one party is in a particularly strong position, compared with the other party, to know the facts. An example of such a contract is an insurance contract. The duty of disclosure laid upon the insured is very heavy. He must disclose "all material facts"; that is, every circumstance "which would influence the judgment of a prudent insurer in fixing the premium or determining whether he will take the risk". In *Woodcott v. Sun Alliance and London Insurance Ltd* (1978), for example, a failure to disclose criminal convictions was held to be material to a contract of fire insurance, since they could affect the moral hazard which the insurers had to assess.

Some fiduciary relationships

A duty of disclosure may arise from the relationship of the parties. There are some relationships which require more than mere disclosure, where there is a fiduciary duty to make full disclosure of all material facts. This arises in the case of contracts between principal and agent, between partners, and between a solicitor and a client. The duty in this class of contract arises from the relationship of the parties, whereas in contracts *uberrimae fidei* the duty arises from the nature of the contract.

THE NATURE OF THE INDUCEMENT

A misstatement is a misrepresentation only if it induces the person to whom it is made to enter into a contract. It cannot be said to induce him if he does not rely on the misstatement. Thus, if a misstatement is made to a person, and that person then makes his own investigations to test the truth of the statement, he cannot claim relief on the ground of misrepresentation. Obviously he cannot if he discovers the truth, but the point is that he still cannot claim even if he does not discover the truth. In *Attwood v. Small* (1838, H.L.) a vendor offered to sell a mine and made exaggerated statements as to its capacity. The buyers appointed expert agents to investigate the mine. The agents reported (wrongly) that the statements were true. The contract of sale was then completed. It was then held that the buyers' subsequent action must fail because they had not relied on the vendor's statements, but on their own independent investigations.

On the other hand, if a person is given an opportunity to test the accuracy of a statement but does not take that opportunity, he is not shut out from relief. In *Redgrave v. Hurd* (1881, C.A.) a man was induced to buy a solicitor's practice by a misstatement of its value. He was given an opportunity to examine the accounts. If he had examined the accounts he would have discovered the truth. He did not examine them. The misstatement was held to be an operative misrepresentation.

If a misstatement is one of the factors that induces a person to enter into a contract, he can claim relief even though there were other inducing factors as well. In *Edgington v. Fitzmaurice* (1885, C.A., above) the plaintiff was induced to take debentures in a company, partly by a misstatement in the prospectus as to how the money was going to be used, and partly by his own incorrect belief that the debenture holders would have a charge on the company's property. He admitted that he would not have lent the money but for his own incorrect belief, but it was held that he was nevertheless entitled to claim the misstatement as an operative misrepresentation.

TYPES OF MISREPRESENTATION AND THEIR EFFECTS

There are three kinds of misrepresentation, depending upon whether the maker of the statement is fraudulent, negligent, or innocent.

Fraudulent Misrepresentation

In *Derry v. Peek* (1889, H.L.) it was decided by the House of Lords that a false statement is fraudulent at common law only if it is made (1) knowingly, or (2) without belief in its truth, or (3) recklessly, careless whether it be true or false.

A fraudulent misrepresentation makes a contract voidable. The party who has been misled may "avoid" the contract. He may also sue for damages. He is not suing for breach of contract; he is suing in tort. Fraud is a tort, in which context it is called "deceit". The case of *Doyle v. Olby* (1969, C.A.) shows very clearly that for fraudulent misrepresentation (and, presumably, for negligent misrepresentation as well) the damages must be calculated on tort principles and not on contract principles.

In addition to suing for damages, the injured party may, as indicated just now, avoid the contract. He need not do so. He may content himself with an action for damages. But he has a choice, to affirm or avoid the contract. If he decides to avoid the contract he need not go to court; all he needs to do is to give notice, by words or conduct, that he refuses to be bound by it. The effect of that notice, if it is justifiable, is that the contract is cancelled. Of course, the most appropriate person to whom to give this notice is the other party to the contract. But it may happen that the other party, being a fraud, disappears. That happened in *Car and Universal Finance Co. Ltd v. Caldwell* (1965, C.A.). A man was induced by fraud to sell his car to a rogue called Norris. Norris's cheque "bounced" and Norris disappeared. The former owner at once notified the police and the Automobile Association and asked them to find the car. It was held that he had done all he could in the circumstances and that his actions had successfully avoided the contract. The importance is this: if a third party in good faith and for value obtains the property which has passed under a voidable contract before the contract is avoided he gets a good title; if he gets the property after it has been avoided he does not (except where section 9 of the Factors Act 1889 or section 25(1) of the Sale of Goods Act 1979 applies).

The party misled by a fraudulent misrepresentation may, instead of, or as well as, merely notifying his "avoidance", apply to the court for a formal order of "rescission". He will want to do this if the other party refuses to hand back what the misled party has paid or transferred under the contract. The word "rescission" (and its verb "to rescind") can mean the order of a court cancelling a contract, and it can also mean the party's act of cancellation without going to court or before going to court. Rescission is available, not only for fraud, but also for negligent and innocent misrepresentation, and will be discussed more fully after the types of misrepresentation have been considered. But there is one feature that applies only in fraud. In general, rescission, whether in court or out of court, involves each party in handing back what he got under the contract; a process which is called restitution. But where a person has been induced by fraud to enter into a contract, he need only hand back what he got under the contract if he himself sues for rescission. If he is taken to court by the other party he can plead fraud as a defence and still refuse to return what he got under the contract. For example, an insurer, where the contract

101

of insurance has been induced by fraud, can deny liability under the policy and keep the premiums.

It is implicit in what has just been said that fraud is a defence to an action brought by the defrauder.

Negligent Misrepresentation

At one time the law made no distinction between negligent misrepresentation and wholly innocent misrepresentation. If a misrepresentation was not fraudulent it was treated as innocent; damages were not obtainable for innocent misrepresentation. The only remedy was the equitable remedy of rescission. But two developments (one at common law and one by statute) have altered all this, and now there is a distinction between negligent and wholly innocent misrepresentation and there is a remedy in damages for negligent misrepresentation.

In *Hedley Byrne & Co. Ltd v. Heller & Partners Ltd* (1964) the House of Lords stated, *obiter*, that the duty of care, which is the foundation of the tort of negligence, can extend to careless statements where a "special relationship" exists between the parties. For some time it was unclear how, if at all, the principle of *Hedley Byrne* applied to a misstatement leading up to a contract. It is now clear from *Esso Petroleum Co. Ltd v. Mardon* (1976, C.A.) that a "special relationship" may exist between the parties in a pre-contractual negotiation if one party has some relevant special knowledge, expertise or skill, and that, if a contract is induced by a careless misstatement made by the expert, the resulting contractual relationship between them does not prevent the non-expert from suing the expert in the tort of negligence. (See also *Banque Financière de la Cité S.A. v. Westgate Insurance Co. Ltd* (1989, C.A.).) But there must be a "relationship of proximity" between the parties giving rise to a duty of care. Thus a person may make a statement which is put into general circulation and may reasonably be relied upon by strangers for a variety of different purposes; but he will not be liable to a person who relied upon the statement unless it is shown that he knew that the statement would be communicated to the person relying upon it (either as an individual or as a member of an identifiable class) specifically in connection with a particular transaction or a transaction of a particular kind and that that person would be very likely to rely on it for the purpose of deciding whether to enter into that transaction. This principle was set out by the House of

Lords in *Caparo Industries plc v. Dickman* (1990). They held that an auditor of a public company's accounts owes no duty of care to a member of the public at large who relies on the accounts to buy shares in the company, nor does the auditor owe a duty of care to an individual shareholder in the company who wishes to buy more shares in the company: the auditor's statutory duty to prepare accounts is owed to the body of shareholders at large to enable them as a body to exercise informed control of the company. (See also *Al Saudi Banque v. Clark Pixley (a firm)* (1989), *Al-Nakib Investments (Jersey) Ltd v. Longcroft* (1990) and *Morgan Crucible plc v. Hill Samuel Bank Ltd* (1991).)

The Misrepresentation Act 1967 distinguishes between negligent and wholly innocent misrepresentation, and gives a remedy in damages for the former. Section 2(1) of the Act provides:

"Where a person has entered into a contract after a misrepresentation has been made to him by another party thereto and as a result thereof he has suffered loss, then, if the person making the misrepresentation would be liable to damages in respect thereof had the misrepresentation been made fraudulently, that person shall be so liable notwithstanding that the misrepresentation was not made fraudulently, unless he proves that he had reasonable ground to believe and did believe up to the time the contract was made that the facts represented were true."

There have not been very many reported cases on the Misrepresentation Act, but *Howard Marine and Dredging Co. Ltd v. A. Ogden and Sons (Excavations) Ltd* (1978, C.A.) is worthy of study. The facts (about the payload of some hired barges) are interesting, and the case shows differences of judicial opinion concerning "reasonable ground to believe" in section 2(1), and also concerning reasonableness in section 3 (exemption clauses). It is clear, however, that the burden on the person making the representation is heavy and not easy to discharge.

It is convenient to refer to the misrepresentation dealt with in section 2(1) as "negligent misrepresentation". But it must be noticed that it bears very little relation to the tort of negligence. The word "negligence" is not used in the subsection, nor is the classic phrase "duty of care". The burden of proof is on the defendant, whereas in tort it is on the plaintiff. Damages are only obtainable if they would have been obtained "had the misrepresentation been made fraudulently".

103

It is not clear whether the subsection can apply to non-disclosure, particularly of the kind which arose in *With v. O'Flanagan* (1936, C.A., above). The difficulty is this: can it be said of the plaintiff in a *With v. O'Flanagan* situation that "a misrepresentation has been made to him"? The decision of the Court of Appeal in *Banque Financière de la Cité v. Westgate Insurance Co. Ltd* (1989) suggests that the answer to this question is "No".

In summary, the present state of the law is that a person induced to enter into a contract by negligent misrepresentation may sue for damages, either under the principle of *Hedley Byrne*, or under section 2(1) of the Misrepresentation Act. The latter course is much the easier, because it places the burden of proof concerning carelessness on the defendant. But where the misrepresentor is not a party to the contract, section 2(1) is not available and the misrepresentee can only sue under the common law principle of *Hedley Byrne*. He would have to show a "special relationship" between himself and the misrepresentor and he would have to prove negligence.

In addition to, or instead of, suing for damages, the misled party may rescind the contract either in court or out of court. We will discuss rescission further when we have considered wholly innocent misrepresentation. Negligent misrepresentation can be used as a defence.

Wholly Innocent Misrepresentation

If the misrepresentor has been neither fraudulent nor negligent, his misrepresentation is wholly innocent. In such a case the misled party has no right to damages; the only remedy is rescission, in or out of court. Notice that I have said that the misled party has no right to damages. That is true, but the court has a *discretion*, where the misled party would be entitled to rescind the contract, to award damages *instead of* rescission. That is laid down by section 2(2) of the Misrepresentation Act. Section 2(2) is absolutely different from section 2(1). Section 2(1) deals only with negligent misrepresentation, and gives the misled party a right to damages in addition to his right of rescission. Section 2(2) deals with both negligent and wholly innocent misrepresentation and it gives the court a discretion to award damages instead of rescission. But notice the overlap: the court has a discretion, even where there is negligent misrepresentation, to say to the misled party: "No, we won't give you rescission, but we will give you damages." So this situation may arise: a misled party sues in respect of negligent misrepresentation for damages and rescission. The court may award him damages under section 2(1), and then, under section 2(2), refuse rescission, awarding damages instead. Section 2(3) deals with this situation by providing that in such a case the damages under section 2(2) should be taken into account in assessing the damages under section 2(1).

The position, then, in wholly innocent misrepresentation is that the misled party starts off with a right to rescission and no right to damages. The court, however, may decide to award him damages instead of rescission. The court may do this "if of opinion that it would be equitable to do so, having regard to the nature of the misrepresentation and the loss that would be caused by it if the contract were upheld, as well as to the loss that rescission would cause to the other party" (s.2(2)). A judge will probably be inclined to award damages and not rescission where the point of fact which has been misrepresented is of only slight importance. An innocent party who claims damages is entitled to recover all his losses: see *Royscot Trust Ltd v. Maidenhead Honda Centre Ltd* (1991), in which the Court of Appeal held that the person making the innocent misrepresentation is liable to damages as if the misrepresentation had been made fraudulently.

It should be noted, as was seen in Chapter 6, that section 3 of the Misrepresentation Act 1967 (as amended) provides that an exemption clause concerning misrepresentation, whether negligent or wholly innocent, is only to have effect in so far as it satisfies the requirement of reasonableness. See page 84 above. (A clause which seeks to exclude liability for fraudulent misrepresentation can, presumably, never satisfy the requirement of reasonableness.)

Wholly innocent misrepresentation can be used as a defence to an action by the other party.

THE RIGHT TO RESCIND

All three kinds of misrepresentation give the misled party a right to rescind. But rescission does not happen automatically when a misrepresentation is made. Misrepresentation makes a contract voidable. This means that the innocent party must take steps to rescind it.

Restitution and Indemnity

Where a court orders rescission it will also order mutual restitution, "a giving back and taking back on both sides". The principle is to put the parties back into their former positions as though the contract had never been made. In some cases this can only be done by ordering a money payment. But such a money payment is not damages. The principle is quite different: with damages, the aim of the court is to put the parties into the positions they would have been in had the contract been performed; with restitution, the aim is to put the parties into the positions they would have been in had the contract never been made. A money payment in connection with rescission is called, to distinguish it from damages, an indemnity.

In *Whittington v. Seale-Hayne* (1900) the plaintiffs, who were poultry breeders, were induced to take a lease of certain premises by the defendant's innocent misrepresentation that the premises were in a thoroughly sanitary condition. The premises turned out to be very insanitary; the water supply was poisoned. The manager of the poultry farm became seriously ill and most of the poultry died. To add to the plaintiffs' troubles, the local council declared the premises unfit for habitation and required the drains to be put in order, which expense, by a term of the lease, fell upon the plaintiffs. The defendant submitted to rescission, and agreed to pay £20 in respect of rent, rates and repairs. The plaintiffs claimed for loss of profits and also loss of stock, removal expenses and medical expenses. The court rejected, not only the claim for loss of profits (which would clearly have amounted to damages), but these other expenses claims as well. It was said that indemnity can only be claimed in respect of obligations which inevitably arise under the contract. The plaintiffs had to pay rent and rates and had to repair the drains, but they did not have to stock up the farm and carry on business. If this case is rightly decided, an indemnity does not even put the plaintiff fully into his pre-contract position. Those expenses which he did not inevitably incur have, so to speak, gone down the drain.

The Right to Rescind may be Lost

Although a party misled by misrepresentation starts off with a right of rescission, that right may be lost. There are now three circumstances which may lead to the loss of the right of rescission. There used to be five, but the Misrepresentation Act 1967 removed two. Thus it used to be the law, possibly, but not certainly, that where a statement began life as a misrepresentation (thus giving a right of rescission) and then became embodied in a contract as a warranty (as distinct from a condition) the right of rescission was lost. That rule was abolished by section 1, paragraph (a) of the Act. Again it used to be the law, at any rate in some kinds of contract, that where a contract had been performed (for example, where a contract for sale of land had been executed), the pre-existing right of rescission was lost (except in fraud). That rule was abolished by section 1, paragraph (b) of the Act.

Affirmation of the contract

If the party who has been misled by a misrepresentation affirms the contract, he cannot afterwards claim rescission. Affirmation occurs when the party misled either declares his intention to proceed with the contract or does some act from which such an intention may be inferred. Lapse of time is not in itself affirmation, but it is some evidence of affirmation. It seems that there is a difference on this point between fraudulent and non-fraudulent misrepresentation. In fraud, time only begins to run from the discovery of the truth. Where the misrepresentation was not fraudulent this seems not to be so, at any rate in sale of goods. In *Leaf v. International Galleries* (1950, C.A.) the plaintiff was induced to buy a picture by a non-fraudulent representation that it was a Constable. Five years later he discovered that it was not by Constable. It was held that he had lost his right of rescission, even though he brought his action as soon as he discovered the truth. At the time when *Leaf's* case was decided the law made no distinction between negligent and wholly innocent misrepresentation. It is likely that today negligent misrepresentation would go along with wholly innocent misrepresentation on this point.

Restitution impossible

The misled party will lose the right of rescission if something happens, in which the misled party has participated, which makes it impossible to restore the parties to their former position. For example, the purchaser of a mine cannot get rescission after he has worked out the mine. But rescission is still available if substantial restoration is possible, even though precise restoration is not. Thus deterioration in the condition or value of

107

property is not a bar to rescission. The court can accompany its order for rescission with financial adjustments between the parties.

Third-party rights

If a third party acquires a right under the contract in good faith and for value the misled party loses the right of rescission. So, for example, A sells goods to B on credit, being induced to do so by B's misrepresentation as to his creditworthiness. B sells the goods to C, who takes them and pays for them and has no knowledge of B's misrepresentation. A, having never been paid by B, now seeks rescission of the contract of sale between himself and B, coupled with restoration of the goods. A will fail in his action. This links up with the point made on page 101, that if a third party in good faith and for value obtains property which had previously passed from A to B under a voidable contract before that contract is avoided, he obtains a good title.

MISREPRESENTATION AND BREACH

An untrue statement may begin life as a non-contractual representation and then later be incorporated into a contract as a term. This may give the innocent party two causes of action; one for misrepresentation and one for breach of contract.

CHAPTER NINE

DURESS AND UNDUE INFLUENCE

WHERE a person is driven into a contract by duress or by undue influence the contract is voidable and may be set aside by a court.

DURESS

Duress traditionally means actual violence or threats of violence to the person; it is a common law doctrine. A threat to the goods of a person is not duress. There are very few instances of duress in the law reports in modern times. Plenty of people suffer violence, but not usually to force them into making a contract. However, in 1976 a case of duress came on appeal to the Privy Council from Australia: *Barton v. Armstrong* (1976, P.C.). Armstrong held the largest shareholding in a company called Landmark and Barton held the next largest. Hostility developed between the two, and in the end Barton executed a deed on behalf of the company buying out Armstrong on terms very favourable to Armstrong and very disastrous to the company and to Barton. During the period leading up to the execution of the deed Armstrong made many threats to Barton. On one occasion he said: "The city is not as safe as you may think between office and home. You will see what I can do against you and you will regret the day when you decided not to work with me." Then Barton began to receive telephone calls in the middle of the night. Generally Barton only heard heavy breathing, but on some occasions he heard a voice say: "You will be killed." Later Armstrong said to Barton: "You had better sign this agreement—or else." The Privy Council, by a majority, held that the deeds were executed by Barton under duress and should be declared void so far as they concerned him. The majority held that duress was like fraud in that the threats need not be the only factor inducing the contract so long as it was *a* factor.

109

Another Privy Council case (from Hong Kong), *Pao On v. Lau Yiu Long* (1980, P.C.), makes it perfectly plain that duress makes a contract voidable, rather than void from the beginning. In the *Pao On* case the Privy Council referred to developments in American law and to two recent English decisions at first instance and accepted in principle that the traditional doctrine of duress (personal violence) could, given strong facts, be extended to provide a remedy in the event of "economic duress" (commercial pressure). This principle was accepted by the House of Lords in *Universe Tankships Inc. of Monrovia v. International Transport Workers Federation* (1983, H.L.), which involved pressure applied by a trade union by "blacking" the plaintiff's ship in port and refusing to release it until they made certain payments. The principle has been applied subsequently to an agreement between two commercial organisations: see *Atlas Express Ltd v. Kafco (Importers and Distributors) Ltd* (1989). In *CTN Cash and Carry Ltd v. Gallaher Ltd* (1994), however, the Court of Appeal emphasised that it would be difficult, though not impossible, to maintain such a claim in the context of arm's length commercial dealings between two trading companies, especially where the party making the threat bona fide believes that its demand is valid.

UNDUE INFLUENCE

Courts of equity regarded the common law doctrine of duress as narrow, and, under the general doctrine of equitable fraud, they developed a much wider jurisdiction over contracts made under pressure. There thus grew up the doctrine of undue influence, designed to give relief where, in circumstances not amounting to duress, a person enters into a disadvantageous transaction either of gift or of contract. But a transaction will not be set aside on the grounds of undue influence unless it was "wrongful"; it must be shown that the transaction was to the obvious and unfair disadvantage of the person subjected to the dominating influence: see *National Westminster Bank plc v. Morgan* (1985, H.L.).

In *Lloyds Bank Ltd v. Bundy* (1975, C.A.), for example, an elderly and ill farmer guaranteed the bank account of his son's ailing company and charged his farm (his only asset) to the bank. The Court of Appeal unanimously set aside the guarantee and the charge and dismissed the bank's action for possession of the farm. Two members of the court reached their decision on the basis of undue influence by the bank. Lord Denning put

110

his judgment on a wider foundation. He said that all the instances where the courts will intervene to set aside a transaction are based on a single principle, that of relief against inequality of bargaining power. In *National Westminster Bank plc v. Morgan* (1985, H.L.) the House of Lords held that Lord Denning's view was not correct and that the doctrine of undue influence is not based on the principle of relief against inequality of bargaining power but the prevention of the victimisation of one party by another. The House of Lords stressed that in exercising its equitable jurisdiction to grant relief against undue influence, a court must look at the facts of each case.

The cases can be divided into two types, according to whether there is or is not a special fiduciary relationship between the parties.

Actual Undue Influence

When there is no special fiduciary relationship between the parties, the person who complains that he was pressed into the contract must prove that actual pressure was applied. Thus a promise to pay money, for example, will be set aside if the promisor proves that he was pressed into the promise by a threat that if he did not promise he would be prosecuted, or his spouse or close relative would be prosecuted, for some criminal offence. The burden of proving the pressure lies upon the complainant.

Williams v. Bayley (1866, H.L.) provides a good illustration. A young man gave to his bank several promissory notes upon which he had forged the indorsements of his father, a colliery owner. There were meetings between son, father, bankers, and solicitors. The bankers made it clear that, unless some arrangements were come to, the son would be prosecuted. The following expressions were used: "We have only one course to pursue; we cannot be parties to compounding a felony"; "This is a serious matter"; "A case of transportation for life." These words made a great impression on Dad. He cried out: "What be I to do? How can I help myself? You see these men will have their money." Eventually Dad agreed to mortgage his colliery to the bank, in return for the bank handing back the promissory notes. This agreement was set aside by the court on the ground that undue pressure had been exerted.

A more recent example of a case of actual undue influence is *Bank of Credit and Commerce International SA v. Aboody* (1992) in which the judge found that the husband had exerted undue influence on the wife.

111

There was evidence that the husband was a bully and that the wife was under pressure and had signed the relevant documents because she wanted peace.

In such cases of actual undue influence, it is not necessary for the victim of the undue influence to prove in addition that he suffered manifest disadvantage, as is required in cases of presumed undue influence: see *CIBC Mortgages plc v. Pitt* (1994, H.L.).

Presumed Undue Influence

In some relationships a presumption of undue influence arises from the relationship. These are all relationships in which one person is in a position of some dominance over the other. The duty of the dominant person is to be faithful to the confidence that is reposed in him by the other. If it comes to litigation, it is his duty to prove that he has not taken unfair advantage of the other person. This duty is imposed by way of presumption. Where a transaction is challenged in the courts, it is for the dominant person, if he wishes to uphold the transaction, to prove that no undue influence was in fact used. If he cannot prove this absence of undue influence he fails, and the transaction will be set aside. In this type of case, a party who proves that there has been undue influence must also prove that the transaction was "manifestly disadvantageous" to him. A manifest disadvantage must be a disadvantage which is obvious as such to any independent and reasonable person who considered the transaction at the time with knowledge of all the relevant facts. It must amount to an "advantage taken of the person subjected to the influence which, failing proof to the contrary, [is] explicable only on the basis that undue influence ha[s] been exercised to procure it": see *National Westminster Bank plc v. Morgan* (1985). In *CIBC Mortgages Ltd v. Pitt* (1993, H.L.), Lord Browne-Wilkinson suggested that this may need to be reconsidered in the future.

The presumption applies even where the person at whose request the gift or promise was made obtained no personal benefit. For example, the presumption applies against a trustee who persuades one beneficiary to enter into some transaction in favour of another beneficiary.

What relationships?

Certain relationships as a matter of law raise the presumption that undue influence has been exercised, for example doctor and patient, solicitor and client, trustee and beneficiary. Even if there is no relationship of this sort, the alleged victim of the undue influence may prove the existence of a relationship under which he generally reposed trust and confidence in the wrongdoer. In that case, the existence of such a relationship raises the presumption of undue influence: see *Barclays Bank plc v. O'Brien* (1993, H.L.). The presumption does not apply as a matter of law between husband and wife, but there may be circumstances in which it does arise, *e.g.* where a wife assumes dominance over an ill husband or the evidence shows that the wife reposed trust and confidence in her husband in relation to their financial affairs. As Lord Browne-Wilkinson said in *Barclays Bank plc v. O'Brien*: ''. . . in those cases . . . where the wife relies in all financial matters on her husband and simply does what he suggests, a presumption of undue influence . . . can be established solely from the proof of such trusts and confidence without proof of actual undue influence.'' The doctrine can apply between parent and child for a short time after the child has come of age. It can even apply after the child has married. The classic phrase is that it only ceases to apply when the child is ''emancipated'' from parental control.

The list of relationships is not closed. In *Re Craig* (1971) Mr Craig was 84 when his wife died. He was then worth about £40,000. He employed a Mrs Middleton as secretary-companion until he died. During the six years of her employment he made gifts to Mrs Middleton amounting to about £30,000. The court set aside the gifts, holding that the circumstances raised a presumption of undue influence which Mrs Middleton had not succeeded in rebutting. See also *Goldsworthy v. Brickell* (1987, C.A.), where the presumption was applied to a relationship of trust and confidence between an elderly farmer and his neighbour.

An interesting (and, in a sense, opposite) case is *Re Brocklehurst* (1978, C.A.). Sir Philip Lee Brocklehurst was the owner of an estate near Macclesfield. In 1972 his second wife left him and his old batman died. He was alone and lonely and in his eighties. He became friendly with a local garage proprietor called John Roberts. Sir Philip made his last will in 1974 and died eight months later. His executors then discovered that Sir Philip had, some six months before he died, severed the shooting rights from the estate by granting a 99-year lease of the shooting rights to Mr Roberts. This had the effect of reducing the value of the estate by some £90,000. A majority of the Court of Appeal (Lord Denning dissenting) held that there was no presumption of undue influence, mainly because, far from Mr Roberts being in a position of dominance, Sir Philip had tended to dominate Mr Roberts. The majority further held that, even if there was a presumption, Mr Roberts had rebutted it by proving that the gift of the shooting rights had been the spontaneous and independent act of Sir Philip.

Rebutting the presumption

The presumption of undue influence can be rebutted if the dominant person can show that the complainant was able to have "the free exercise of independent will". The usual way of doing this is to show that the complainant had independent advice. But the mere fact of independent advice will not necessarily save the transaction, and conversely the mere absence of independent advice is not necessarily fatal to the transaction. For recent examples of this, see *Massey v. Midland Bank Ltd* (1995), *Banco Exterior Internacional v. Mann* (1995) and *TSB Bank plc v. Camfield* (1994).

How the Right to Relief may be Lost

A contract affected by undue influence is voidable, rather than void. This means that the person alleging undue influence must bring an action for rescission to avoid it. The action will fail in the following circumstances: (1) it can be shown that the plaintiff affirmed the transaction after the influence, or that the relationship giving rise to the presumption of influence had ceased; (2) if there has been "laches"; and (3) if third parties have acquired rights from the transaction, provided that they have acted in good faith, for value and without knowledge of the undue influence.

Laches is an equitable idea, meaning a person's prolonged neglect to assert his rights. An example is *Allcard v. Skinner* (1887), in which undue influence was found to have been exerted, but the plaintiff was unable to recover the balance of the money paid as a result of the influence because she waited for six years before claiming; during that time the influence would have ceased to affect her and she could have taken independent advice.

CHAPTER TEN

MISTAKE

THE types of mistake are classified in different ways. Here, mistake is considered under three heads: "Agreement Mistake", "Possibility Mistake" and "Mistakes in Documents".

AGREEMENT MISTAKE

If two (or more) persons agree in the same terms on the same subject-matter they are bound. A person will also generally be bound if his conduct would lead a reasonable man to suppose that he had agreed, even though he has not in his own mind agreed. But a court will depart from this usual objective view if it is satisfied that in reality there is no agreement. Agreement mistake, therefore, is a mistake as to the offer or the acceptance; mistake, that is, as to the agreement. This kind of mistake is sometimes called "mistake negativing consent", because it tends to arise either where it appears that the parties were at cross-purposes or where one party entered the agreement after being deceived by the other.

Agreement mistake may arise in one of three ways. There may, first, be mistake as to the person. A may intend to contract with B, only to find that the other party to the apparent agreement is C. Secondly, there may be mistake as to the subject-matter. A may intend to contract about a thing (X), whereas B intends to contract about another thing (Y). Thirdly, there may be mistake about terms. A may intend to buy a horse for £500, whereas B intends to sell it for £800. These three types of mistakes will now be examined in turn. It should be noted that where the court decides to uphold the mistake, the effect is that there is no contract; in other words, the contract will be void.

Mistake as to the Person

This type of case usually involves fraudulent activity by a rogue who acquires property fraudulently and resells it to an innocent third party. For example, in *Cundy v. Lindsay* (1878, H.L.) the plaintiffs, Messrs Lindsay, linen manufacturers, received an order for a large quantity of handkerchiefs from a rogue called Blenkarn, who gave his address as "37, Wood Street, Cheapside, London; entrance, second door in Little Love Lane". He signed his name to look like "Blenkiron & Co.", a respectable firm, known by reputation to the plaintiffs and carrying on business at 123, Wood Street. The plaintiffs sent the goods on credit addressed to "Blenkiron Co., 37 Wood Street". In that way Blenkarn got possession of the handkerchiefs. He did not pay for them and he sold 250 dozen of them to the defendants, Messrs Cundy. The plaintiffs sued the defendants in conversion. It was held by the House of Lords that there was no contract between the plaintiffs and Blenkarn, as the plaintiffs had no intention of dealing with him but with someone else. As there was no contract with Blenkarn he obtained no title to the goods and so could pass none to the defendants, who were liable in conversion. It makes no matter whether one thinks of the plaintiffs as offerors or as offerees. Either their offer was accepted by someone for whom it was not intended, or their acceptance was made to someone for whom it was not intended.

In *King's Norton Metal Co. v. Edridge, Merrett & Co. Ltd* (1897, C.A.) the plaintiffs received by letter an order for wire from "Hallam & Co". On the note-paper was a picture of a large factory with numerous chimneys, and in one corner was a printed statement that "Hallam & Co." had depots and agencies at Belfast, Lille and Ghent. In fact "Hallam & Co." was simply an alias of a penniless rogue called Wallis. The plaintiffs, relying on the description of "Hallam & Co." contained in the letter, sent the goods on credit. Wallis thus got possession of them. He did not pay for them, and he sold them to the defendants. The plaintiffs sued for conversion. It was held by the Court of Appeal that the plaintiffs "had intended to contract with the writer of the letter". So there was a contract between the plaintiffs and Wallis, and thus Wallis was able to pass a good title to the defendants, who were not liable in conversion.

The distinction between *Cundy v. Lindsay* and the *King's Norton* case is that in *Cundy v. Lindsay* the plaintiffs made a mistake as to the identity of the person they were dealing with; they thought they were dealing with a different entity. In the *King's Norton* case the plaintiffs were not mistaken as to the identity of the person they were dealing with, only as to his attributes, particularly his creditworthiness. They did not think they were dealing with a different entity; there was no other entity.

There is a difference in effect. If there is no contract, as in *Cundy v. Lindsay*, the innocent third party obtains no title, and suffers the loss. If there is a contract, as in the *King's Norton* case, it is voidable for fraud, but provided the innocent third-party buyer obtains the goods before the contract has in fact been avoided, he is secure. Reference may be made back to Chapter 8, to the section on fraudulent misrepresentation, on the question of avoidance. (See also *Citibank NA v. Brown Shipley & Co. Ltd* (1991).)

The distinction between a mistake as to the person which prevents a contract coming into existence at all and a mistake as to the person which renders the contract voidable for fraud is a difficult distinction to make, and it is particularly difficult when the parties are not dealing by letter, but face to face. For example, in *Phillips v. Brooks Ltd* (1919) a man whose real name was North went into the plaintiff's shop and asked to see pearls and rings. He selected pearls costing £2,550 and a ring costing £450. He took out a cheque-book and said that he was Sir George Bullough. The jeweller (the plaintiff) had heard of Sir George Bullough as a wealthy man. North gave Sir George's address. The jeweller checked the address in a directory. He then allowed North to take away the ring in exchange for a cheque for £3,000. The cheque bounced (*i.e.* was dishonoured by non-payment). North pawned the ring with the defendant, a pawnbroker. The plaintiff jeweller sued the defendant pawnbroker, arguing that there was never any contract between himself and North, so that North had no title to the ring, and so the defendant had no title either. But the defendant won. The judge said that the plaintiff "had contracted to sell and deliver the ring to the person who came into his shop . . . who obtained the sale and delivery by means of the false pretence that he was Sir George Bullough. His intention was to sell to the person present and identified by sight and hearing". The contract of sale was voidable for fraud, but it had not been avoided at the time when the defendant acquired his interest in the ring.

The more recent case of *Ingram v. Little* (1961, C.A.) involved another rogue. The plaintiffs were three sisters, living in Surrey. They were joint owners of a car, and they advertised it for sale. The rogue, introducing himself as "Hutchinson", came to the house and negotiated for the purchase of the car. He eventually offered £717 for it. This price was agreed, and "Hutchinson" produced his cheque-book. Elsie Ingram, who was conducting the negotiations, said she would not in any circumstances accept a cheque and the proposed deal was finished. The rogue then said that he was P. G. M. Hutchinson, with business interests in Guildford and living at Stanstead House, Caterham. Hilda Ingram, one of the sisters, went along the street to the local post office and checked in the telephone directory that there was such a person as P. G. M. Hutchinson living at that address. The sisters then let the rogue have the car in exchange for his cheque. The rogue was not P. G. M. Hutchinson, who had nothing whatsoever to do with the transaction. The cheque was dishonoured. The rogue sold the car to the defendant and disappeared. The plaintiffs sued the defendant in conversion. They won at first instance and the Court of Appeal, by a majority, affirmed this decision, on the ground that there was no contract between the plaintiffs and the rogue. The plaintiffs intended to deal with the Hutchinson of Stanstead House, and not with the separate entity, the so-called "Hutchinson" who was before their eyes. Thus they were mistaken, not merely as to his attributes (such as creditworthiness), but as to his identity.

In *Lewis v. Averay* (1972, C.A.) the plaintiff advertised a car for sale. A man telephoned about it and subsequently called. He was a rogue, of course. Having said that he liked the car, the rogue introduced himself as "Richard Green", making the plaintiff believe that he was the well-known film actor of that name. They agreed on a price of £450. The rogue wrote out a cheque for that amount, signing it "R. A. Green". The plaintiff was hesitant and asked for proof of identity. The rogue produced an admission pass to Pinewood Studios, bearing the name "Richard A. Green", and a photograph which was plainly that of the rogue. The plaintiff then let the rogue have the car and log-book. A few days later the plaintiff was told by his bank that the cheque was worthless. Meanwhile the rogue had sold the car to the defendant, who bought it in good faith and without knowledge of the fraud. The plaintiff sued the defendant for conversion of the car. The Court of Appeal gave judgment for the defendant, holding that the rogue's fraud did not prevent there being a contract (albeit a voidable one) between him and the plaintiff. Consequently, as the contract had not been avoided in time, the rogue was able to pass a good title to the defendant.

The Court of Appeal made very plain their preference for *Phillips v. Brooks* over *Ingram v. Little*. Lord Denning said that he could see no valid distinction of fact between the two cases. He thought there was no substance in the idea (suggested by the majority of the Court of Appeal in *Ingram v.*

Little) that in *Phillips v. Brooks* the contract of sale was concluded before the rogue made his misrepresentation, whereas in *Ingram v. Little* the rogue made his misrepresentation before the contract was concluded. In Lord Denning's view the property in the goods did not pass in either case until the seller let the rogue have the goods. Lord Denning also said that the alleged distinction between a mistake as to identity and a mistake as to attributes was a distinction without a difference. If this view prevails, the distinction between *Cundy v. Lindsay* and the *King's Norton* case will disappear and the courts will have to decide which of these two cases is right and which is wrong. The interest of *Lewis v. Averay* goes beyond the bounds of contract law in that it is a very clear instance of the Court of Appeal refusing to follow a previous decision of its own, *Ingram v. Little*.

For mistake as to the person to have any effect in law the mistake must be known to the other party. In *Upton R.D.C. v. Powell* (1942, C.A.), a farmer, whose barn was on fire, rang up the Upton police and asked for "the fire brigade". The police summoned the Upton Fire Brigade. It later turned out that though the farm was in the Upton police area, it was in the Pershore fire area. If the police had summoned the Pershore Fire Brigade it would have come to Farmer Powell's fire without charge. The Upton Fire Brigade was entitled to go to fires outside its own area and, if it did so, to charge for its services. The Upton Fire Brigade went to the fire, neither party knowing that there was any mistake. The court held that the Upton Fire Brigade was entitled, on an implied contract, to remuneration for its work. Similarly, if Blenkarn (see *Cundy v. Lindsay*) had acted quite innocently—had had a genuine address in Wood Street and had ordered handkerchiefs over an unadorned signature "Blenkarn"—and really believed that the plaintiffs meant to contract with him, there would have been a contract.

For mistake as to the person to have any effect, it must also be a material mistake. That means that it must matter to the mistaken party. In *Mackie v. European Assurance Society* (1869) the plaintiff instructed a man called Waddell to take out an insurance policy for him. Waddell had been agent for the X assurance society and the plaintiff thought that his policy would be effected with that society. In fact Waddell had just ceased to be agent for the X society and effected the policy with the defendant society. The defendant society argued that the contract of insurance was void because of this mistake. This argument was rejected by the court on the ground that it did not matter to the plaintiff which insurance society issued the policy; it was a matter of indifference to him. But on the other side of the line lies *Boulton v. Jones* (1857). Jones had had dealings with a man called Brocklehurst and, at a time when Brocklehurst owed money to Jones, Jones sent to Brocklehurst a written order for 50 feet of leather hose. On that very day Brocklehurst had transferred his business to his foreman, Boulton. Boulton executed the order by sending the goods to Jones on credit. Jones accepted and used the goods in the belief that they had been sent by Brocklehurst. When, later, Jones was asked for payment he refused. His argument was that he had intended to contract with Brocklehurst, and that it mattered to him because of the set-off which he had against Brocklehurst and which he wished to utilise. The court held that Jones was not liable for the price of the goods.

Mistake as to the Subject-Matter

This kind of case arises where the parties are at cross-purposes. An example is *Scriven v. Hindley* (1913). A man made a bid at an auction sale, thinking that he was bidding for hemp. In fact the bales in question contained tow. The bidder was sued for the price. The court held that there was no contract. "The parties were never *ad idem* as to the subject-matter of the proposed sale."

Raffles v. Wichelhaus (1864) may also be treated as a case of cross-purpose mistake. In that case, R agreed to sell, and W agreed to buy, a consignment of cotton which was to arrive "*ex Peerless* from Bombay". There happened to be two ships called *Peerless* sailing from Bombay, one in October and one in December. The seller tendered the cotton from the December *Peerless*. The buyer refused to accept it, on the ground that he had intended to buy cotton from the October *Peerless*. Judgment was given for the defendant. The court gave no reasons for its decision, but one would think that since there was an ambiguity and since, apparently, there were no circumstances which pointed to one meaning rather than the other, there was no contract, because the offer and acceptance did not match.

Mistake as to the Terms of the Contract

Mistake as to the terms of the contract is only rarely upheld. In *Wood v. Scarth* (1858) the defendant offered in writing to let a public house to the plaintiff for £63 a year. The plaintiff had a conversation about it with the defendant's clerk and then accepted the offer by letter. The defendant intended that a premium of £500 should be payable in addition to the rent, and he believed that his clerk had made this clear to the plaintiff. The plaintiff believed that the £63 a year was all that would be payable. It was held that the contract must stand; and the plaintiff was awarded damages for the defendant's refusal to grant the lease. It is interesting to note that the plaintiff, before bringing this action in a common law court, had sued for specific performance in an equity court. There he failed. Specific performance, along with other equitable remedies, is not given as of right but lies in the discretion of the court. A court may, instead of refusing specific performance outright, grant it on terms. This happened in *Baskomb v. Beckwith* (1869). An estate was sold in lots on the terms that the purchaser of each lot should covenant not to build a public house on it. The vendor kept one of the lots himself, and proposed to build a public house on it. The plan of the lots did not make this clear. It was held that the vendor could have specific performance but only on terms that he covenanted not to build a public house on the land retained by himself. A more recent example of the court holding a party to mistakenly agreed terms is *Centrovincial Estates plc v. Merchant Investors Assurance Company Ltd* (1983).

The refusal of specific performance, or the refusal of it except upon terms, does not amount to the court declaring there is no contract. But a court will, on occasion, make such a declaration. In *Hartog v. Colin and Shields* (1939) the defendants intended to offer for sale to the plaintiffs some hareskins at a certain price "per piece". By a slip they offered to sell them at that price "per pound". The value of a piece was about one-third that of a pound. The prior negotiations had been conducted on the understanding that the skins would be sold at so much per piece. The plaintiffs sued for non-delivery of the skins. They failed. It was held that there was no contract. The plaintiffs must have known, from the previous negotiations, that "pound" was a slip for "piece". The judge stressed that the defendant had to establish that the plaintiff must have realised the mistake.

Thus the usual rule, as stated above, does not apply where the offeree knows (or should be taken as knowing) that the offeror has made a mistake as to the terms of the offer.

Mistake as to Quality is not Operative

In *Smith v. Hughes* (1871) the defendant was shown a sample of oats by the plaintiff, and bought them. The defendant thought they were old oats; new oats were no use to him. They were in fact new oats, and he refused to accept them. It was held that, if that was all his mistake, it was a mistake merely as to the quality of the oats and was without any legal effect, even if the other party knew of his mistake. But the court ordered a new trial so that another point could be investigated, whether there had been a mistake going further than quality, going indeed to the terms of the contract. The case is not a very clear authority on that point, which in any case is covered by *Hartog v. Colin and Shields* (above). It is clear that mistake by one party as to the quality of the subject-matter, even if that mistake is known to the other party, does not affect the contract.

POSSIBILITY MISTAKE

This kind of mistake has nothing to do with a failure of the acceptance to correspond to the offer. In this situation there has been undoubted agreement. But the parties have made a common mistake about some underlying fact. To take the simplest example, suppose A has agreed with B for the sale of some article to B; unknown to both A and B the article does not exist. That particular mistake has the effect of rendering the contract void. The question here is what mistakes do have this effect and are "operative".

A party to a contract may make all manner of mistakes. In particular he may think that he is getting a good bargain, and then later discover that the facts are not as he thought them to be, and that he has got a thoroughly bad bargain. Many such mistakes do not have any legal effect at all. Mistake in the legal sense is a very much narrower idea than it is in popular speech. Because mistake as a legal idea is so narrow, a lawyer acting for a client who has not obtained from a contract what he expected to does not think first of launching an action based on mistake. That is a last resort. He will consider, first, whether there has been a misrepresentation by the other party, and, secondly, whether, having regard to the express and the implied terms of the contract, there has been a breach of contract. Only if there has been no misrepresentation (or if the right to rescission has been lost) and if there has been no breach of contract will the idea of suing for mistake be resorted to.

This kind of mistake is called possibility mistake because the parties have made a mistake as to the possibility of the contract's object being achieved. Thus, in the example given, the object of the contract was to transfer the ownership of an article from A to B in return for a sum of money. If the article does not exist, that object cannot be achieved. The impossibility here is antecedent impossibility or initial impossibility, because the impossibility already exists at the time the contract is made. There can also arise in a contract subsequent impossibility; that is where the impossibility only arises after the contract has been made (but before it has been carried out). Thus, going back to the example, if the article perishes after A and B have made their contract for its sale (but before the sale has gone through), that is a case of subsequent impossibility. That kind of impossibility is called "frustration", and will be discussed in Chapter 18. The underlying idea is the same in both cases; whether the article perishes before the contract is made or after it is made, the object of the contract is frustrated. But it is better to confine the word "frustration" to mean subsequent impossibility. There is another similarity underlying both cases; antecedent impossibility and subsequent impossibility both excuse the parties. Since A is unable to deliver the article it looks as though this must be a breach of contract, but it is not. A is excused from his obligation to deliver the article, and, of course, B is excused from his obligation to pay the price. It is because impossibility excuses the parties that it is so important to determine the limits of the doctrine of impossibility. The rest of this section will consider antecedent, not subsequent, impossibility. But when reading Chapter 18 reference should be made back to this chapter. For a case where antecedent impossibility (common mistake) and frustration were pleaded in the alternative see *Amalgamated Investment & Property Co. Ltd v. John Walker & Sons Ltd* (1977, C.A.).

Mistake as to Existence

It is clear law that if, unknown to the parties, the subject-matter of the contract does not exist at the time that they make their agreement, the contract is void; in the older cases, this is called *res extincta*. So, for example, in *Strickland v. Turner* (1852) A bought from B an annuity on the life of X. Unknown to both A and B, X was already dead. It was held that as the annuity was not in existence at the time of the contract, the contract was void, and A was entitled to have his purchase money back. Similarly, in *Galloway v. Galloway* (1914), a man and a woman entered into a separation deed, believing that they were husband and wife. This was not so, because the prior spouse of the husband turned out to be still alive. The separation deed was held to be void, because the "marriage" which was the basis of the deed did not exist.

It is sometimes suggested that there is a separate category of operative mistake, mistake as to quantity. In *Barrow, Lane & Ballard Ltd v. Phillip Phillips & Co. Ltd* (1929) there was a contract for the sale of 700 bags of nuts, believed to be lying in certain warehouses. In fact 109 of the bags had disappeared, presumably by theft, at the time when the contract was made. The court held the contract void, the judge emphasising that he regarded the 700 bags as an "indivisible parcel" of goods. It is clear, therefore, that mistake as to quantity is just a particular aspect of mistake as to existence.

A mistake as to existence does not always amount to an operative mistake, and consequently it does not always excuse the parties. This is because the contract may, by its terms, lay the responsibility for non-existence on one party or the other. If A agrees to sell something to B it may be clear from the terms of the contract that, if that something does not exist, A is to be liable to B for failure to deliver it; alternatively, it may be clear that B is willing to take a risk, so that if it does not exist B is to be liable to A for the price. It is only where the contract does not lay the responsibility on either party that non-existence excuses the parties. In an Australian case, *McRae v. Commonwealth Disposals Commission* (1951), the Commission contracted to sell to the plaintiff a wrecked oil tanker described as lying on Jourmaund Reef, 100 miles north of Samarai. In fact there was no tanker lying anywhere near the latitude and longitude stated, and indeed there was no place known as Jourmaund Reef. In the High Court of Australia the plaintiff was awarded damages for breach of contract. The court held that the only proper construction of this particular contract was that it included a promise by the Commission that there was a tanker in the position specified.

Mistake as to Ownership

In *Cooper v. Phibbs* (1867) A agreed to let a fishery to B. Unknown to both parties, the fishery already belonged to B. The agreement was set aside by the House of Lords. The object of the contract—transfer of rights from A to B—was just as impossible of achievement as it would have been if the thing contracted about had been non-existent. Thus the principle applicable to a case of *res extincta* has been extended to the case of what is called *"res sua"* ("the thing was already his").

The mistake in *Cooper v. Phibbs* was not regarded as a question of law, but rather of the private rights of B. Similarly in *Galloway v. Galloway*, the mistake was regarded as being not one of law, but of the private status of the parties. But a mistake as to the general law is never an operative mistake, just as a misstatement of law is never an operative mis-representation.

The Problem of Quality

If A contracts with B for the sale of a thing from A to B, the contract (subject to the construction point) is void for mistake if the thing does not exist or if the thing already belongs to B. The question now arises, can the contract be held void simply because A and B were mistaken about the *quality* of the thing? We have seen that a mistake as to quality cannot cause an operative agreement mistake. Here the question is whether it can cause an operative possibility mistake. Can it be said that a contract's object is impossible of achievement if the thing contracted about does not have some quality which the parties thought it had?

The answer to this question depends upon the correct interpretation of *Bell v. Lever Brothers Ltd* (1932, H.L.). In 1923, the Lever Company, which had a controlling interest in the Niger Company, appointed Bell as chairman of the Niger Company at a salary of £8,000 a year. In 1926 the contract was renewed for another five years. Bell, by speculating in the company's business, committed breaches of duty which would have justi-fied the Lever Company in terminating his appointment. In 1929 the Niger Company amalgamated with another company, and Bell became redund-ant. The Lever Company agreed to pay Bell, and did pay him, £30,000 as compensation for terminating his service contract. Later the Lever Com-pany found out about Bell's breaches of duty. They brought an action claiming rescission of the compensation agreement and return of the £30,000. The jury found that Bell was not fraudulent; when he entered into the compensation agreement he had forgotten his breaches of duty. The trial judge held that the compensation agreement was void for mis-take. The mistake was the belief of both parties that they were bargaining about a service contract which could only be terminated with compensa-tion, whereas in fact it could have been terminated without compensation.

125

The Court of Appeal affirmed this decision. The House of Lords allowed the appeal, holding that there was no operative mistake. The House so decided by a majority of three to two. Two Law Lords said that there was an operative mistake, as did the trial judge and the three Lords Justices in the Court of Appeal.

It is not at all clear from the speeches of the majority Law Lords what the true meaning of the decision is. The case is open to two interpretations: (1) that there is a doctrine of operative mistake as to quality, but that the mistake in the instant case was not great enough to bring the doctrine into play; and (2) that there is no such doctrine.

The true meaning of the decision in *Bell v. Lever* is still open to argument, but in the 50 years which have gone by since it was given the courts have really decided to adopt the second interpretation; that is, that there is no doctrine of operative mistake as to quality. In *Solle v. Butcher* (1950, C.A.) the Court of Appeal held that a contract of letting was not void where the parties had both assumed, wrongly, that the premises were not subject to the Rent Restriction Acts. This was a fundamental mistake as to quality, yet the contract was held not to be void, in the light of *Bell v. Lever*. In *Leaf v. International Galleries* (1950, C.A.) the plaintiff bought from the defendants a picture which they both believed, mistakenly, to have been painted by Constable. The plaintiff sued for the return of the price. He based his claim on misrepresentation, so the issue of mistake did not have to be decided, but the Court of Appeal indicated that the contract was not void for mistake.

There are, however, a few cases which suggest that a contract can be rendered void by a mistake as to quality. In *Griffith v. Brymer* (1903) a contract was made at 11 a.m. on June 24, 1902, for the hire of a room which overlooked the route of the Coronation procession, due to be held on June 26. At 10 a.m. on June 24, his doctors decided to operate upon King Edward VII, and, of course, this rendered the procession impossible. This decision was not known to the parties when the contract was made. The court held the contract void. This was a kind of mistake as to quality; the room which was the subject of the contract lacked a quality which it was thought to have. There was a similar mistake in *The Salvador* (1909). The defendant undertook to take a tug and two lighters in tow from Milford Haven to Rio de Janeiro for £570, of which £350 was to be paid in advance. This sum was paid, and the procession started off. Four days later it put back into Milford Haven. Both parties believed, at the time the contract was made, that the tug was capable of towing the lighters to South

126

America. The court held that there was no contract, as the supposed contract had been entered into "on the mistaken assumption that it could be performed". The plaintiff recovered back his £350. I do not think these cases would be followed today. As Lord Denning said in *Solle v. Butcher*: "All previous decisions on this subject must now be read in the light of *Bell v. Lever*."

But there are two cases decided since *Bell v. Lever* in which a contract was held void for what was, in effect, a mistake of quality. In *Sheikh Bros. Ltd v. Ochsner* (1957, P.C.) a contract was made for the exploitation of sisal (a fibre used for ropes) growing on land belonging to A, which was to be cut and processed by B. It was a term of the contract that B should deliver to A an average minimum of 50 tons of sisal fibre a month. The profits were to be split between them. It turned out the land was not capable of producing 50 tons of sisal a month. So there was a mistake as to the quality of the land. The Privy Council, supposedly applying the principles laid down in *Bell v. Lever*, held the contract to be void. The same result was reached in *Associated Japanese Bank (International) Ltd v. Crédit du Nord S.A.* (1988), in which a guarantee of an agreement relating to four non-existent machines was held to be void for common mistake. Also, in *R. v. Williams* (1980, C.A.) the Court of Appeal in a criminal case apparently took a similar view of *Bell v. Lever*. But in the later case of *Sybron Corporation v. Rochem* (1984, C.A.) the Court of Appeal, in a civil case, took the view that a mistake as to quality does not render a contract void. The case of *R v. Williams* was not cited.

Contracts Voidable for Mistake

Although a mistake as to quality cannot make a contract *void*, it can make a contract *voidable*. This is so in equity but not at common law. In matters of agreement mistake, equity and common law marched in step. So they did in matters of possibility mistake, so far as concerned mistake as to existence and mistake as to ownership. But in dealing with mistake as to quality, equity diverged from the common law. That divergence is now only a matter of history, since all courts have for over a century been able to administer both common law and equity.

So the question may arise in any court as to whether a contract is void for mistake or, if not, whether it is voidable for mistake. In *Associated Japanese Bank (International) Ltd v. Crédit du Nord* (1988), Steyn J. said that the court must first decide whether the contract is void at common law. It will be void if its subject-matter is essentially and radically different from what both contracting parties believed it to be, provided that the party relying on the mistake had reasonable grounds for his mistaken belief. If the contract is void at common law, no question of mistake in equity arises. If, on the other hand, the contract is valid at common law, the court must go on to consider whether it can be set aside in equity. This is what happened in *Solle v. Butcher* (1950, C.A., above). In that case the Court of Appeal held that the contract was not void, but *voidable*. The defendant had let a flat to the plaintiff at £250 a year. Both parties thought that the flat was not subject to the Rent Restriction Acts. This was because it had been so drastically reconstructed as to be virtually a new flat. If it really was a new flat the Acts would not apply. But it was held later that it was not a new flat within the meaning of the legislation and that therefore the Acts did apply. So the parties had been under a mistake as to a quality of the flat. One of the judges in the Court of Appeal thought that that was a mistake of law. The other two judges thought it was a mistake of fact. On the footing that the Acts applied, the maximum permissible rent was only £140. After he had been in possession for about two years the tenant sued to recover back the rent that he had overpaid. The landlord counterclaimed to have the contract set aside. The Court of Appeal held, first, that the contract of letting was not void, and, secondly, that it was voidable. They set aside the contract on terms by which, in effect, the tenant was given the choice of giving up the flat or staying on and paying rent at £250.

Solle v. Butcher was followed in *Grist v. Bailey* (1967). The defendant agreed to sell a house to the plaintiff, subject to an existing tenancy. The value of the house with vacant possession would have been about £2,250, but the purchase price was agreed at £850 because both parties believed that the tenancy was protected by the Rent Acts. This was a mistake. In fact the tenant did not claim the protection of the Rent Acts, and left. The plaintiff sued for specific performance, and the defendant counterclaimed to have the contract set aside. The judge held that the contract was not void, but was voidable, and he set the contract aside on terms that the defendant undertook to permit the plaintiff to buy the house (if he wanted to) at the proper vacant possession price, £2,250.

In *Magee v. Pennine Insurance Co. Ltd* (1969, C.A.) there was a dispute between an insurance company and the insured as to the proper amount due under a claim. The parties compromised the dispute, the insurance company agreeing to pay £385 to the insured. Later, but before they had actually paid this amount, the insurers discovered that some statements made in the insured's proposal form, some years before, were incorrect. They refused to pay the amount which had been agreed under the compromise. The Court of Appeal, by a majority, held that the compromise had been reached under a fundamental mistake that the policy was good and binding. Lord Denning M.R. held that such a mistake, with regard to *Bell v. Lever*, did not make the contract (that is, the compromise) void but, following *Solle v. Butcher*, it did make it voidable. Fenton Atkinson L.J. held that the insurance company were "entitled to avoid" the contract under *Bell v. Lever*, but it is not clear whether he was treating the contract as void or as voidable, nor whether he was treating the mistake as one of quality or as one of existence (existence of the policy). The court, Winn L.J. dissenting, gave judgment for the insurance company.

So a contract may be *voidable* for mistake in circumstances where it is *not void* for mistake. Exactly what circumstances will permit a court to set aside a contract has never been precisely stated. In *Huddersfield Banking Co. Ltd v. Henry Lister and Son Ltd* (1895, C.A.) Kay L.J. stated the principle in this way: "It seems to me that, both on principle and authority, when once the court finds that an agreement has been come to between parties who were under a common mistake of a material fact, the court may set it aside." "Common" here means "shared by both parties"; it does not mean "prevalent".

So the court has power to set aside a contract whenever the parties are under a mistake of a material fact. The extent of the court's power to impose terms is not entirely clear. It is clear that the court can impose terms when setting aside a contract which is not void at law. It is not clear whether the court can impose terms when the contract is void at law. There are dicta pointing each way. On principle one would think that if the contract is void the court cannot impose terms; it is as though the contract had never been made, and the parties (and even third parties) must suffer whatever consequences flow from its voidness.

A claim to have a contract set aside for mistake under this equity jurisdiction may be lost in any of the ways in which a claim to rescind a contract for misrepresentation may be lost: affirmation, inability to restore the status quo, and the existence of third party rights. in relation to this last point it should be noted that if a contract is *void* for mistake, and the court declares it to be so, the rights acquired by a third party, even if he acquired them in good faith and for value, are defeated; if a contract is only *voidable* for mistake, a court will preserve the rights of third parties by declining to set the contract aside.

In one circumstance the appropriate remedy may be rectification (on which see p. 57, above) rather than setting aside the contract. If the parties have reached an agreement and then a written document is drawn up which, by mistake, does not truly reflect their agreement, the court may rectify the document to bring it into line with the earlier agreement. Suppose A agrees to let a flat to B for £2,000 a year. The lease, when drawn up, states the rent to be £1,000 a year. The court may order rectification of the lease, by the substitution of "£2,000" for "£1,000". If justice so requires, the court may offer to B the choice of submitting to rectification or having the lease cancelled altogether.

MISTAKES IN DOCUMENTS

Where a person signs a document, he is, as a general rule, bound by his signature. If he has not read the document he is still, in general, bound by it. Of course, he may be able to prove that he has been induced to sign it by fraud or other misrepresentation, or he may be able to prove the presence of a mistake; either an agreement mistake or a possibility mistake. If he can prove any of these things his possible remedies are as already discussed.

But there is one further remedy which may possibly be open to him. This is what is called the plea of *non est factum* ("this is not my deed"). This plea is peculiar to signed documents, and the law relating to it is quite separate from the general law of misrepresentation and mistake.

The plea of *non est factum* first made its appearance at the end of the sixteenth century. If a person who could not read had a deed "read over" to him, and the "reading" did not correctly state what was in the writing, he was not bound by the deed. The deed was not merely voidable for the fraud of the "reader", but was altogether void, with the consequence that if it came into the hands of even an innocent third party he could not acquire any rights under it. Later the plea was extended to written documents not under seal, and it was extended to persons who could have read, but did not read, the document.

At this stage in its development, the plea was very wide indeed, and the courts set about trying to bring it within more reasonable bounds. It became established law that the plea was not available to a signer who was mistaken merely as to the *contents* of the document, not as to its *character* or *class*. It was also established that the plea was not available to a signer who was negligent in signing.

The most important recent case on *non est factum* is the House of Lords decision in *Saunders v. Anglia Building Society* (1971, H.L.). The plaintiff was Mrs Gallie, an old lady of 78, who owned a house held on long leasehold. She had a nephew called Wally Parkin. She had made a will leaving the house to Parkin, and she had handed over the deeds of the house to him. Parkin had a friend called Lee. Parkin and Lee together came to Mrs Gallie's house and asked her to sign a document. She got the impression that the point of the document was to enable Parkin and Lee to raise money jointly on the security of the house, and she had no objection to that. She thought that the document was an assignment of the leasehold by gift from herself to Parkin. She did not read the document because she had broken her spectacles. She signed it unread. In fact the document was an assignment from Mrs Gallie to Lee for £3,000. Lee did not pay Mrs Gallie the £3,000 or anything at all. Lee mortgaged the house to a building society and used the proceeds entirely for his own purposes, to the exclusion of Parkin. He defaulted on the mortgage payments, and the building society sought possession of the house. Mrs Gallie sued for a declaration that the assignment was void, on the basis of *non est factum*. Lee was the first defendant, and the building society was the second defendant.

The trial judge gave judgment for Mrs Gallie. The Court of Appeal unanimously reversed his decision and the House of Lords unanimously affirmed the Court of Appeal. At first instance and in the Court of Appeal the case is called *Gallie v. Lee and Another*. In the House of Lords it is called *Saunders v. Anglia Building Society*. Mrs Gallie had died before the case reached the House of Lords, and Saunders was the name of her executrix. Lee ceased to be a party to the proceedings after the first instance decision.

The views of the House of Lords can be summarised as follows:

(1) The plea of *non est factum* can only succeed where the person who signed the document can show that there was a *radical difference* between what he signed and what he thought he was signing, and this test should replace the former distinction between the contents of a document and its *character* or *class*.

(2) The plea is not open to a signer who was careless in signing. The word "careless" is preferable to the word "negligent", because "negli-

gent'' has come to have a technical meaning (involving the breach of a duty of care) which is not appropriate in this context.

Mrs Gallie's executrix failed on the first point because, given Mrs Gallie's wish to enable Parkin and Lee to raise money on the security of the house, there was not a radical difference between what she signed and what she thought she was signing. Two of the Law Lords expressly approved the way Russell L.J. had put it in the Court of Appeal; namely, that Mrs Gallie was not mistaken as to the very ''object of the exercise'' as distinct from the details of the document or its parties.

In *United Dominions Trust Ltd v. Western* (1976, C.A.) the Court of Appeal held that no valid distinction can be drawn between the carelessness of a person who signs a document without reading it and the carelessness of a person who signs a document in blank leaving the details to be filled in by a third party.

The most recent case involving a plea of *non est factum* confirms the narrow limits of the rule: see *Norwich and Peterborough Building Society v. Steed* (No.2) (1992).

CHAPTER ELEVEN

CONFLICT WITH A LEGAL RULE

THIS chapter is concerned with the situation where a contract, perfectly valid in other respects, comes into conflict with some legal rule. The rule in question may be a rule laid down by a statute or it may be a rule of common law. Some contracts are prohibited by statute; some are prohibited by a rule of common law. Other contracts, though not absolutely prohibited, are denied their full validity by a statute or by a rule of common law. Where a contract is prohibited it is said to be "illegal"; where a contract is merely denied its full validity it is said to be "void". This nomenclature will be used in this chapter but it should be noted that not all writers, and not all judges, use the words in exactly this way. In some cases of high authority the word "unenforceable" is used rather than the word "void".

VOID CONTRACTS

Void contracts may be divided into those which are void by statute and those which are void at common law.

Contracts Void by Statute

It would be impossible in this book to go through all the contracts which are made void by different statutes and only wagering contracts will be dealt with here.

Wagering contracts

A bet upon some future event or upon some past or present fact is a wager if it has the following features: (1) there are two parties, or groups of parties, and not more; (2) each party stands to win or lose; and (3) neither party has any financial interest in the outcome other than the sum in issue. Because of point (1) a football pool is not a wager; because of point (2) a bet with "The Tote" is not a wager, since "The Tote" cannot lose: see *Tote Investors Ltd v. Smoker* (1968, C.A.); because of point (3) a contract of insurance is not a wager, provided that the assured has a genuine "insurable interest".

Rights of the parties under a wagering contract

Section 18 of the Gaming Act 1845 provides as follows:

> "All contracts or agreements, whether by parole or in writing, by way of gaming or wagering, shall be null and void; and no suit shall be brought or maintained in any court of law or equity for recovering any sum of money or valuable thing alleged to be won upon any wager, or which shall have been deposited in the hands of any person to abide the event on which any wager shall have been made. Provided always that this enactment shall not be deemed to apply to any subscription or contribution or agreement to subscribe or contribute for or towards any plate, prize or sum of money to be awarded to the winner or winners of any lawful game, sport, pastime or exercise."

The section thus makes a wagering contract *void*, but not *illegal*. If the loser does not pay, the winner cannot sue. If the loser pays by cheque and then stops the cheque, the winner cannot sue on the cheque. If the loser does pay, he cannot sue to recover back his money. Under most void contracts money paid can be recovered back, but it has been held that in this context it cannot because the payer has, by paying, waived the "benefit which the statute has given to him". The section also makes collateral contracts associated with gambling contracts unenforceable. In *Hill v. William Hill (Park Lane) Ltd* (1949, H.L.), for example, the defendant owed some £3,600 to the plaintiffs for lost bets. The committee of Tattersalls ordered the defendant to pay his debt by stated instalments. The defendant did not pay. Then, in consideration that the plaintiffs would not enforce the order, the defendant made a fresh promise to pay. He still did not pay. The plaintiffs sued him. The House of Lords held that the fresh promise was invalidated by section 18, as being the promise of a "sum of money alleged to be won upon a wager".

A third effect of the section is that it prevents the winner from suing the stakeholder if the stakeholder declines to pay over the money deposited with him by the loser. It does not prevent the winner or the loser suing the stakeholder to recover back *his own* stake.

Cases involving the Gaming Act 1845 are rare. A recent example is *City Index Ltd v. Leslie* (1992) which involved wagers on stock market index movements. The case in fact turned on the construction of the relevant provisions of the Financial Services Act 1986, section 63 of which excludes from the ambit of section 18 of the 1845 Act activities listed in the Schedule 1 to the 1986 Act. The Court of Appeal held that this type of bet fell within the 1986 Act and was therefore enforceable.

Rights on cheques and other securities

The winner of a wager cannot sue on the cheque if the loser pays by a cheque which bounces. But can a third party, to whom such a cheque is negotiated, sue on it? It is necessary to distinguish here between gaming wagers and non-gaming wagers. Cheques given for money won on a game are deemed to be given for an "illegal consideration", by virtue of the Gaming Act 1835. The third-party holder of a cheque can sue on it if he can prove that he or some previous holder gave value for it and that he personally, when he took the cheque, had no notice of its origin. A cheque given on a non-gaming wager is given without consideration, since the wager itself is void, but it is not tainted with illegality. The third-party holder of such a cheque will succeed unless the defendant can prove that at no stage in its career has the cheque been transferred for value. It does not matter if the holder knew of its origin.

Contracts Void at Common Law

From at least the time of Elizabeth I judges have regarded themselves as having jurisdiction to rule that certain contracts (and certain non-contractual transactions) are injurious to society. There has thus grown up what is called the doctrine of "public policy", enabling judges to refuse relief to litigants claiming under contracts which are considered to be injurious to the public good. This is a vague and uncertain doctrine and was described by a judge in 1824 as being "a very unruly horse".

It is now settled that it is no longer open to the courts to invent a new head of public policy. But the courts continue to act on the heads of public policy established by earlier decisions. Thus the doctrine has now crystallised and the heads of public policy can be enumerated. There is scope for disagreement as to whether a particular point of public policy should be regarded as a separate head or should more properly come under some wider head. Three kinds of void contracts will be considered here: contracts to oust the jurisdiction of the courts; contracts damaging to the institution of marriage; and contracts in restraint of trade.

Contracts to oust the jurisdiction of the courts

A contract which has the effect of taking away the right of one party, or both parties, to submit questions of law to the courts is contrary to public policy and is, to that extent, void. Notice "to that extent"; the rest of the contract may be perfectly valid. In Chapter 3, it was said that it is permissible for two (or more) persons to make an agreement and to provide in it that it shall not be enforceable at all; that it shall be a "gentleman's agreement". It is not permissible, however, to provide that it is to be enforceable and yet not open to the supervision of the courts.

An example is *Baker v. Jones* (1954), which involved an association formed to promote the sport of weightlifting. The association's rules, which constituted a contract between the members, provided that its council should be the sole interpreter of the rules and that the council's decision should in all cases be final. A member applied to the court for a declaration that the use of the association's funds for a particular purpose was against the rules. Lynskey J. held that the court had jurisdiction to entertain the action, and to consider whether the council's interpretation of the rules in a given case was correct in law. The rules, so far as they purported to oust the court's jurisdiction, were contrary to public policy and void.

An agreement between husband and wife for maintenance sometimes contains a term purporting to oust the jurisdiction of the courts. The wife, in return for an allowance, may promise not to apply to the court for maintenance. In *Hyman v. Hyman* (1929, H.L.) the House of Lords held that such an agreement did not prevent the wife from applying to the court for maintenance. The effect of this decision has been overtaken by legislation.

It is possible, however, for parties to agree to submit a dispute to arbitration and arbitration clauses are enforceable. Under the Arbitration Act

1979 it is permissible, in certain circumstances, for the parties to agree that neither of them will appeal to the courts from the award of the arbitrator.

Contracts damaging to the institution of marriage

The sanctity of marriage is regarded by the law as a matter of public interest. Under this principle the following contracts are void as being against public policy.

Contract in restraint of marriage

A contract is void if it restrains a person from marrying at all, or if it requires someone to marry a particular person without a reciprocal obligation on that person. In *Lowe v. Peers* (1768) a man made a contract under seal in these terms: "I do truly promise Mrs Catherine Lowe that I will not marry with any person besides herself: if I do, I agree to pay the said Catherine Lowe £1,000 within three months next after I shall marry anybody else." The contract was held void.

An ordinary engagement to marry never was affected by this principle, because in an engagement there was a reciprocal obligation. Now an engagement to marry is not an obligation in the legal sense at all. Section 1 of the Law Reform (Miscellaneous Provisions) Act 1970 provides that engagements to marry are not to be enforceable at law.

Marriage brokage contract

The contract struck at here is a contract by which A undertakes for a fee to procure a marriage for B. Thus a contract between a client and a "marriage bureau" is void: see *Hermann v. Charlesworth* (1905).

Contract for future separation

A contract between husband and wife for immediate separation is valid and enforceable if it is in fact followed by immediate separation. But a contract between husband and wife for possible separation in the future is void, as, for example, where a husband promises his wife that he will make provision for her if she should ever live apart from him. There is one exemption to this principle: if spouses have been separated and then come together again, the reconciliation agreement may make provision for the possibility of a renewed separation in the future.

Contracts in restraint of trade

The doctrine of restraint of trade is to the effect that a contract which comes within its ambit, and which restricts the liberty of a person to carry on his trade, business or profession in any manner he chooses, is contrary to public policy and void, unless it is justifiable as being reasonable.

The following general propositions of law may be stated:

1. The doctrine of restraint of trade does not apply to every contract which, in any circumstances whatever, restricts a man's liberty to trade. It does not apply to restrictions which are part of the "accepted and normal currency of commercial or contractual or conveyancing relations". Thus an agreement by the lessee of a public house that he will not sell beer on the premises except that brewed by his lessor is outside the doctrine of restraint of trade, as also is a negative covenant by which a lessee or purchaser of land agrees not to use the premises for trading purposes. The doctrine undoubtedly does apply to (1) contracts under which an employee restricts his liberty to compete against his employer after he has left his present employment, and (2) contracts by which the vendor of a business restricts his liberty to compete against the purchaser. There is a middle ground where the doctrine may or may not apply, depending upon the terms of the contract and the surrounding circumstances. "The classification must remain fluid and the categories can never be closed." This is not inconsistent with the point made earlier that the heads of public policy are closed; what we are considering here is not new heads, but new applications of the head "restraint of trade". Notice that it is usually the promisor who will be arguing that the doctrine applies, because it offers the possibility of escape from an otherwise binding obligation.

2. If a particular contract comes within the ambit of the doctrine, and contains restrictions on a person's liberty to trade, it is prima facie void, and will only be saved if it is reasonable.

3. To pass the test of reasonableness the restraint must be reasonable as between the parties and reasonable in the public interest.

4. To be held reasonable, the restraint must protect, and protect only, some proprietary or other legitimate interest of the promisee; and consequently the restraint must not be excessive as regards its area, time of operation or the trades which it forbids.

Restraints in a contract of employment

A restraint imposed on an employee is never reasonable unless there is some proprietary interest of the employer which requires protection. The only matters in which he will be held to have such an interest are his trade secrets (if any) and his business connection. In *Eastham v. Newcastle United Football Club* (1964) it was held that the rules of the Football Association and Football League relating to the retention and transfer of professional footballers did not protect any interest of the employer which the law would recognise for this purpose, and consequently they were void.

A good example of a trade secrets case is *Forster & Sons Ltd v. Suggett* (1918). The works manager of the plaintiff company was instructed in certain confidential methods concerning the correct mixture of gas and air in the furnaces for the manufacture of glass and glass bottles. He entered into a contract which contained a covenant that he would not, during the five years following the end of his employment, carry on in the United Kingdom, or be interested in, glass bottle manufacture or any other business connected with glass-making as conducted by the plaintiff company. This restraint was held to be valid.

A good example of a case concerning business connection is *Fitch v. Dewes* (1921, H.L.). A solicitor's managing clerk at Tamworth entered into a covenant that after leaving his employer he would not, for the rest of his life, practise as a solicitor within seven miles of Tamworth Town Hall. This restraint was upheld.

It will be observed that in *Forster v. Suggett* the area of the restraint was the whole of the United Kingdom, and that in *Fitch v. Dewes* the duration of the restraint was a life-time. But it must be borne in mind that there are very many cases where a restraint has been held void because it was too wide in area or too long in duration. It all depends on the circumstances, for they determine what is *reasonable*. Recent cases have tended to strike down covenants which prevent a former employee trading at all within a given area, and to uphold covenants which merely prevent him from soliciting the customers of his former employer.

If a restraint is imposed, not by a direct covenant, but by some indirect means, the doctrine still applies, and the restraint will be void if it is not reasonable. In *Bull v. Pitney-Bowes Ltd* (1967) the plaintiff was employed by the defendant company. It was a condition of his employment that he should become a member of a non-contributory pension scheme. Rule 16 of this scheme provided that a retired member should be liable to forfeit his pension rights if he engaged in any occupation which was in competition with the interests of the defendant company. After 26 years' service, the plaintiff voluntarily retired. He joined another company carrying on a business similar to that of the defendant company. He was warned that he might lose his pension if he did not leave his new employment. He sued for a declaration that rule 16 was in unreasonable restraint of trade and therefore void. Thesiger J. held that rule 16 was void. It was equivalent to a covenant in restraint of trade and was unreasonable. This is one of the comparatively rare cases where the court has stressed the public aspect of the unreasonableness, as distinct from the "party and party" aspect. The judge held that it was contrary to public policy that the community should be deprived of the services of a man skilled in a particular trade.

In *Kores Manufacturing Co. Ltd v. Kolok Manufacturing Co. Ltd* (1959, C.A.) two companies, manufacturing similar products, agreed that neither would employ any person who had been employed by the other during the last five years. The defendant company broke its promise. The Court of Appeal held that the plaintiff company's action must fail. The agreement was in restraint of trade and was unreasonable. More recently, the Court of Appeal has again considered such covenants, which in effect prevent the poaching of employees: see *Hanover Insurance Brokers v. Schapiro* (1994), in which the court refused to enforce such a covenant. It is clear that if it is to have any chance of enforcement it should be very narrowly drawn so as to be applicable to a small group or class of employees.

Restraints in a contract of sale of a business

The courts are more willing to uphold a restraint on the vendor of a business than one on an employee. The idea behind this is that buyers of a business would not be forthcoming if they could not have protection against competition by the vendor. Who would buy a grocer's shop if the vendor was to be left free to start up a new grocer's shop next door?

Such a restraint is valid, but only if it is connected with the proprietary interest which has been bought. In *British Reinforced Concrete Engineering Co. Ltd v. Schelff* (1921) the plaintiff company carried on a large business for the manufacture and sale of "B.R.C." road reinforcements. The defendant had a small business for the sale of "Loop" road reinforcements. The defendant sold his business to the plaintiff company and agreed not to compete with them in the manufacture or sale of road reinforcements. The covenant was held void. The interest which the plaintiff company had bought was the business of selling (not making) "Loop" reinforcements. It was therefore not justifiable to restrain the defendant from competing with the plaintiff company in road reinforcements in general. This case is a good example of unreasonableness residing in the excessive wideness of the forbidden trades: see proposition 4, above. But many more cases turn on unreasonableness of area or duration.

Restraints in other contracts

Proposition 1, above, said that there is a "middle ground", where there is no rigid rule of law that the doctrine of restraint of trade does apply, and no rigid rule of law that it does not. There are at least three fields in which the doctrine has been held to apply: in connection with trade associations; "solus" trading agreements; and agreements for exclusive services.

Trade associations. Sometimes a restraint is imposed by the rules of a trade association. One could call these "multilateral" restraints, as distinct from the unilateral restraints we have been considering. The principles are the same—the restrictions are prima facie void, and can only be enforced if they are reasonable.

In *English Hop Growers v. Dering* (1928, C.A.) the defendant was a member of the plaintiff association. He agreed to deliver to the association all the hops grown on his land in 1926. He did not do so, and he was sued. He pleaded that the restraint was unreasonable. The restraint was upheld. He had joined the association voluntarily. It was a sensible attempt to spread the loss caused by excessive stocks of hops having been accumulated during the First World War.

On the other side of the line of reasonableness lies *McEllistrim v. Ballymacelligott Co-operative Agricultural and Dairy Society* (1919, H.L.). The Society manufactured cheese and butter from milk supplied by members. The rules provided that no member should sell milk otherwise than to the Society without consent of the committee; that no member could withdraw from the Society unless his shares were transferred or cancelled; that there could be no transfer or cancellation of shares without consent of the committee; and that such consent could be refused without giving reasons. The restraint was held to be unreasonable.

"Solus" trading agreements. It is common for oil companies to enter into "solus" agreements with garage owners. An oil company advances money to help with the purchase or development of a garage, and/or offers a rebate on the price of the fuel, and the garage owner undertakes in return to sell only the company's products at the garage. A similar situation obtains in some other trades.

141

In *Esso Petroleum Co. Ltd v. Harper's Garage (Stourport) Ltd* (1968, H.L.) the garage company owned two garages and had entered into a solus agreement with Esso in respect of each garage. The garage company agreed to buy all its motor fuel from Esso; to keep the garage open at all reasonable hours; and not to sell the garage without ensuring that the purchaser entered into a similar agreement with Esso. Esso agreed to allow a rebate on all fuels bought. The agreement in respect of one garage was to operate for four years and five months; that in respect of the other garage was to operate for 21 years. The latter garage was mortgaged to Esso in return for an advance of £7,000, and the mortgage was not redeemable before the end of the 21 years. The House of Lords held that both agreements were within the ambit of the doctrine of restraint of trade: see proposition 1, above. In particular, the fact that one of the agreements was by way of covenant in a mortgage of land did not exclude the doctrine. The agreements were therefore prima facie void, and could only be enforced if they were reasonable. In the particular circumstances of the case, the crucial consideration in determining reasonableness was the duration of restraints. The agreement which was to last for four years and five months was reasonable; the agreement which was to last for 21 years was not.

In *Alec Lobb (Garages) Ltd v. Total Oil (Great Britain) Ltd* (1985, C.A.), on the other hand, the Court of Appeal, in rather special circumstances, upheld as valid a restraint operating for 21 years.

In *Cleveland Petroleum Co. Ltd v. Dartstone Ltd* (1969, C.A.) the Court of Appeal held that the doctrine of restraint of trade does not apply where a person is let into possession of land on the express term that he "ties" himself; consequently, such a person cannot argue that the tie is void. This situation was sharply distinguished from the situation where a person who is *already* in possession of land ties himself. Whereas in the second case the person is giving up a freedom which he previously had, in the first case he is not; he never had freedom to trade in any manner at all from that land.

Agreements for exclusive services. In *A. Schroeder Music Publishing Co. Ltd v. Macaulay* (1974, H.L.) Macaulay, who at the time was an unknown song-writer, aged 21, entered into a standard form agreement with a publishing company; the agreement was very one-sidedly in favour of the publishers. Macaulay was to hand over all his musical compositions to the publishers, who were to have the full world copyright in the compositions in return for a fixed percentage of any royalties. The term of the agreement was five years, with automatic extension for another five years if the royalties payable to Macaulay within the first five years should exceed £5,000. The publishers could terminate the agreement or assign the benefit of it; Macaulay could not terminate the agreement and could only assign his rights under it with the publishers' consent. The agreement did not put the publishers under any obligation to publish or promote any of Macaulay's compositions. Macaulay sued for a declaration that the agreement was contrary to public policy, as being in unreasonable restraint of trade, and void. The trial judge granted the declaration sought, and this decision was affirmed by the Court of Appeal and the House of Lords.

The *Schroeder* case is important, because the ground on which the House of Lords decided the case was that where there is clear inequality of bargaining power between the parties the courts can and should inquire into the circumstances to see whether the contract is fair. It follows that the restraint of trade doctrine can apply (as in the *Schroeder* case itself) to contracts for services as well as to contracts of service (contracts of employment strictly so-called), and the courts can investigate the fairness of restraints operating during the currency of the employment as well as the restraints which are to operate after the termination of the employment. It follows also that any contract, whether it imposes a restraint or not, can be struck down by the courts for unfairness where there is inequality of bargaining power. But it should be noted that in *National Westminster Bank plc v. Morgan* (1985, H.L.) (see p. 111, above) Lord Scarman, in a speech concurred in by the other four Law Lords, said: "... in the field of contract I question whether there is any need in the modern law to erect a general principle of relief against inequality of bargaining power. Parliament has undertaken the task (and it is essentially a legislative task) of enacting such restrictions upon freedom of contract as are in its judgment necessary to relieve against the mischief... I doubt whether the courts should assume the burden of formulating further restrictions."

General observations on restraint of trade

Three points should be made here. First, where a court holds that a restraint is valid it generally grants an injunction. This is one of the rare instances in the law of contract where an injunction, rather than damages, is the primary remedy.

Secondly, Article 85 of the Treaty of Rome has the force of law in the United Kingdom. Article 85 makes void (unless they are specifically exempted) agreements, decisions and concerted practices which have as their object or effect the prevention, restriction or distortion of competition within the Common Market. This Article would clearly apply to a restrictive agreement between a body in the United Kingdom and a body in another Member State of the E.U., and it could even apply to an agreement between two or more bodies within the United Kingdom if that agreement adversely affected competition within the Common Market.

Thirdly, just as the doctrine of public policy does not apply only to contracts, so the doctrine of restraint of trade (which is an aspect of the public policy doctrine) does not apply only to contracts. This point was emphasised by the House of Lords in *Pharmaceutical Society of G.B. v. Dickson* (1970, H.L.). A motion passed by a majority of members of the Society was held to be subject to the doctrine even though it was binding in honour only. It was further held to be in unreasonable restraint of trade and so void.

The Effects where a Contract is held Void

The legal effects of a contract being held to be void are broadly the same whether a contract is void by statute or void at common law. But where a contract is void by statute, one cannot really generalise about the effects, because they will depend upon the precise wording of the statute in question and the code of case law that grows up around it. Thus, for example, the effects of a wagering contract have to be studied separately. In what follows the effects of a contract void at common law will be considered, though many of the principles are applied by analogy when a court is dealing with the effects of a contract void by statute.

The extent of the voidness

The contract is void *in so far as* it contravenes public policy. The contravention does not render the whole contract void. Provided that there is something left in the contract when the void part of it is put on one side, that "something" is valid and can be sued on. For instance, suppose there is a contract of employment which contains, amongst other clauses, a restraint clause which is unreasonable and therefore void. Neither party can sue successfully on the restraint clause. But despite the presence of that void clause, the employee can sue for his wages (for example).

Severance

Severance means the separating of the void part of the contract from the valid part. Severance may involve the cutting out of a whole promise from the contract, or it may only require the cutting out of a part of a promise. Thus, in the example just given, severance involves the cutting out of the whole of the restraint clause. If, to stay with that example, the employer was seeking to enforce the restraint clause, it might be possible to cut out from that clause the objectionable part, leaving the reasonable part enforceable.

If a whole promise is void as being contrary to public policy, severance will have a markedly different effect according to whether there is or is not any consideration other than that promise. The point is neatly illustrated by two cases on restraint of trade. In *Bull v. Pitney-Bowes Ltd* (1967), the facts of which have already been given at p. 139, above, the non-competition clause in the pension scheme rules was held to be void, and was severed. As the employee had given other consideration as well as that promise, the result was that he was held entitled to his pension free of any restriction. In an earlier case, *Wyatt v. Kreglinger and Fernau* (1933, C.A.), the facts were similar. Just before the plaintiff retired from employment with the defendants they told him that they were going to give him an annual pension of £200 a year subject to the condition that he did not compete against them in the wool trade. After paying the pension for some years the defendants refused to make any further payments. The plaintiff sued them. The defendants pleaded that, if there was a contract at all, it was void as being in unreasonable restraint of trade. The Court of Appeal held the contract void. The plaintiff lost his pension; when the non-competition clause was severed there was no other consideration moving from the plaintiff, and consequently he could not enforce the defendants' promise to pay the pension.

An example of severance in the more limited sense of cutting out part of a promise is to be found in *Goldsoll v. Goldman* (1915, C.A.). There, the defendant carried on business in London, selling imitation jewellery. He sold the business to the plaintiff and agreed that for a period of two years he would not deal in real or imitation jewellery in any part of the United Kingdom or in France, the United States, Russia or Spain, or within 25 miles of Potsdammerstrasse, Berlin, or St Stefans Kirche, Vienna. The restraint over the whole United Kingdom was reasonable, as the business gained most of its customers from advertisements in national newspapers. The restraint relating to areas outside the United Kingdom was unreasonable. Also, whilst the prohibition against dealing in imitation jewellery was reasonable, the prohibition against dealing in real jewellery was not, since the business which the defendant had sold to the plaintiff was not concerned with real jewellery. The Court of Appeal held that the restraint clause could and should be severed in two ways: the references to places outside the United Kingdom were deleted, as also was the reference to real jewellery. That left a valid restraint against dealing in imitation jewellery in the United Kingdom.

In *Attwood v. Lamont* (1920, C.A.) the plaintiffs had a general outfitters' business at Kidderminster. It was divided into several departments, each of which was supervised by one of their employees. The head of each department signed a contract promising that he would not, after leaving the plaintiffs' service, ''be concerned in any of the following trades or businesses: that is to say, the trade or business of a tailor, dressmaker, general draper, milliner, hatter, haberdasher, gentlemen's, ladies' or children's outfitter'' within 10 miles of Kidderminster. The plaintiffs were seeking to enforce this covenant against the former head of the tailoring department. They had to admit that the covenant was too wide in subject-matter to be enforced as it stood. But they argued that everything except the reference to tailoring should be cut out, thus leaving a valid covenant which they could enforce. This argument was rejected by the Court of Appeal. Severance would have altered the whole nature of the covenant. After severance the covenant would protect only that part of the business in which the defendant had worked, whereas the original covenant was ''part of a scheme by which every head of a department was to be restrained from competition with the plaintiffs, even in the business of departments with which he had no connection''. This was not a case of several distinct covenants; ''. . . there is in truth but one covenant for the protection of the respondent's entire business, and not several covenants for the protection of his several businesses. The respondent is, on the evidence, not carrying on several businesses but one business, and in my opinion this covenant must stand or fall in its unaltered form''. It fell.

The main point of distinction between the two cases is that in *Goldsoll's* case the deletions which the court made did not alter the whole nature of the covenant, but merely cut down its extent, whereas in *Attwood's* case the deletions that were asked for, and refused, would have meant making, in effect, a new contract.

Recovering back

When money is paid, or property is transferred, by one party to the other, and the contract is held to be void as being contrary to public policy, it can probably be recovered back by the payer or transferor. In *Hermann v. Charlesworth* (1905, C.A.) there was a marriage brokage contract. The defendant agreed to introduce gentlemen to Miss Hermann with a view to marriage. He took a fee of £52, and was to receive a further £250 on the day of the marriage. He introduced her to several men, and corresponded with others, but nothing came of it. Miss Hermann sued for the return of the £52. She succeeded.

ILLEGAL CONTRACTS

As with void contracts, the legal rule may be a rule laid down by a statute or may be a rule of common law. These two situations will be looked at separately, and the effects of illegality will then be examined.

Contracts Illegal by Statute

A contract is illegal if it is prohibited by a statute. "Statute" for this purpose includes delegated legislation, such as a statutory instrument.

Express or implied prohibition

Express prohibition

An example of an express prohibition is to be found in Part I of the Resale Prices Act 1976, which prohibits and makes unlawful an agreement for the collective enforcement of conditions regulating the price at which goods may be resold. Another example of express prohibition is to be found in the case of *Re Mahmoud and Ispahani* (1921, C.A.). A statutory order provided that no one should buy or sell linseed oil without a licence. The plaintiff had a licence to sell to other licensed dealers, and he was induced to sell to the defendant by the latter's fraudulent statement that he also had a licence. Subsequently, the defendant refused to take delivery and the plaintiff sued him for damages. Although the plaintiff was entirely innocent, he failed in his action. The order expressly prohibited any contract of sale if either party to it was unlicensed.

Implied prohibition

Cope v. Rowlands (1836) provides an example of an implied prohibition. A statute provided that any person who acted as broker in the City of London without a licence should forfeit the sum of £25 to the City. The plaintiff, who was unlicensed, did some work for the defendant in buying and selling stock. He failed in an action for his fee. Park B. said: "the legislature had in view, as one object, the benefit and security of the public in those important transactions which are negotiated by brokers. The clause, therefore, which imposes a penalty, must be taken . . . to imply a prohibition of all unadmitted persons to act as brokers, and consequently to prohibit by necessary inference all contracts which such persons make for compensation to themselves for so acting."

The courts will not lightly hold that a statute impliedly prohibits a contract. In *Archbolds (Freightage) Ltd v. S. Spanglett Ltd* (1961, C.A.) the Road and Rail Traffic Act 1933 was in issue. That statute provided that no person should use a vehicle for the carriage of goods unless he held an "A" or "C" licence. An "A" licence entitled him to carry other people's goods for reward; a "C" licence entitled him to carry his own goods only. The defendants, who held only a "C" licence, agreed to carry for the plaintiffs 200 crates of whisky belonging to third parties from Leeds to London. The plaintiffs did not know that the defendants had not got an "A" licence. The whisky was stolen on the way, and the plaintiffs sued for damages. The defendants argued that the contract was prohibited under the Act, since the vehicle used for carriage had only a "C" licence. The Court of Appeal rejected this argument, and held that the Act did not prohibit the contract expressly, and did not even prohibit it by implication. The object of the statute was to promote the efficiency of transport services, and that object could be attained without invalidating every contract made by carriers in breach of its provisions; it could be attained by imposing penalties on such carriers.

Contracts illegal in themselves and contracts illegal in their performance

It is necessary to distinguish between a contract which is illegal in itself and a contract which becomes illegal in its performance. The importance of the distinction will be seen when the effects of illegality are discussed.

A contract illegal in itself

The case of *Re Mahmoud and Ispahani* (1921, C.A.), considered above, illustrates this situation. Since Ispahani was an unlicensed person, the con-

148

tract to sell linseed oil to him was illegal in itself. It could not be performed in any way that would not be illegal.

A contract illegal in its performance

It is possible for a contract to be legal in itself, and yet to become illegal by reason of the way in which it is performed. This happened in *Anderson Ltd v. Daniel* (1924, C.A.). A statute required every seller of artificial manure to give to the buyer an invoice stating the proportion of certain chemicals contained in the manure. The plaintiffs sold 10 tons of artificial manure to the defendant without giving him these particulars. They sued for the contract price, and they failed, because the way in which they had performed the contract made it illegal.

This principle, by which the manner of performance can make a contract illegal, applies only where the prohibited act lies at the centre of the contract. It does not apply where the prohibited act is merely incidental to the performance of the contract. In *St John Shipping Corporation v. Joseph Rank Ltd* (1957), a shipowner, in performing a contract of carriage, overloaded his ship to such an extent that the load line became submerged. This was a breach of the Merchant Shipping Act 1932. The master of the ship was prosecuted for this offence, and was fined £1,200. The defendants withheld part of the freight due, and, when sued, they contended that the plaintiff shipowner could not enforce the contract because it had been performed in an illegal manner. This argument was rejected by the court, because the illegal loading was merely incidental to the performance of the contract.

Shaw v. Groom (1970, C.A.) was decided on similar lines. It was held that a landlord who, in breach of section 4 of the Landlord and Tenant Act 1962, fails to provide his tenant with a rent book, is not precluded from suing the tenant for rent. The Court of Appeal distinguished *Anderson Ltd v. Daniel* (1924, C.A.) on somewhat narrow grounds. *Shaw v. Groom* is important as showing that in the (almost) half-century that separated these two cases the courts had become very much more sensitive to the injustices which tend to flow from holding contracts to be illegal.

Contracts Illegal at Common Law

Seven kinds of contract which are illegal at common law will now be considered. These all stem from the doctrine of public policy, discussed above in connection with contracts which are void at common law. The contracts to be considered here are held to be contrary to public policy, and are held to be so objectionable that they are not merely void but are illegal.

A contract to commit a crime, tort or fraud

A contract which has as its object the commission of a crime, or of a tort, or of a fraud upon third parties, is illegal. A clear example is *Everet v. Williams* (1725), where a contract between two highwaymen to rob a coach and then share the takings was held to be illegal, so that one highwayman could not sue the other for his share.

A more modern example is *Scott v. Brown, Doering, McNab & Co.* (1892, C.A.). There there was a contract to "rig the market", that is, to enhance artificially the price of shares, by purchasing some of them at a fictitious premium. The plaintiff was unable to recover back money that he had paid to a firm of stockbrokers in pursuance of that contract.

A contract damaging to the country's safety

The most important example of this class of contract is a trading contract between a British subject and an alien enemy in time of war. If such a contract is *made* during war it is wholly illegal. If it is made in peacetime and then war comes, it can give rise to no further rights or obligations. But existing rights and obligations are only suspended; after hostilities cease they can be enforced.

A contract damaging to the country's foreign relations

A contract which tends to disturb this country's good relations with a friendly country is illegal. In *Regazzoni v. K.C. Sethia (1944) Ltd* (1958, H.L.) the defendants agreed to sell to the plaintiffs jute twills, with the intention that they should be exported from India to Europe for resale in South Africa. Indian law prohibited the export of goods from India if they were destined for South Africa. The plaintiffs claimed damages for non-delivery of the goods. They failed. It was the common intent of both parties to violate the law of India, and, since India was a friendly country, the contract was contrary to public policy in this country. See also *Lemenda Trading Co. v. African Middle East Petroleum Co. Ltd* (1988).

A contract damaging to the administration of justice

The most important example of this class is a contract to stifle a prosecution, that is, to compromise a prosecution or to prevent a prosecution which has begun from taking its normal course. See *R v. Andrews* (1973).

Another example of a contract damaging to the administration of justice is a contract which involves maintenance or champerty. Maintenance in this context means stirring up litigation by giving aid to a plaintiff or defendant without just cause or excuse. Champerty is the maintenance of an action coupled with a bargain that the maintainer shall receive a share of whatever is recovered in the action. Both maintenance and champerty used to be criminal and tortious. The Criminal Law Act 1967 provides that neither shall any longer be criminal or tortious. But by section 14(2) it is provided that this abolition of liability "shall not affect any rule of . . . law as to the cases in which a contract is to be treated as contrary to public policy or otherwise illegal". So the rule still stands that contracts involving maintenance or champerty are illegal. In *Giles v. Thompson* (1994) the House of Lords refused to treat as champertous an agreement between a car hire company and a potential plaintiff whose car needed repairs as a result of a motor accident by which the potential plaintiff received free car hire in return for agreeing that the company could bring an action for damages in the plaintiff's name.

More recently, however, in *Grovewood Holdings plc v. James Capel & Co. Ltd* (1994) Lightman J. held to be champertous and an abuse of the process of the court an agreement by which a liquidator of a company engaged in litigation agreed with backers that, in return for funding to continue with litigation, they should receive a share of the recoveries of the action. The judge drew a distinction between selling a "bare" cause of action, which is permitted by the Insolvency Act 1986, and a sale of the fruits of litigation, which remains subject to the law of maintenance and champerty. So he ordered the action to be stayed.

A contract tending to promote corruption in public life

This is a fairly wide principle, but one example will suffice. In *Parkinson v. College of Ambulance* (1925) the secretary of the defendant charity told the plaintiff that the charity was in a position to procure him a knighthood if he would make an adequate donation. After a certain amount of bargaining, the plaintiff paid £3,000 to the charity and undertook to do more when the knighthood was forthcoming. The plaintiff did not get a knighthood, and he sued for the return of his money. His action failed. See also *Lemenda Trading Co. Ltd v. African Middle East Petroleum Co. Ltd* (1988).

151

A contract to defraud the revenue authorities

A contract to defraud the revenue authorities, whether national or local, is illegal. In *Miller v. Karlinski* (1945, C.A.) the plaintiff was employed by the defendant. He was to receive a salary of £10 a week and repayment of his expenses. He was also entitled to include in his expense account the amount of income tax due in respect of his weekly salary. The plaintiff brought an action to recover 10 weeks' arrears of salary and £21 2s. 8d. for expenses. It emerged at the trial that about £17 of this latter sum represented his liability for income tax. It was held that the contract was illegal since it constituted a fraud on the revenue, and the plaintiff's action therefore failed. He was not only unable to recover the illegal "expenses"; he could not even recover his ordinary salary.

A contract to promote sexual immorality

A contract tending to promote sexual immorality is illegal at common law. In *Upfill v. Wright* (1911) a landlord let a flat to a woman whom he knew to be the mistress of a certain man. He also knew, or could be presumed to know, that the money for the rent would be given to her "as the price of her immorality". When the landlord sued for the rent, his action failed. In *Pearce v. Brooks* (1866) the plaintiffs agreed to supply the defendant with a new miniature brougham. The defendant was a prostitute, and she intended to use the carriage, which was said to be "ornamental", in plying her trade, or plying for hire. The Court Exchequer Chamber were satisfied that the plaintiffs were aware of the defendant's intention. The plaintiffs' action for money due under the contract failed.

Contracts illegal in themselves and contracts illegal in their performance

In connection with contracts illegal by statute a distinction was made between contracts illegal in themselves and contracts illegal in their performance. A similar distinction falls to be made in contracts illegal at common law. In this context a contract may be illegal in itself in either of two ways. It may be illegal in itself in that it is a contract to do something which is prohibited by a rule of common law. An example is a contract of trade between a British subject and an enemy alien in time of war. Or a contract may be illegal in itself in that both parties intend to execute an illegal purpose. Thus a contract to let a flat is illegal in itself if both parties intend that the flat shall be used for the commission of crime. But a contract to let a flat where the landlord is unaware that the tenant intends to use it for criminal purposes is not in itself illegal; it becomes illegal in its performance if the tenant carries out his intention.

The Effects where a Contract is held Illegal

Where a contract is held to be illegal, the effects are broadly the same whether the contract is illegal by statute or illegal at common law; but the effects differ sharply according to whether the contract is illegal in itself or illegal in its performance.

First, however, severance will be considered, since that concerns equally contracts which are illegal in themselves and contracts which are illegal in their performance. It will be remembered that a contract which is merely void (not illegal) may be subjected to severance, so that the objectionable part of a promise—or even a whole promise—is cut out, leaving the rest of the contract valid and enforceable. The conventional view has been that that process is not possible with an illegal contract. If the contract is affected by illegality at all, the whole contract is invalid; it is all or nothing. There is clear authority, *e.g. Bennett v. Bennett* (1952, C.A.), to that effect, but this position is changing. In *Fielding and Platt Ltd v. Najjar* (1969, C.A.) Lord Denning said, *obiter*, of a particular term in a contract: "That term would be void for illegality. But it can clearly be severed from the rest of the contract. It can be rejected, leaving the rest of the contract good and enforceable." In *Ailion v. Spiekermann* (1976) Templeman J. expressly held that the illegal part of the contract he was dealing with could be severed, and the legal part enforced. The contract was for the assignment of the lease of a protected tenancy. The contract provided for the purchasers to pay an excess sum for certain chattels, which provision was illegal under the Rent Acts. Lord Denning was dealing with common law illegality; Templeman J. was dealing with statutory illegality. The line of thought is towards allowing severance where one party is innocent or in a weak bargaining position.

Where a contract is illegal in itself

The consequences where a contract is illegal in itself are as follows:

(1) Neither party can sue on the contract, unless (see above) severance is possible. For example, in *Keir v. Leeman* (1846) the plaintiff, though he had performed his promise not to pursue a prosecution, could not sue on the counter-promise made by his friends to pay the debt owed to him.

Leeman and his friend obtained what they promised to pay for and then got away without paying. This is often the case with illegal contracts. Sometimes it is possible for a wholly innocent party to an illegal contract to obtain redress by suing the villain for fraud as a tort. Until recently this was only possible where the fraud related to the illegality, but in *Shelley v. Paddock* (1980, C.A.) an innocent victim of fraud successfully sued in tort even though the fraud was not connected with the illegality. Miss Shelley, of Lowestoft, wanted to buy a house in Spain. Mr and Mrs Paddock, who were resident in Spain, showed her a house near Alicante, telling her fraudulently that they were authorised agents of the owner to sell it. She agreed to buy the house, and paid a deposit of £80, and subsequently paid £9,320 into the Paddocks' bank account in England. These payments, without the consent of the Treasury, were illegal under the exchange control legislation, but Miss Shelley did not know that there was such a thing. (Exchange control, with minor exceptions, was abolished in 1979, but the facts of this case occurred in 1974.) Miss Shelley never got the house. In an action for fraud she recovered as damages a sum equal to the amount she had paid to the Paddocks, plus damages for mental and physical suffering and plus her expenses. See also *Saunders v. Edwards* (1987, C.A.) and *Howard v. Shirlstar Container Transport Ltd* (1990, C.A.).

(2) Property or other rights transferred under an illegal contract become vested in the transferee: *Belvoir Finance Co. Ltd v. Stapleton* (1971, C.A.). Consequently neither party can, in general, sue to recover back what he has paid or transferred under the contract. It will be remembered that Mr Parkinson could not get his money back from the College of Ambulance. That is the general rule, but there are three exceptions.

(i) A party can recover back money or property if he can establish his case without reliance on the illegal contract. In *Bowmakers Ltd v. Barnet Instruments Ltd* (1945, C.A.) the defendants obtained some machine tools from the plaintiffs under three hire-purchase contracts. These contracts were illegal as contravening various war-time regulations. The defendants failed to pay the periodical hire charges. They sold some of the goods, and so "converted them to their own use", and the other goods they also "converted to their own use" by refusing to deliver them up to the plaintiffs on demand. The owners successfully claimed damages for the conversion of all the goods. A hirer under a hire-purchase contract has a "special property" in the goods, which he loses if he sells the goods. Thus the plaintiffs, in suing in respect of the goods which had been sold, were not relying on the contract of hire-purchase; they were simply asserting their rights in respect of goods owned by them. It is not entirely clear from the report how the court reached the same result in relation to the goods which the defendants kept in their own hands. The most likely explanation is that the hire-purchase contract contained a clause under which the contract terminated automatically on non-payment of hire, with the consequence that the hirer's "special property" ceased automatically. (See also *Euro-Diam Ltd v. Bathurst* (1988, C.A.).) The House of Lords came to the same conclusion in *Tinsley v. Milligan* (1993). The case involved a claim to a house which had been put into the name of only one of the parties to assist in a fraud on the Department of Social Security. The House of Lords said that a party to the illegality could enforce his property right provided that he could establish title without relying on his own illegality, even if it emerged that the title on which he relied was acquired in the course of carrying through an illegal transaction.

(ii) A party can recover back money or property if he is not *in pari delicto*, not equally guilty. For example, some statutes have as their object the protection of a class or group of persons. So a tenant can recover back an illegal premium paid to a landlord. Under the Rent Acts, this right of recovery is expressly enacted. But in *Kiriri Cotton Co. Ltd v. Dewani* (1960, P.C.) the Privy Council were dealing with a foreign ordinance which, though it made the taking of a premium illegal, did not expressly say that the premium could be recovered back by the tenant. The Privy Council held that the tenant could recover back the premium by virtue of this common law principle.

(iii) A party can recover back what he has transferred to the other if he repents before the contract has been substantially performed. In *Taylor v. Bowers* (1876, C.A.) the plaintiff was being pressed by his creditors. To prevent certain machinery from falling into his creditors' hands, he made a fictitious assignment of it to a man called Alcock. He then called two meetings of creditors in an attempt to reach a settlement, but no composition agreement in fact resulted. In the meantime Alcock had mortgaged the machinery to Bowers, who took it with notice of the fraudulent scheme. The plaintiff sued to recover back the machinery, and he won. The illegal purpose had not been carried out; no creditor had in fact been defrauded.

(3) Related transactions between the parties are also illegal. Thus if A gives B a promissory note in respect of money due from A to B under an illegal contract, the promissory note is as illegal, and so as unenforceable,

as the original contract: see *Fisher v. Bridges* (1854). But where a contract between A and B is illegal, a related contract between B and C will only be illegal if C knew of the illegality in the first contract. Thus, if B borrows money from C, to pay what he owes to A on an illegal contract, C will not be able to sue on the contract of loan if he knew that his loan was to be used to pay an illegal debt. On the other hand, if C did not know that his money was to be used in this way, he will be able to sue for money lent. see *Spector v. Ageda* (1973).

Where a contract is illegal in its performance

In this situation one of the parties may be guilty and the other innocent. But this is not always so; probably both may be innocent, and certainly both may be guilty, in the sense of participating in the illegal design. On the last point, see *Ashmore, Benson, Pease & Co. Ltd v. A.V. Dawson Ltd* (1973, C.A.).

A guilty party cannot sue on the contract, and he cannot, in general, recover back the money paid or property transferred. He presumably can do so where he can establish his case without reliance on the illegal contract, and, possibly, where he is not *in pari delicto*, in the sense that he is not as guilty as the other party. The third possibility of recovering back which applies in the case of a contract illegal in itself, namely, repentance in time, cannot really arise here. This is because, given that the contract is only illegal in its performance, if the guilty party repents before it is in fact performed, no illegality arises.

An innocent party has full remedies. He can sue on the contract, and he can, in appropriate circumstances, recover back money paid or property transferred. An example of the innocent party successfully suing is to be found in *Marles v. Trant* (1954, C.A.). The defendants sold some seed to the plaintiff. They believed it to be spring wheat, and they sold it as spring wheat. In fact it was winter wheat. This contract was illegal as performed, because the defendants failed to comply with a statute which required an invoice to be delivered with the goods. The plaintiff, when he discovered that the wheat was winter wheat, sued the defendants for breach of contract. He won; the contract was illegal, but it was not illegal in itself, only in its performance, and he was innocent. The facts of *Marles v. Trant* are extremely similar to those of *Anderson Ltd v. Daniel*, which was considered at page 149. In that case the sellers were suing on the contract, and they failed, because they were not innocent; it was they who had contravened the statute. In *Marles v. Trant* it was the buyer who was suing, and he succeeded, because he was innocent.

So far as related transactions are concerned, there is very little authority. It is thought that a guilty party cannot sue on a related transaction, but an innocent party can. For example, if the sellers in *Anderson v. Daniel* had received a promissory note from the buyer in respect of the purchase price of the manure, they could not have sued on the note any more than they could sue on the contract of sale. If the buyer in *Marles v. Trant* had received a promissory note from the sellers in respect of the sellers' breach of contract, the buyer could have sued on the note, just as he could sue on the contract of sale.

A guilty party cannot sue on the contract. But the device of the collateral contract (which was discussed in Chapter 4) sometimes comes into play here. In *Strongman (1945) Ltd v. Sincock* (1955, C.A.) the plaintiff builders contracted to modernise some houses belonging to the defendant, who was an architect. It was illegal at the time to carry out the work without a licence from the Ministry of Works. Before the contract was made, the defendant promised the plaintiffs that he would make himself responsible for obtaining the necessary licences. The plaintiffs did work to the value of over £6,000. The defendant paid about half this sum, and then took the point that, since licences had only in fact been obtained to the amount of £2,150, the contract had been illegally performed. The Court of Appeal held that the builders should succeed in their action for the unpaid balance. The builders could not succeed on the main contract, because they had taken part in the illegal performance of it. But since they were only technically (not morally) guilty, they could succeed on the collateral contract; that is to say, the promise of the architect to obtain the licences in return for the implied promise of the builders to do the work on that understanding. In *Shelley v. Paddock* (1980) (discussed at p. 154, above), the court was prepared to allow an innocent party to an illegal contract to recover damages in tort for fraudulent misrepresentation. A similar result was arrived at in *Saunders v. Edwards* (1987, C.A.). More recently, the Court of Appeal has applied this line of reasoning to a claim by the guilty party. In *Euro-Diam Ltd v. Bathurst* (1988, C.A.), the plaintiffs (diamond suppliers) sent diamonds to suppliers in West Germany (as it then was). The accompanying invoice understated the value of the goods with the intention of enabling the customers to avoid payment of German customs duty. Some of the diamonds were later stolen in Germany. The

157

plaintiffs sued their insurers to recover the agreed value of the diamonds, but the insurers argued that the plaintiffs' claim was tainted with illegality, the avoidance of German customs duty. The judge found in the plaintiffs' favour; the Court of Appeal dismissed the insurers' appeal on the grounds that there was no direct, proximate connection between the plaintiffs' claim and the understated invoice. This was because (a) the invoice was wholly unconnected with the plaintiffs' cause of action (which relied on the contract of insurance), (b) the invoice involved no deception on the insurers, since the value of the diamonds was agreed for the purposes of insurance and was thus unaffected by the value of the invoice, (c) the plaintiffs obtained no tangible benefit from the illegality, and (d) the fact that the invoice might prove an embarrassment to the plaintiffs in any other proceedings concerning the diamonds was not sufficient to enable the insurers to rely on illegality. See also *Howard v. Shirlstar Container Transport Ltd* (1990, C.A.).

CHAPTER TWELVE

INCAPACITY

IN general all persons have full legal power to enter into any contract they wish and thus bind themselves; but a few groups of persons do not have this power in full, and they are said to be under incapacity. The groups concerned are minors, persons lacking mental capacity, drunkards and corporations. Different rules apply to these groups, which will be considered separately.

MINORS

Incapacity is imposed by law upon a minor in an attempt to protect him from the consequences of his inexperience. A minor is a person under the age of 18.

Minors' contracts are divisible into two groups: (1) some contracts are valid; and (2) some contracts are voidable in the sense that they are binding on the minor unless he repudiates them. Apart from these two groups, the general common law rule was that minors were not bound by contracts they entered into unless they ratified them after reaching majority.

Two points are common to all kinds of minors' contracts: (a) a parent is not liable on his child's contracts, unless the child was acting as the parent's agent; (b) a minor's contracts cannot be validated by the consent or authorisation of his parent.

Valid Contracts

Contract for necessaries

Contracts for necessaries are not affected by the Minors' Contracts Act 1987 and therefore remain subject to the common law rules. Necessaries may be goods or services. A minor is bound by a contract for necessaries only if it is on the whole for his benefit; if it is not, the minor is not bound by it, unless he ratifies it after reaching his majority. He is not bound by one entire contract comprising necessaries and non-necessaries.

So far as goods are concerned, necessaries are statutorily defined in section 3(3) of the Sale of Goods Act 1979 as "goods suitable to the condition in life of the minor ... and to his actual requirements at the time of the sale and delivery". Thus whether a particular article is a necessary or not depends upon two factors: the condition in life of the minor and his actual requirements at the time.

In the nineteenth century juries showed a marked tendency to find that luxuries supplied to young men of high social standing were necessaries. It was stated in the House of Commons that in one case an Oxford jury held that champagne and wild ducks were necessaries to an infant undergraduate. The courts gradually overcame this tendency by laying it down as a rule of law that "mere luxuries" could not be necessaries, and by holding that the question whether other goods were or were not necessaries was a question of mixed law and fact. Thus it was for the judge to rule whether a particular article in a particular case *could* be a necessary, and for the jury to say whether it *was* a necessary.

In considering this question, the jury had to consider not only the condition in life of the minor but also his actual requirements. In *Nash v. Inman* (1908, C.A.), a Savile Row tailor sued a minor, a Cambridge undergraduate, for the price of clothes supplied, including 11 fancy waistcoats. The tailor failed in his action because he did not prove that the minor was not already adequately supplied with clothes. If it turns out that the minor was already adequately supplied, the plaintiff will fail even though he did not know this. See, however, section 3 of the Minors' Contracts Act 1987, considered below.

Necessary goods have been defined by statute. On the other hand, necessary services have not been defined, but the tests are the same as for necessary goods. Necessary services include education (both liberal and vocational) and medical and legal advice. In *Chapple v. Cooper* (1844) it was held that the provision of a funeral ordered by a minor widow for her deceased husband was a necessary.

If money is lent to a minor to buy necessaries, the loan as such is not recoverable, but the lender can sue for such part of the loans as represents a reasonable price for any necessaries which have in fact been bought by the minor.

A minor's contract for necessaries is a valid contract. There is no doubt that it is valid in the sense that the minor himself can sue on it, and there is no doubt that the other party can sue on it when he has performed his part. But there is some doubt whether the other party can sue on the contract where it is executory; that is, where the other party has not performed his part. Suppose a minor orders a (necessary) suit, and then, before it has been delivered he says he does not want it. Can he be sued for non-acceptance?

There are three points in favour of the view that a minor is not liable on an executory contract for necessaries. (1) In *Nash v. Inman* (above) Fletcher Moulton L.J. said that a minor was liable *re* (because he had been supplied with the thing), and not *consensu* (because he had contracted). In the same case, however, Buckley L.J. said that a minor is liable *in contract*. (2) The minor is liable to pay a reasonable price, not necessarily the price agreed in the contract. Section 3(2) of the Sale of Goods Act 1979 provides: "Where necessaries are sold and delivered to a minor . . . he must pay a reasonable price for them." That does not look like a consensual contract. But it is not conclusive: a possible analysis would be that the law is interfering with one particular term, the price, without destroying the contract as such. (3) Section 3(3) of the Sale of Goods Act says: " 'necessaries' means goods suitable to the condition in life of the minor . . . and to his actual requirements *at the time of the sale and delivery*." It is arguable that this means that a minor can only be sued on a contract for necessary goods where they have been delivered. But the section does not say that in terms; it is dealing with the situation where necessaries have been sold and delivered, not with the situation where necessaries have been contracted for but not yet sold and delivered, which is the case with an executory contract.

There is one case in favour of the view that a minor can be liable on an executory contract for necessaries. In *Roberts v. Gray* (1913, C.A.) the plaintiff was a famous billiards player, who agreed to take the infant defendant on a world billiards tour, and to pay for his board and lodging and travelling expenses. This was a contract for necessaries in the sense that its object was to teach the defendant the profession of a billiards player; a kind of education. Roberts expended time and trouble and incurred certain liabilities in making preparations. A dispute arose between the parties, and, before the tour began, Gray repudiated the contract. He was held liable in damages. Hamilton L.J. said "I am unable to appreciate

161

why a contract which is in itself binding, because it is a contract for necessaries not qualified by unreasonable terms, can cease to be binding merely because it is still executory.'' The contract in the case was not *wholly* executory, but that point was not relied on in the decision.

It may be that one has to draw a distinction and say that contracts for necessary *goods* are not enforceable against the minor if executory, and that contracts for necessary *services* (which is what *Roberts v. Gray* was about) are.

Contracts of employment

A contract of employment is binding on a minor if, viewed as a whole, it is for his benefit. Consequently, this type of contract is often referred to as a "beneficial contract of service". If a contract of service is not beneficial it will only be binding on the minor if he ratifies it on attaining his majority. The minor may be bound even though some of the clauses of the contract are to his disadvantage. In *Clements v. London and N.W. Rail Co.* (1894, C.A.) a minor porter agreed to join an insurance scheme, to which his employers contributed, and to give up his right to sue for personal injuries under the Employers' Liability Act 1880. Under the insurance scheme he could get compensation without proving negligence, and without litigation; on the other hand compensation under the scheme might be smaller than the amount recoverable under the Act. It was held that the contract was on the whole beneficial to him, and binding on him.

On the other hand, in *De Francesco v. Barnum* (1890) a girl was apprenticed for stage dancing by a deed which provided that she should be entirely at the disposal of the master; that she should get no pay unless he actually employed her, which he was not bound to do; that he could send her abroad; that he could put an end to the contract if, after fair trial, he found her unsuitable; and that she should not accept any professional engagement or contract matrimony without his consent. It was held that the contract was unreasonably harsh and was invalid.

The same principles have been extended by analogy to contracts which are similar to employment contracts. In *Doyle v. White City Stadium Ltd* (1935, C.A.) a minor professional boxer was engaged to fight for £3,000, win, draw or lose, subject to the rules of the British Boxing Board of Control. Under these rules a boxer who was disqualified forfeited his "purse". Doyle was disqualified. He sued for the £3,000. He failed. It was held that his contract with the Board was on the whole beneficial to him. This was so, even though in the particular case it operated against

162

him. In *Chaplin v. Leslie Frewin (Publishers) Ltd* (1966, C.A.) the Court of Appeal unanimously held that a contract whereby a minor agreed to tell his life story to a publishing company in return for royalties on the resulting book was a contract analogous to a service contract. The majority of the court (Lord Denning dissenting) held that the particular contract was beneficial to the minor, and was therefore binding on him.

But these principles do not apply to a minor's *trading* contracts. It has long been settled that a minor is not bound by a trading contract, even if it is beneficial. He is not liable for the price of goods supplied to him for the purpose of trade; he is not liable for non-delivery of goods which he has sold as a trader; and he cannot be made bankrupt for trade debts. There is no precise definition of "trade" for this purpose. The principle seems to be that it is trade if the minor's *capital* is at risk.

Whatever may be the true position with regard to contracts for necessaries, there is no doubt that beneficial contracts of employment, and analogous contracts, are binding on the minor even when they are executory.

Voidable Contracts

The contracts in this group are voidable in the sense that the minor can repudiate them before majority or within a reasonable time afterwards. The other party cannot repudiate. The most common types of contract of this sort are contracts to buy or rent land and contracts to acquire shares in a company.

When a minor repudiates such a contract he is relieved of all liabilities (*e.g.* rent) which accrue after the repudiation, but he can be sued for liabilities (rent is a good example again) which have already accrued.

The minor can recover back money which he has paid under the contract only if there has been a total failure of consideration. In *Corpe v. Overton* (1833) a minor agreed to enter into a partnership and paid a deposit of £100, the deposit to be forfeited if he failed to execute the partnership deed. He repudiated the contract, never did execute the partnership deed, and sued to recover back the £100. He won, as there had been a total failure of consideration. In *Steinberg v. Scala (Leeds) Ltd* (1923, C.A.) a minor applied for shares in a company, and then, after they had been allotted to her, repudiated the contract. She was freed from liability for future calls on the shares, but she failed in her action to recover back the money she had already paid. There was not total failure of consideration; she had got the very shares she had contracted for.

The possibility of recovering back money paid if there is a total failure of consideration is a feature of contract law generally, but the point which distinguishes minors' voidable contracts is that the minor can recover back even where the total failure of consideration is caused by his own act, as in *Corpe v. Overton*.

The Minors' Contracts Act 1987

Until the Minors' Contracts Act 1987 was passed, contracts entered into by minors were affected by the Infants Relief Act 1874. Section 1(1)(a) of the 1987 Act provides that the 1874 Act is not to apply to any contract entered into by a minor after the commencement of the Act (June 9, 1987). This means that the common law rules considered earlier in this chapter will prevail. There are two substantive provisions in the Act: section 2 affects guarantees and section 3 makes provision for restitution in certain circumstances. These are considered in turn below.

Guarantees

Section 2 makes a guarantee of a minor's contractual obligations enforceable against a guarantor irrespective of the fact that the main contractual obligation is not enforceable against the minor. This means that the guarantee of an unenforceable minor's contract is as effective as if the minor had been an adult. It does not affect contracts for necessaries, since, as was seen earlier, a minor is obliged to pay a reasonable price for them.

Restitution

Section 3 provides that where a contract is unenforceable against a minor, or he repudiates it, the court may require the minor to transfer to the other party any "property acquired" by him under the contract or any property "representing it"; but the court must consider that it is "just and equitable to do so". This means that in a case like *Nash v. Inman* (where the minor was supplied with fancy waistcoats) the court would now have the power to order the minor to restore to the vendor the fancy waistcoats. If the minor has disposed of the property for value, he could still be ordered to give up the money or property representing the original property; if he has consumed or disposed of the goods and obtained nothing in return, he cannot be required to compensate the other person.

Quasi-contract and Restitution

The doctrine of quasi-contract has grown up over the years to provide a remedy where one person has become unjustly enriched at the expense of another. One type of action in quasi-contract is an "action for money had and received by the defendant to the plaintiff's use". These rules are preserved by section 3(2) of the Minors' Contracts Act 1987.

The principles which govern a minor's liability in tort also govern his liability in quasi-contract. Just as an action in tort can be brought against a minor except where that would be an indirect way of enforcing a contract, so an action in quasi-contract can be brought against a minor except where that would be an indirect way of enforcing a contract against him. Thus in *Bristow v. Eastman* (1794) a minor apprentice who had embezzled his master's property was held liable in quasi-contract.

That is the common law position, but equity has developed a principle which requires the minor to give up what he has got under the contract if the contract was fraudulently induced. This principle of restitution, however, operates on rather a narrow front. Where the minor is still in possession of the thing transferred to him under the contract, there is no doubt that an order for restitution can and will be made.

Where the minor obtains goods by fraud and then ceases to possess them, the position is more doubtful. In *Stocks v. Wilson* (1913) the minor defendant, by fraudulently misrepresenting that he was of full age, induced the plaintiff to sell some goods to him. When he had obtained the goods, the defendant sold some of them. Lush J. held him liable to account to the plaintiff for the proceeds. But in *Leslie v. Sheill* (1914, C.A.), *Stocks v. Wilson* was criticised, though it was not formally overruled. In *Leslie v. Sheill* an infant obtained a loan of £400 by fraudulently misrepresenting that he was of full age. It was held by the Court of Appeal that the equitable doctrine of restitution did not extend to the restoration of money borrowed. Lord Sumner said: "Restitution stopped where repayment began." It is difficult to reconcile *Stocks v. Wilson* with *Leslie v. Sheill*. One can say that the former case deals with goods sold to the infant, and the latter with money lent to the infant; but that does not seem to be a difference in principle. It is probably better to go by *Leslie v. Sheill* now, and say that where the goods have been resold or the money spent, restitution will not be granted. If the goods bought, or the actual notes or coins borrowed, are still in the hands of the infant, restitution will be granted.

PERSONS LACKING MENTAL CAPACITY

A person whose property is subject to the control of the court under Part VII of the Mental Health Act 1983 appears to be incapable of entering into a contract. In the case of a person whose property is not subject to the control of the court under the Act, mental incapacity is not a ground for setting aside the contract, unless the incapacity was known to the other party. Where the incapacity is not known to the other party and the affliction is not apparent, the validity of the contract must be judged by the same standards as a contract made by a person of sound mind and may only be set aside on the same principles. See *Hart v. O'Connor* (1985, P.C.).

Section 3 of the Sale of Goods Act 1979, as well as dealing with minors, deals also with "a person who by reason of mental incapacity . . . is incompetent to contract". The section provides that, where necessaries are sold and delivered to such a person, "he must pay a reasonable price for them".

DRUNKEN PERSONS

If a person, when he enters into a contract, is in such a state of drunkenness as not to know what he is doing, and if this fact is appreciated by the other party, the contract is *voidable* at his instance. The question of having to prove the other party's knowledge of the drunkenness can hardly arise, because it is virtually impossible that a person could be so drunk as not to know what he is doing without that fact being obvious to the other party. In relation to necessaries section 3 of the Sale of Goods Act applies to drunkenness in the same way as it does to mental incapacity.

CORPORATIONS

A corporation is, in law, a person; it is an artificial legal person. A corporation may be a "corporation sole", such as the vicar of a parish, or a "corporation aggregate" such as the mayor and corporation of a borough. Some corporations are created by Royal Charter from the Crown, such as universities. Some are created by special Act of Parliament, such as new universities, which were formerly polytechnics. Some corporations are set up under the provisions of a general Act of Parliament, notably trading companies set up under successive Companies Acts. The current statute is the Companies Act 1985.

A corporation created by charter has the same contractual powers as a natural person of full age and capacity. The contractual capacity of a statutory corporation is subject to the doctrine of *ultra vires*.

The powers of a corporation set up by a special Act of Parliament are invariably set out in the creating Act. The powers of a corporation, such as a normal trading company, set up under the Companies Act, are limited by the objects as set forth in the memorandum of association. This is a compulsory document, without which no company can be set up under the Companies Act. It must be registered, and it is open to public inspection. Any activity outside the objects clause in the memorandum of association is *ultra vires* (beyond its powers) and void.

The doctrine of *ultra vires* was intended to protect investors in, and creditors of, the company, by enabling them, to know that their money could only be spent on certain specified objects. In practice the doctrine's main effect has been to deny a remedy to outside persons dealing with the company by way of trade. The position is now largely covered by section 35(1) of the Companies Act 1985 (as amended by the Companies Act 1989) which states: "The validity of an act done by a company shall not be called into question on the ground of lack of capacity by reason of the fact that it is beyond the objects of the company stated in the memorandum of association." (See also sections 35A and 35B.) The object of this section is to abolish the *ultra vires* rule as regards innocent third parties who deal in good faith with the company, but to retain it for internal purposes concerning the relationship between the shareholders and the company; see also section 35(2) and (3). So contracts made by third parties who deal in good faith with the company remain valid and enforceable.

PART FOUR

WHO IS WITHIN THE BOND

CHAPTER THIRTEEN

PRIVITY OF CONTRACT

THE doctrine of privity is to the effect that a person who is not a party to a contract cannot enjoy the benefits or suffer the burdens of that contract. It has been mentioned earlier in this book in Chapter 2, in connection with the rule that consideration must move from the promisee, and in Chapter 6, in connection with exemption clauses. It will thus be seen that the doctrine of privity has wide ramifications in the law of contract. But it is important to appreciate its limits.

WHAT THE DOCTRINE IS

The doctrine is often stated in this way: a contract cannot confer benefits on strangers, nor can it impose burdens on strangers. A "stranger" in this context simply means a person who is not a party to the contract.

In the case of *Tweddle v. Atkinson* (1861) an agreement was made between William Guy and John Tweddle by which each promised to pay a sum of money to William Tweddle. William Tweddle was the son of John Tweddle, and he was about to marry the daughter of William Guy. William Guy died without having paid, and William Tweddle sued his executors. His action failed, on the ground that William Tweddle was "a stranger to the consideration". See also Chapter 2, p. 30.

In *Dunlop Pneumatic Tyre Co. Ltd v. Selfridge* (1915, H.L.) the plaintiff company sold some tyres to Dew & Co. on the terms that Dew & Co. would not resell them below certain prices and that when Dew & Co. came to resell the tyres they would extract a similar undertaking from their purchaser. Dew & Co. sold the tyres to Selfridge, who agreed to observe the restrictions and to pay to Dunlop the sum of £5 for each tyre sold in breach of the agreement. Selfridge sold some of the tyres below the fixed price, and Dunlop sued him. Dunlop were met by the defence that they were not parties to the agreement with Selfridge and had furnished no consideration. The House of Lords gave judgment for the defendant. Lord Haldane L.C. said: "My Lords, in the law of England certain principles are fundamental. One is that only a person who is a party to a contract can sue on it. ... A second principle is that if a person with whom a contract not under seal has been made is to be able to enforce it consideration must have been given by him." It will be noticed that Lord Haldane referred to two principles: that a stranger to a contract cannot sue on it, and that a stranger to the consideration cannot sue. The tendency nowadays is to regard these two statements as two aspects of the same principle. This is because of the notion of contract as bargain. Even if a person is mentioned in an agreement and stated to be the promisee, if he gives no consideration he will be not able to sue; though he is a party to the agreement, he is not a party to the bargain, and so is not a party to the contract. *Dunlop v. Selfridge* put the stamp of House of Lords authority on the doctrine of privity. In *Scruttons Ltd v. Midland Silicones Ltd* (1962) the House reaffirmed the doctrine in the context of exemption clauses: see page 81, above.

THE LIMITS OF THE DOCTRINE

1. The doctrine of privity does not forbid assignment of contractual rights. Assignment is a big subject, and the whole of the next chapter will be devoted to it.

2. The doctrine does not forbid agency. That is another big topic, which forms the subject-matter of Chapter 15.

3. There are many instances in land law where the doctrine does not apply. For example, a lease is a contract, but it also creates proprietary rights. Thus, if A grants a lease of land to B, the lease will contain a number of covenants (promises) by the tenant, *e.g.* to pay the rent, and a number of covenants by the landlord, *e.g.* to keep the premises in repair. As between A and B there is privity of contract, and so there is no difficulty about the enforcement of the covenants. But suppose A sells the freehold of the land to X, and B assigns the lease to Y. The law is that, although there is no privity of contract between X and Y, either may enforce a covenant in the original lease against the other. Similarly, when a freeholder sells his land, he can, subject to certain conditions, impose restrictions on its use which will be binding, not only on the immediate

purchaser, but also on his successors in title. A restrictive covenant of this kind is a species of property, and is said to "run with the land". Attempts have been made to extend the idea from land to goods, as will be seen.

4. In the law of trusts the doctrine of privity has no application. If A and B by contract create a trust for the benefit of C, C has a proprietary right in the trust property and can directly enforce his right, though he was not a party to the contract. Attempts have been made to extend this trust idea into the field of pure contract by arguing in various situations that a notional trust has been created: see page 174.

5. The legislature has intervened, in a rather piecemeal fashion, to provide some exceptions to the doctrine of privity. This has been notably so in the field of insurance.

6. Where there is a contract between A and C to which B is not a party, there may also be another contract, between B and A. Where that is so, B will of course be able to sue on the A–B contract. That was the situation in *Shanklin Pier Ltd v. Detel Products Ltd* (1951), which was looked at in Chapter 4 at page 60. In that case the pier company, although shut out by the doctrine of privity from suing the suppliers of the defective paint on the contract for the sale of the paint, were able to obtain a complete remedy by suing them on the collateral contract. Similarly, in *Charnock v. Liverpool Corporation* (1968, C.A.) the plaintiff's car was damaged in a collision with another car, whose driver was solely to blame. The plaintiff took his car to a garage to be repaired. His insurance company's assessor attended. The insurance company later told the garage that it was in order for them to carry out the repair "as per your estimate". The garage took eight weeks to do the repairs, whereas a reasonable time would have been five weeks. The plaintiff sued the garage for £53, the cost of hiring another car for three weeks. The garage argued that there was only one contract, between them and the insurers, and that, as the plaintiff was not a party to that contract, he could not sue them. It was held by the Court of Appeal that that was not the only contract; although there was a contract between the insurers and the garage to pay for the repairs, there was also a contract between the garage and the plaintiff to carry out the repairs, and it was an implied term of that contract that the garage would carry out the repairs within a reasonable time. So the plaintiff won.

7. Inducing a breach of contract is a tort. If C induces B to break his (B's) contract with A, A can sue C in tort. Thus, whilst the doctrine of

privity ensures that no contractual duty can be imposed by the A–B contract on C, the law of tort does impose on C the negative duty of not interfering with the A–B contract.

The doctrine of privity often causes inconvenience in practice, and many attempts have been made to evade it. These attempts have centred on three ideas, which will be considered in turn.

The Trust Idea

In the first 30 years of this century it looked as though the idea of the trust was going to provide a path round the doctrine of privity. In *Les Affreteurs Réunis S.A. v. Walford* (1919, H.L.) Walford, a broker, negotiated a charterparty between shipowners and charterers. By a clause in the charterparty the owners promised the charterers to pay Walford a commission of 3 per cent on the estimated gross amount of hire. Walford sued the owners for his commission. The charterers were not made parties to the action. Walford applied to join them as parties, and the owners then agreed that the case should proceed as though the charters were co-plaintiffs. Walford won. Lord Birkenhead said: "... in such cases charterers can sue as trustees on behalf of the broker." The significant point is that, as the charterers were treated as trustees for the broker, the broker could ask them to sue the owners on his behalf, and, if they refused to sue, the broker could then join the charterers as co-defendants, and proceed with the action as sole plaintiff. Thus, where the court is willing to find a trust, the beneficiary may himself enforce the contract by which that trust was set up, even though he was not a party to that contract.

In later cases, however, the courts have set their faces against this idea. In *Vandepitte v. Preferred Accident Insurance Corporation of New York* (1933, P.C.) the plaintiff was injured by a car driven by a young lady who was a minor. The car belonged to her father, and she was driving it with his consent. The plaintiff obtained judgment against the girl, but this judgment remained unsatisfied. The plaintiff therefore began another action against the insurance company. The father held a policy of insurance by which the company undertook to indemnify him and anyone driving the car with his permission. Judgment was given in Canada for the insurance company, and this was affirmed by the Judicial Committee of the Privy Council. One of the plaintiff's arguments was that the company's promise to indemnify was the subject of a trust of which the father was trustee and the daughter beneficiary. If that argument had been upheld the daughter would have been, via the trust, a party to the insurance contract, and so an "insured person". Then the plaintiff could have relied on a British Columbia statute which provided that where a person obtained judgment against an "insured person" and the judgment was unsatisfied, the judgment creditor could proceed against the insurers for the amount of the judgment. But that argument never got off the ground, because the Privy Council held that there was no trust. There cannot be a trust without an *intention* to create a trust. It was held that such intention must be affirmatively proved, and that in the instant case it had not been proved that the father intended to create a trust. By the law of British Columbia a father was liable for the torts of his minor children. Thus if the daughter, while driving the father's car, injured a person, the father might expect that he, not she, would be sued. From that it followed that it was not clear, when the father took out the insurance policy, that he had the intention to benefit his daughter, because it was not clear that she would need the protection of the policy.

Although *Vandepitte's* case is a decision of the Privy Council, and although it turned to some extent on the law of British Columbia, the fact is that since that time there has been no finding of a trust in a comparable case in any English court.

One factor in this situation is that if it is held that a contract between A and B has created a trust in favour of C, then the terms of the A–B contract cannot be altered, however much A and B may want to alter them. This point was emphasised in *Re Schebsman* (1944, C.A.). Schebsman was employed by two companies. By a contract made between him and them, one of the companies agreed to pay £5,500 in six annual instalments. The money was to be paid to Schebsman, or, if he died, to his widow, or, if she died, to his daughter. During the instalment period, Schebsman first went bankrupt and then died. His trustee in bankruptcy claimed a declaration that all sums payable under the agreement formed part of the estate of the debtor (Schebsman). The trial judge dismissed the claim, and the Court of Appeal affirmed his decision. One of the arguments in the case was that Schebsman was a trustee of the company's promise, holding it on behalf of his wife and daughter. This argument was rejected. Du Parcq L.J. said:

175

"... unless an intention to create a trust is clearly to be collected from the language used and the circumstances of the case, I think that the court ought not to be astute to discover indications of such an intention. I have little doubt that in the present case both parties (and certainly the debtor) intended to keep alive their common law right to vary consensually the terms of the obligation undertaken by the company, and if circumstances had changed in the debtor's lifetime injustice might have been done by holding that a trust had been created and that those terms were accordingly unalterable."

Lord Greene M.R. in the same case said: "... it is not legitimate to import into the contract the idea of a trust when the parties have given no indication that such was their intention. To interpret this contract as creating a trust would, in my judgment, be to disregard the dividing line between the case of a trust and the simple case of a contract made between two persons for the benefit of a third." In *Re Schebsman* the company was quite willing to pay instalments to Mrs Schebsman and so it did not matter to her that there was held to be no trust in her favour; it was sufficient that, as the court held, payment by the company to her was due performance of the contract. That stopped the trustee in bankruptcy getting his hands on the money. But if the company had refused to pay her, that would have shown up the difference between a trust in favour of Mrs Schebsman and a mere contract for the benefit of Mrs Schebsman. In the former case she would have been able to sue; in the latter she would not.

The Restrictive Covenant Idea

Another attack on the doctrine of privity has taken the form of trying to carry over into the general law of contract the land law notion of covenants running with the land.

The land law case which has been most strongly relied on for this purpose is *Tulk v. Moxhay* (1848). In that case the purchaser of the garden in the centre of Leicester Square entered into a covenant with the vendor promising not to build on the garden. The covenant was held to be binding in equity on a subsequent purchaser of the garden. At the time it was given, this decision was based on the fact that the subsequent purchaser had notice of the covenant. But in later years "the rule in *Tulk v. Moxhay*" (as it came to be called) ceased to be based solely upon notice and became limited to situations where the original vendor or his successors retained a proprietary interest in other land in the neighbourhood which stood to benefit from the restrictive covenant.

This development made it very difficult to argue that the rule in *Tulk v. Moxhay* could apply to contracts not concerned with land. In *Taddy v. Sterious* (1904) the argument was tried. The plaintiffs were tobacco manufacturers, and they wanted to prevent retailers from selling the tobacco below a certain minimum price. They attached to each packet a printed notice stating that the tobacco was sold "on the express condition that retail dealers do not sell it below the prices above set forth". The plaintiffs sold some of the tobacco to a firm of wholesalers, and that firm resold it to the defendants, who were retailers. The defendants had notice of the condition, but they nevertheless sold the tobacco at a price below the minimum laid down. The plaintiffs sued for a declaration that the defendants were bound by the condition. They argued that the rule in *Tulk v. Moxhay* should be applied. This argument was rejected by the judge. He said: "Conditions of this kind do not run with goods and cannot be imposed upon them. Subsequent purchasers, therefore, do not take subject to any conditions which the court can enforce." (Resale price maintenance is now governed by statute.)

Nevertheless, the argument from analogy with covenants running with the land found favour with the Privy Council in *Lord Strathcona Steamship Co. v. Dominion Coal Co.* (1926, P.C.). The owners of the steamer Lord Strathcona chartered her to X. The contract provided that X should be free to use the ship on the St Lawrence River for each summer season and should surrender her to the owners in the November of each year. During the currency of the charterparty, while the ship was in the possession of the owners, they sold her to Y, who in turn resold her to Z. Z knew of the charterparty but refused to deliver the ship to X for the summer season. X obtained an injunction in the Canadian courts restraining Z from using the ship in any way inconsistent with the charterparty; the Judicial Committee of the Privy Council affirmed this decision. They held in effect that Z was caught by the rule in *Tulk v. Moxhay*. The Privy Council recognised that, for the rule to apply, the person seeking to enforce the restriction must have a proprietary interest in its subject-matter. They said that this condition was satisfied because X had an interest in the ship. But there are two difficulties in that reasoning. First, that interest was merely conferred on X by the very contract which he was seeking to enforce against a third party; it was nothing like the independent proprietary interest which the rule in *Tulk v. Moxhay* requires. Secondly, there is clear authority for the proposition that a charterparty does not give the charterer any right of property in the ship.

It is not surprising that Lord Wright M.R. said, in *Clore v. Theatrical Properties Ltd* (1936), that the *Strathcona* principle must in any event be confined to "the very special case of a ship under a charterparty". In *Port Line Ltd v. Ben Line Steamers Ltd* (1958) Diplock J. (as he then was) went further; he declared that the *Strathcona* case was wrongly decided. In the later case of *Swiss Bank Corporation v. Lloyds Bank Ltd* (1981), the judge said that the *Strathcona* principle had continuing validity. More recently, in *Law Debenture Trust Corporation plc v. Ural Caspian Oil Corporation Ltd* (1993), Hoffman J. proceeded on the basis that this was correct.

The Section 56 Idea

Section 56(1) of the Law of Property Act 1925 declares: "A person may take an immediate or other interest in land or other property, or the benefit of any condition, right of entry, covenant or agreement over or respecting land or other property, although he may not be named as a party to the conveyance or other instrument." This enactment has been used as a weapon with which to attack the doctrine of privity. It was argued in several cases that the subsection had destroyed the doctrine. The argument was that the phrase "other property" included a contractual right, and that the phrase "not . . . named as a party" was equivalent to not being a party; therefore the subsection empowered a person to sue on a contract even though he was not a party to it. This argument gained the support of Lord Denning, but it was rejected by other judges in a number of cases and was finally killed off by the decision of the House of Lords in *Beswick v. Beswick* (1968). Peter Beswick was a coal merchant. As he was getting on in years he contracted to sell the business to his nephew John. The consideration was a promise by John to pay Peter £6 10s. a week for as long as he lived, and, if Peter's wife survived him, to pay her £5 a week for as long as she lived. John did pay Peter's widow one sum of £5 and then refused to pay any more. The widow sued John for arrears and for specific performance of the contract. She sued in two capacities; as administratrix of Peter's estate, and in her personal capacity. The House of Lords held that, as administratrix, the widow could obtain specific performance, but not in her personal capacity. The argument founded on section 56(1) was rejected. The majority in the House took the view that section 56(1) was confined in its application to covenants relating to land, and the whole House were of the opinion that it did not diminish the doctrine of privity in the field of general contract law.

THE PRESENT STATE OF THE LAW

Although the House of Lords, by their decision in *Beswick v. Beswick*, decisively rejected the section 56(1) attack on the doctrine of privity, they cleared up one of the more objectionable features of the doctrine. It was argued for the nephew that, though the widow might be entitled, in her capacity as administratrix, to damages for breach of the contract which the nephew made with her husband, she should not have substantial damages, but only nominal damages, and that she should not have specific performance. The basis of this argument was that, in her capacity as administratrix, the widow could only sue for loss which had been suffered by her husband's estate, and that the estate had not suffered any loss. The nephew's failure to make payment to the widow was no loss to the estate. The House of Lords rejected this argument. Granted that the estate had suffered no loss, the estate nevertheless had the right to enforce the contract. In the circumstances of the case the most just way of enforcing the contract was to order specific performance, and there was no impediment to the making of that order. The House also indicated that if, in other circumstances, justice required the making of an order for substantial damages, that order could be made.

An interesting application occurred in *Jackson v. Horizon Holidays Ltd* (1975, C.A.). A family man took his wife and children on a holiday, which turned out to be disastrous; he recovered damages not only for his own disappointment but also for the disappointment of his wife and children. But in *Woodar Investment Development Ltd v. Wimpey Construction U.K. Ltd* (1980, H.L.) the House of Lords, though not overruling *Jackson's* case, severely criticised some of its reasoning. Three of their Lordships also expressed the hope that the House would get an opportunity to review the rule that a third party cannot enforce a contractual promise taken by another for his benefit. Lord Scarman said: "if the opportunity arises, I hope the House will reconsider *Tweddle v. Atkinson* and the other cases which stand guard over this unjust rule."

There was a time in the early 1980s when the rule of privity appeared to lose some of its significance through a development in the law of tort. The doctrine of privity only matters where a remedy in contract is the only possible remedy. It used to be the law that a plaintiff could not obtain damages in the tort of negligence for pure economic loss. The House of Lords decision in *Junior Books Ltd v. Veitchi Co. Ltd* (1983, H.L.) appeared to change that. By a majority, they held that a building owner who was in close proximity to a sub-contractor, but not in contractual relationship with him, could recover damages in tort for the economic loss caused by the sub-contractor's negligence in laying a defective floor in the building owner's premises. Later cases, however, have indicated a reluctance to follow this approach. In *Simaan General Contracting Co. v. Pilkington Glass Ltd (No. 2)* (1988, C.A.), for example, the plaintiffs were the main contractors for a building, whose plans and specifications stipulated that a particular type of glass manufactured by the defendants should be used in the curtain walling of the building. The supply and erection of the curtain walling was sub-contracted to another company which, as required, ordered the glass from the defendants. The glass supplied was not right; so the building owner withheld payment from the plaintiffs who sued the defendants for economic loss caused by the withholding of payment. The Court of Appeal refused to allow the claim to proceed. They said that in the absence of a contract between the parties the plaintiffs could not bring a direct claim against the defendants for economic loss alone, because the defendants had not voluntarily assumed direct responsibility to the plaintiffs for the quality of the glass and the plaintiffs had not relied on the defendants. The Court of Appeal also pointed out that the plaintiffs had a remedy against the sub-contractor who in turn could claim against the defendants; at each stage liability could be determined in the light of the exemption clause, if any, applying to each contract. (See also *Muirhead v. Industrial Tank Specialities Ltd* (1985, C.A.) and *Greater Nottingham Co-operative Society v. Cementation Piling & Foundations Ltd* (1988, C.A.).) In *D. & F. Estates Ltd v. Church Commissioners for England* (1988, H.L.), the House of Lords stressed that where a defect in a chattel or structure makes the chattel or structure less valuable but is discovered before it causes personal injury or physical damage to other property, the remedy, if any, for the economic loss lies in contract not tort.

It can be said for the present, then, that the courts have set their faces against pursuing the possibilities suggested by *Junior Books Ltd v. Veitchi*.

CHAPTER FOURTEEN

ASSIGNMENT

A person who is entitled to the benefit of a contract may transfer that benefit to another person by a transaction known as assignment.

WHAT ASSIGNMENT IS

Assignment is the transfer of the benefit of a contract, by the party entitled to that benefit, to a third party. The effect of the transfer is that the third party becomes entitled to sue the person bearing the burden of the contract. For example, if A makes a contract with B by which A undertakes to paint B's house for £1,000, A may assign to C the right to receive from B the £1,000. B's consent to the assignment is not necessary. If B declines to pay C, C can sue him. In this example, A is the "creditor" and the "assignor", B is the "debtor" and C is the "assignee". The words "creditor" and "debtor" are sometimes, in connection with assignment, used in a wider sense than in ordinary speech. Thus "creditor" can mean the party who has any right (not necessarily a money right) under a contract and "debtor" can mean the party who owes any duty under a contract.

The right to receive the £1,000 is a "chose in action" or "thing in action". That is a form of property distinct from a "thing in possession". The meaning is that it is something which can be enforced, if the debtor proves difficult, only by action, that is, by suing for it. Assignment is concerned with things in action, and not with things in possession. Things in action include shares, rights under a trust, legacies, policies of insurance, patents, copyrights, rights of action in tort, debts and other contractual rights.

In the last chapter it was said that the doctrine of privity does not forbid assignment. In the example above, A gave C the right to sue B for the £1,000, by assignment to C of an existing contractual right. But if A had, in the original contract, stipulated that B should pay the £1,000 to C, the

181

doctrine of privity would prevent C from suing B. The explanation of this lies in history. The doctrine of privity is a common law doctrine; assignment is an invention of equity.

METHODS OF ASSIGNMENT

Assignment is a branch of the law which really has to be examined under the separate heads of common law, equity and statute.

Common Law

At common law, it was not possible for A to assign to C his contractual right against B. A could give C a "power of attorney" enabling C to sue B, but that was a very cumbrous and imperfect procedure. An exception was made in favour of the Crown; the Crown could make and take assignments.

Equity

The inability to transfer a chose in action, such as a contractual right, was a considerable inconvenience and equity soon decided to recognise such transfers; that is, assignments. In equity, no particular formality is required to render an assignment valid, except that the assignment of an equitable interest (as distinct from a legal interest) must be in writing. This provision is now contained in section 53(1)(c) of the Law of Property Act 1925. What *is* required is intention. There cannot be an assignment without an intention to assign.

The exact effect of an equitable assignment depends upon two factors: (1) whether the chose in action which is being assigned is legal or equitable; and (2) whether the assignment is absolute or non-absolute. The best example of a legal chose in action is a debt due under a contract; the best example of an equitable chose in action is a legacy or an interest in a trust fund. An absolute assignment is one by which the assignor divests himself of his whole interest in the thing assigned. An assignment may be absolute, however, even though it provides for the assignor to regain his interest at some time in the future. Thus it is well settled that a mortgage of

182

a chose in action can be an absolute assignment. In *Tancred v. Delagoa Bay and East Africa Rly. Co.* (1889) a debt was assigned as security for a loan of money, with the provision that if the assignor repaid the loan, the debt should be reassigned to him. This was held to be an absolute assignment.

An absolute assignment must be distinguished from (a) a conditional assignment, (b) an assignment by way of charge, and (c) an assignment of part of a debt. A conditional assignment is one which is to become operative or to cease to be operative upon the happening of some uncertain event. In *Durham Brothers v. Robertson* (1898, C.A.) a firm of builders assigned a debt as security for a loan of money. The assignment was expressed to last "until the money with added interest be repaid to you". This was held to be a conditional, not an absolute, assignment. The difference between this case and *Tancred's* case (above) is that, whereas in *Tancred's* case the debtor could safely pay the assignee until he received notice of the reassignment, in *Durham Brothers v. Robertson* the debtor would not know whether he ought to pay his debt to the assignee or to the assignor, because this would depend on whether or not the assignor had repaid the loan, and that the debtor could not know. It comes to this: where the assignment provides for automatic reversion to the assignor the assignment is not absolute; where the assignment provides for a reassignment it is absolute.

An assignment by way of charge is one which merely entitles the assignee to pay out of a fund, without transferring the fund itself. In *Jones v. Humphreys* (1902) a schoolmaster assigned to a money-lender so much of his salary as should be necessary to repay a sum of £22 10s. which he had borrowed and any further sums which he might borrow. This was held to be not an absolute assignment. Here again the debtor (schoolmaster's employer) would not know whom he ought to pay, because he would not know the state of accounts between the schoolmaster and the money-lender.

The assignment of part of a debt is not an absolute assignment. If A assigns to C £50 out of the £75 which B owes to A, that is not an absolute agreement.

The effect of an equitable assignment can be stated in three rules. First, where the chose in action assigned is legal the assignee can sue the debtor, but only if he joins the assignor as a party to the action. He must first ask the assignor to sue as a co-plaintiff with him. If the assignor refuses, the assignee may join him as a co-defendant with the debtor. This rule applies wherever a legal chose in action is assigned, whether the assignment is absolute or non-absolute. The reason for the rule is historical, arising from the different views of assignment taken by common law and equity.

Secondly, where the chose in action assigned is equitable and the assignment is non-absolute, again the assignee can only sue if he joins the assignor—either as co-plaintiff or co-defendant. There is a good practical reason for this rule. Since the assignment is not absolute—being conditional, or by way of charge, or of part of a debt—the court cannot safely adjudicate unless all three parties (assignor, assignee and debtor) are before the court.

Thirdly, where the chose in action assigned is equitable and the assignment is absolute, the assignee may sue by himself in his own name without making the assignor a party to the action. There is no reason why the assignor should be a party to the action: since the chose is equitable there is no historical reason for him to be present; and since the assignment is absolute, the assignor has given up all his rights in the chose.

Notice

In order to perfect the title of the equitable assignee as against the assignor it is not necessary that notice should be given to the debtor. But if the case of *Warner Bros Records Inc. v. Rollgreen Ltd* (1976, C.A.) is rightly decided, it seems that such notice is necessary in order to give the assignee any rights against the debtor. The Court of Appeal held, on a preliminary issue, that the equitable assignee of a contractual option who has not given notice of the assignment to the grantor of the option cannot exercise the option in his own name so as to bind the grantor of the option. The principle of this case does not seem to be confined to options, but would apply to the equitable assignment of any kind of contractual right.

It is well settled that the assignee cannot sue the debtor if the debtor, not having had notice of the assignment, makes payment to the assignor. Notice is also important where there is more than one assignee, because they take priority in the order in which they give notice to the debtor. This is known as the rule in *Dearle v. Hall* (1828). But the rule cannot benefit a person who takes an assignment knowing of a previous assignment.

Notice may be given by the assignor or by the assignee. It need not be in any particular form, but where an equitable chose in action is assigned notice will not give priority over later assignees unless it is in writing: see section 137(3) of the Law of Property Act 1925.

Consideration

The question arises whether consideration is necessary to an equitable assignment. This question arises only as between the assignor and assignee; the debtor cannot refuse to pay the assignee on the ground that the assignee gave no consideration to the assignor. The point most often arises when the assignor is dead or bankrupt; his personal representative or trustee in bankruptcy may wish to challenge the validity of the assignment. Bear in mind that an assignment for no consideration is a *gift* of a chose in action.

A gift of a chose in action, just like the gift of a chose in possession, is only irrevocable if it is completed, or perfected. If a gift is not perfected, the donor can change his mind and revoke it. So it is only an incomplete assignment that requires consideration to make it irrevocable. An assignment is incomplete if the assignor has not done all that he needs to do to transfer the right of action to the assignee. At first sight it looks as though the distinction between a complete and an incomplete assignment is the same as that between an absolute and a non-absolute assignment. But this is not so. It is true that an absolute assignment is necessarily complete, but it is not true that a non-absolute assignment is necessarily incomplete. In *Re McArdle* (1951, C.A.) the Court of Appeal indicated that the assignment of part of a debt can be a completed assignment. But assignments which are conditional or by way of charge are not completed assignments, and thus require consideration, because something remains to be done (such as settling the state of accounts between assignor and assignee) before the assignee can bring an action.

An assignment is the transfer of an existing right. Consequently, a promise to transfer a right which does not yet exist (sometimes called "future property") is not an assignment. For example, A may promise to transfer to B what he expects to get under the will of X, who is still living. That is not an assignment, it is an agreement to assign, and it requires consideration just like any ordinary contract. The same is true of a promise to transfer, *in the future*, an existing right.

Statute

Section 136(1) of the Law of Property Act 1925 provides that an absolute assignment in writing of any debt or other legal thing in action, of which express notice in writing has been given to the debtor, is effectual in law to pass to the assignee the legal right to the debt or chose in action. The phrase "legal thing in action" has been held to include an equitable thing in action.

There are three conditions which must be satisfied to make an assignment valid under the statute: (1) it must be absolute; (2) it must be written; and (3) written notice must be given to the debtor. So there is no such thing as a non-absolute statutory assignment; there is no such thing as an oral statutory assignment; and there is no such thing as a statutory assignment without notice to the debtor. Notice to the debtor is an essential part of the statutory transfer of the debt. But no very high standard of formality is required. In *Van Lynn Developments Ltd v. Pelias Construction Co. Ltd* (1969, C.A.) a notice of assignment was held to be good though it did not give the date of the assignment which was being referred to, and though it contained an incorrect statement.

It is not a necessary condition of a valid statutory assignment that there should be consideration. It has been held that an assignment which satisfies the requirement of the statute transfers the chose in action by virtue of the statute itself, so that consideration is irrelevant.

The statute does not destroy, or affect in any way, the possibility of equitable assignment. Thus an assignment which fails to meet the requirements of the statute—because it is non-absolute, or because it is oral, or because written notice is not given to the debtor—may yet be an equitable assignment.

"SUBJECT TO EQUITIES"

An assignee is said to take "subject to equities". That is the classic phrase. But it is misleading, because the principle embraces legal as well as equitable defences. The debtor can plead against the assignee any defences that he could have pleaded against the assignor. This is true both of equitable and statutory assignments. In *Roxburghe v. Cox* (1881, C.A.) Lord Charles Ker assigned to the Duke of Roxburghe the money that would accrue to him from the sale of his commission in the army. This money (£3,000) was paid, on December 18, to the credit of Lord Charles Ker's account at his bank. On that date the account was overdrawn to the extent of £647. On December 19 the Duke gave notice of the assignment to the bank. It was held that the bank could set off the sum of £647 against the right of the Duke to the £3,000.

186

In *Roxburghe v. Cox* the defence took the form of a set-off of a quantified sum. But a debtor can equally rely, by way of counterclaim, on an unliquidated amount. Suppose A, a builder, assigns to C money to become due to him from B at the conclusion of a building contract. C, the assignee, sues B, the debtor. B can defend the action by pleading (if it be so) that he has suffered damage by reason of defective work by A. In this situation, because the debtor's claim arises out of the contract assigned, it matters not whether the claim arises before or after notice of the assignment has been given. But where, as in *Roxburghe v. Cox*, the debtor's claim arises out of some transaction other than the contract assigned, it can only be set up against the assignee if it arose before notice of the assignment. Thus, if Lord Charles Ker had drawn another £100 on December 20, the bank could not have increased their set-off; they would still have been limited to £647. A more recent (and more complicated) case in which these rules are expounded and applied is *Business Computers Ltd v. Anglo-African Leasing Ltd* (1977).

The defence available to the debtor may be something much broader than a mere set-off or counterclaim. Any defect in the title of the assignor effects the title of the assignee. Thus misrepresentation, mistake, illegality, incapacity, and non-performance may all be pleaded by the debtor.

RIGHTS WHICH CANNOT BE ASSIGNED

1. Public policy forbids the assignment of some contractual rights. In particular, a public officer cannot assign his salary; and a wife cannot assign maintenance and similar payments to which she may become entitled in matrimonial proceedings.

2. Parties to a contract are free, if they so wish, to make it a term of the contract that the rights under it shall not be assignable. See, for example, *Linden Gardens Trust Ltd v. Lenesta Sludge Disposals Ltd* (1994), in which the House of Lords refused to hold void as being contrary to public policy a clause in the JCT Standard Form of Building Contract prohibiting the assignment of any benefit of the contract, including not only the assignment of the right to future performance but also the assignment of accrued rights of action.

3. A bare right of action is not assignable. This is because it savours of maintenance. ("Maintenance", of course, in this context is linked with champerty; it is nothing whatever to do with the "maintenance" payable

to a wife, which has just been mentioned above. It is the same word, but a totally different meaning.) The only problem is, when is a right of action "bare"? It is not bare if the assignee has a genuine commercial interest in the enforcement of the assignor's claim or if that claim is coupled with some other property which is assigned along with it. Thus if A sells his land to C, and assigns to him the right to sue for damages for breach of covenant committed by B (the tenant) before the sale, C gets a perfectly good right of action against B. But if A, whilst keeping the land, purported to assign to C the right to sue the tenant for breach of covenant, that would be the attempted assignment of a bare right of action and the "assignment" would be void.

4. The benefit of a contract cannot be assigned if the "debtor" is reasonable in wishing to perform his contractual duty only in favour of one particular "creditor". If A, an author, contracts with B, a publisher, that A shall write a book for B to publish, B cannot assign to C the right to publish the book. A may reasonably have relied on B's skill and judgment as a publisher.

WHAT ASSIGNMENT IS NOT

To complete this study of assignment, it is necessary to look at two transactions which are similar to, but not the same as, assignment.

Novation

Novation is a transaction by which a new contract is substituted for an existing contract. This can happen between the original parties but it can also happen (and this is where it becomes relevant to the present discussion) between the original parties and a new party. Suppose there is a contract between A and B under which A owes B £50, and a contract between B and C under which B owes C £50. By agreement between all three of them, the A–B contract and the B–C contract may be discharged and a new contract may be made under which A is to pay C £50. The essential point about novation is that it requires the agreement of all the parties concerned, whereas assignment does not require the agreement of the debtor. Novation can be used in connection with rights. In the example just given, B gives up his right to receive £50 from A. But he could more easily have done that by assignment to C, which would not have needed the consent of A. The real importance of novation is that it can be used in connection with duties, whereas assignment cannot. By novation (as in the example) B can get out of his duty to pay £50 to C. He could not have done that by assigning his duty to A. Duties cannot be assigned; only rights can.

Negotiable Instruments

Some written contracts are not merely assignable, they are negotiable. Such contracts are called negotiable instruments. The most important kinds of negotiable instrument are bills of exchange (including cheques) and promissory notes. Since a cheque is the commonest of these, we will discuss that. A cheque is a written order by a person (called the drawer) addressed to a banker (the drawee) to pay on demand a sum of money to someone. That "someone" may be the drawer himself, or a named third person, or "bearer". A cheque can pass from one person to another, and the holder can sue on it.

The negotiation (transfer) of a negotiable instrument differs from assignment in three main ways:

1. There is never any need to give notice to the debtor that there has been a transfer. (In the case of a cheque the debtor is the banker.)

2. The ordinary rules of consideration do not apply. Past consideration is sufficient. The plaintiff need not himself have given consideration, provided that some prior party has. There is a presumption that consideration has been given.

3. The transferee does not take subject to equities: he takes free from equities, provided he takes in good faith; and there is a presumption of good faith.

It is curious, therefore, that whereas assignment was not possible at common law, negotiation was. The negotiability of the three instruments mentioned above is now governed by the Bills of Exchange Act 1882. But it originated in the custom of merchants, and was then incorporated into the common law, and then put into statutory form.

TRANSFER BY OPERATION OF LAW

Assignment is the transfer of a right by the *voluntary* act of the transferor. It is now necessary to consider the involuntary transfer of both rights and duties which may arise by operation of law on the death or insolvency of a party to a contract.

Death

If A and B have entered into a contract which is not of a personal nature, and A or B dies during the currency of the contract, his rights and duties pass automatically to his personal representatives. Where A has contracted to sell goods to B, and A dies before he has delivered the goods, his personal representatives acquire, by operation of law, the duty to deliver the goods and the right to sue for the price.

This procedure does not apply, however, to a contract of a personal nature. Thus, if A has entered into a contract of employment with B (the employer), and A dies during the term of employment, A's personal representatives do not acquire any rights or duties; they have no duty to perform the service and no right to (post-death) wages. If B, the employer, dies, B's personal representatives do not acquire any rights or duties; they have no right to A's service and no duty to pay A any (post-death) wages. In a personal contract, the death of either party puts an end to the contract. It is a form of frustration, as will be seen in Chapter 18.

Insolvency

When a person becomes insolvent, his trustee in bankruptcy must get in all his property and distribute it fairly amongst his creditors. The rule, therefore, is that any right of action relating to the property of the insolvent person passes automatically to the trustee in bankruptcy. If A (who becomes insolvent) has a contract with B under which B had to deliver goods or pay money to A, C (the trustee) can sue B if he fails to deliver the goods or pay the money. Similarly with duties. If A had a contract with B under which it was A's duty to deliver goods, his trustee in bankruptcy must go on with the contract and deliver the goods (and then claim the price). There is a qualification to this rule; if an executory contract is onerous or unprofitable, the trustee is permitted to disclaim the contract. That means that he need not go on with the contract, but the bankrupt's estate will be liable for breach of it.

Personal contracts are not, as such, transferred. Thus, if an employee becomes insolvent, he will probably be able to go on serving, in which case there is no question of transferring his duties. If the insolvency makes it impossible for him to continue in his employment, the trustee in bankruptcy need not and cannot take up his duties. The contract is at an end. So far as rights are concerned, special rules apply. The right to sue for wages already earned, or for breach of contract already committed before insolvency, passes to the trustee. Post-insolvency wages, and damages for post-insolvency breach of contract, can be sued for by the insolvent person himself, but he must hand over to the trustee any part of such wages or damages which is not needed to support him and his family. The trustee's right to sue for pre-insolvency wrongs is limited to wrongs against the insolvent person's property in a narrow sense. Thus a right of action for personal injury, or for injury to the feelings or reputation of the insolvent person, remains with him and does not pass to the trustee.

CHAPTER FIFTEEN

AGENCY

THE third and last topic to be studied in this examination of "Who is within the Bond" is agency.

WHAT AGENCY IS

Agency is the relationship which arises when one person is authorised to act as the representative of another person. The person authorised is the agent (A); the person authorising is the principal (P).

Usually, the agent is authorised to make a contract with a third party on behalf of the principal. In that situation agency involves two contracts: the contract of agency between P and A, and the contract—of sale, or hire, or carriage, or whatever it may be—which A makes on behalf of P with X (a third party). In this book on the general principles of contract it is naturally the latter contract with which we are primarily concerned, though the contract of agency will also be considered, particularly as regards formation and termination.

A common form of agency is where A buys or sells goods (or land, or shares or anything else) on behalf of P. It is important to distinguish an agent of this kind from a person who buys goods on his own account and then resells them. Thus a shopkeeper is not usually an agent in the legal sense, though he may call himself "agent" of some well-known manufacturer.

HOW AGENCY ARISES

Agency arises wherever one person acquires authority to act as the representative of another. An agent's authority may be "actual," or "apparent" (or "ostensible"), or "usual", or it may arise from "necessity", or it may be conferred retrospectively by "ratification".

Actual Authority

Actual authority may be express or it may be implied.

Express authority

This arises when express words are used, to the effect that P specifically appoints A as his agent. In general no formality is required. An agent who has been appointed orally, not in writing, has power to make a contract which the law requires to be in writing or to be evidenced in writing. But an agent cannot execute a deed unless he has been appointed by deed. The appointment of an agent by deed is called a "power of attorney".

Implied authority

Authority may be implied from some other relationship. Thus, for example, a wife living with her husband has authority, implied by law, to "pledge his credit" for necessary household expenses. This means that she can order goods and services necessary and appropriate to the husband's lifestyle, and the supplier can sue the husband for the price. The authority derives from the family unit, that is, the cohabitation. On the other hand, where there is a cohabitation and a family unit exists, the authority attaches to a mistress no less than to a wife. The husband can forbid his wife to pledge his credit, and this is effective, except that he may be estopped (see "apparent" authority, below) as against a tradesman whose bills the husband has paid in the past. To such a tradesman the husband should give express notice that the authority is withdrawn.

Another form of implied authority is that which is incidental to some larger agency where the terms of the agency are incomplete or where the agent has a discretion as to how he should act. An example of this is where P instructs A to insure goods but leaves A to select a suitable policy. Here A has implied authority to select a particular policy, and P will then be bound by its terms. Should that policy not cover the risk that arises then (assuming the agent acted in good faith) the principal bears the loss.

Apparent Authority

Apparent authority arises where circumstances make it appear to others that a person has authority to act as agent of another person. In *Hely-Hutchinson v. Brayhead Ltd* (1968, C.A., above) Lord Denning M.R. said:

> "Ostensible or apparent authority is the authority of an agent as it *appears* to others. .... [S]ometimes ostensible authority exceeds actual authority. For instance, when the board appoint the managing director, they may expressly limit his authority by saying he is not to order goods worth more than £500 without the sanction of the board. In that case his actual authority is subject to the £500 limitation, but his ostensible authority includes all the usual authority of a managing director. The company is bound by his ostensible authority in his dealings with those who do not know of the limitation."

If, therefore, the board appointed A to be managing director, but with an express limit on his authority, (for example, that he is not to order goods worth more than £500 without the sanction of the board and A nevertheless orders goods worth £1,000) he will have apparent authority to make this contract if it can be shown that £1,000 is within the usual authority of a managing director of that type of company.

Apparent authority rests upon a representation by P to X that A has authority. This representation more often arises from conduct than from words. The representation cannot come from the agent alone; some act of the principal is necessary. Further the representation will be considered from the perspective of the third party. The principal's representation sets up an "estoppel". P (the company in Lord Denning's example) is estopped from denying to X (a third party from whom A has ordered £1,000 worth of goods on behalf of the company) that A (the managing director) had authority to do so. Whilst it is true that A did not have authority the equitable rule of estoppel protects X by prohibiting P from denying that he made the representation which X has relied upon. P will be estopped where by words or conduct he represents facts which are intended to be acted upon by X and where X does act in reliance on them.

In the recent case of *First Energy v. Hungarian International Bank* (1993, C.A.) Nourse L.J. said: "A question of ostensible authority is primarily one of fact. Did the principal hold out the agent as having his authority to ... do the act on which the other party relies?"

Usual Authority

The phrase "usual authority" denotes the authority which agents of the type concerned usually have in a particular trade or business. Usual authority arises where the agent is appointed by the principal to some position or office. There is an overlap with "implied" and "apparent" authority, as can be seen in Lord Denning's example above.

In *Watteau v. Fenwick* (1893) the manager of a public house bought some cigars despite being instructed not to do so by the brewer who was the owner of the house. The manager ordered the cigars in his own name, and the supplier believed that the manager was contracting on his own behalf. So this was not a case of apparent authority, because it did not appear to the supplier that the manager had the owner's authority. Nevertheless, the supplier successfully sued the owner on the basis that it was usual for managers of public houses to buy cigars.

Whilst a bank manager does not have usual authority to bind his bank, in *First Energy v. Hungarian International Bank* (above) the bank was held to have authorised its manager to communicate the offer of finance made by others in the bank with authority to contract on its behalf. Thus this case distinguished between the making of an offer (or acceptance) and the communication of that offer to a third party.

Authority of Necessity

There is a limited class of case in which a person may acquire authority to act for another even without his consent in circumstances of necessity. Thus the master of a ship, where it is necessary for the continuance of the voyage, may borrow money on the shipowner's credit, and so bind the shipowner. Or he may even bind the cargo-owners where the cargo is in danger (*e.g.* of perishable goods perishing) by borrowing money on the security of the cargo, or by selling part of the cargo. The same power is possessed by a carrier by land in respect of perishable goods. The "principal" is bound in such cases only if (1) there is an unforseen risk to the goods, (2) the course adopted is reasonably necessary in the circumstances and (3) it was practically impossible to communicate with the owners. In the present state of world-wide communications the third condition will not often be fulfilled.

Ratification

If A, without authority, purports to contract with X on behalf of P, P can subsequently adopt the contract. This subsequent adoption is called ratification. It relates back to the contract which A made with X. Ratification has a double effect: it sets up (retrospectively) a relation of agency between P and A, and it sets up (also retrospectively) a contractual relation between P and X. Ratification is usually express, but implied ratification is possible. In *Cornwal v. Wilson* (1750) A, claiming to act on behalf of P, bought some hemp from X. A did not have authority to buy the hemp. P purported to repudiate the purchase, but he then sold the hemp. It was held that his selling the hemp amounted to implied ratification of the purchase contract, since he could not sell the hemp unless he had first bought it.

In the light of the doctrine of privity of contract, the permissibility of ratification is somewhat surprising, since by means of it P becomes entitled to the benefits of a contract which he had no intention of making. But equally he becomes liable on the contract, so that sometimes ratification is a positive gain to the third party. Moreover, ratification is subject to a number of conditions.

1. The agent must purport to act on behalf of the principal. If A gives the impression that he is acting on his own behalf, then ratification is not open to P, so that even if P purports to ratify it will not be effective. In *Keighley, Maxsted & Co. v. Durrant* (1901, H.L.) A was authorised by P to buy wheat at 44s. 3d. a quarter on a joint account for A and P. A could not get wheat at that price, and (exceeding his authority) he bought from X at 44s. 6d. a quarter. A intended to purchase on the joint account, but he did not disclose this fact to X. Next day P "ratified" the purchase, but later refused to accept delivery. X sued P. He failed, on the ground that the purchase had not been professedly made on behalf of P. Indeed, for ratification to be possible not only must A expressly contract as agent, but the principal must be capable of being ascertained (*i.e.* identified). It is not necessary that the principal should be named. However, there must be such a description of him as shall amount to a reasonable designation of the person intended to be bound by the contract.

2. The principal must have the legal capacity to do the act at the time the agent makes the contract with the third party. In *Ashbury Railway Carriage Company v. Riche* (1875, H.L.), for example, the directors of a company entered into an *ultra vires* contract on behalf of the company.

That contract could not be ratified even by the unanimous vote of the shareholders since the principal did not have the necessary capacity at the time when the contract was made. Although the *ultra vires* rule no longer applies to third party dealings with companies, this case remains important as an illustration of the principle. If a company has not been formally incorporated at the time a person purports to contract as its agent, ratification cannot be effected subsequently after the company has been incorporated: see *Kelner v. Baxter* (1866). In such a case the agent becomes personally liable on the contract. This rule is now enacted as section 36C of the Companies Act 1985.

3. The principal must ratify in time. A contract cannot be ratified after the time fixed for its performance has passed. If no time is fixed for its ratification the contract must be ratified within a reasonable time.

RELATIONS OF THE PARTIES

Where A, on behalf of P, makes a contract with X, the transaction may set up a relation between P and X and/or a relation between A and X.

It is sometimes supposed that there can only be rights and liabilities between P and X or between A and X, and that these two contractual relationships are mutually exclusive. This is not correct. There may well arise a contract between P and X *and* between A and X. This is clear from *Teheran-Europe Co. Ltd v. S.T. Belton (Tractors) Ltd* (1968, C.A.), more particularly in the judgment of Donaldson J. at first instance, and from *The Swan* (1968). It all depends on the words used, the conduct engaged in, and the surrounding circumstances.

Principal and Third Party

It is necessary to distinguish here between two situations: where the principal is disclosed, and where the principal is undisclosed.

Where the principal is disclosed

A principal is called a disclosed principal when his existence is known to the third party at the time A enters into the contract with X. If the third party knew his name he is called a named principal. If the third party did not know his name, but knew that there was a principal, such a principal is called an unnamed principal.

The general rule is that a disclosed principal, whether named or unnamed, is liable and entitled on the contract, and the agent is not. Thus the principal, rather than the agent, can sue and be sued on the contract. The agent having made the contract on behalf of the principal is not liable on it and plays no further part in its performance. However words, conduct or surrounding circumstances may show that the agent is liable and entitled, either instead of, or as well as, the principal.

The fact that P is a foreigner abroad does not prevent a contract arising between him and X. In the *Teheran-Europe* case (1968, C.A., above) the Court of Appeal held that the fact that P was a foreigner abroad was simply one factor in determining whether a contract between P and X had been brought into existence.

Where the principal is undisclosed

A principal is said to be undisclosed where his existence is not known to the third party at the time of contracting. Thus, if A (who is P's agent) makes a contract with X, as though he were acting for himself, and without saying anything about agency so that X is unaware of the agency, P is an undisclosed principal. Nevertheless, an "undisclosed principal" can sue and be sued on the contract. This is surprising (and indeed has been criticised) because it is hard to reconcile with the doctrine of privity of contract. Diplock L.J. suggested in *Freeman & Lockyer v. Buckhurst Park Properties* (1964, C.A.) that it could be explained as being for the avoidance of circuity of action: ". . . the principal could in equity compel the agent to lend his name in an action to enforce the contract against the contractor, and would at common law be liable to indemnify the agent in respect of the performance of the obligations assumed by the agent under the contract."

P's right to come into the contract, however, is subject to several conditions.

1. A must have had authority from P to make the contract when he did. This rule is vitally important. If it were not so, *anyone* could come in to *any* contract. The ratification rule and the "undisclosed principal" rule are the converse of each other. P may come into a contract by ratification, though authority was absent, provided a disclosure of agency was present; P may come into a contract by the "undisclosed principal" rule, though disclosure of agency was absent, provided authority was present.

These rules are, however, mutually exclusive; an undisclosed principal cannot ratify an agent's excess of authority.

2. An undisclosed principal cannot intervene if this would be inconsistent with the terms of the contract. In *Humble v. Hunter* (1848) a person signed a charterparty as "owner of the good ship or vessel called *The Ann*". Clearly, acting in this manner is incompatible with the concept of agency. The undisclosed principal was not allowed to sue on the contract. It was held that the word "owner" implied that the person signing was the principal.

3. An undisclosed principal cannot come in if the third party can show that he wanted to deal with A and with no one else. Such a situation arises where the personality of the agent is of importance to the third party. In *Collins v. Associated Greyhound Racecourses Ltd* (1930) A agreed to underwrite a new issue of shares to be made by a company. (To underwrite shares means to agree to take up any shares which are not subscribed for by the public.) P, the undisclosed principal of A, was not allowed to come into the contract. The contract was held to involve exclusive reliance by the other party on A's business reputation and integrity.

Where an undisclosed principal is permitted to come into the contract, the agent nevertheless remains liable and entitled along with the principal.

Agent and Third Party

The general rule is that an agent is neither liable nor entitled under a contract which he makes on behalf of his principal. He just fades out of the picture. There are exceptions, however, to this general rule.

1. An agent is liable on the contract if he shows an intention to undertake personal liability. In the case of a written contract, if there is no mention of agency in the body of the contract or in the signature, it is almost certain that a court will hold A to be a party to the contract. If A is referred to, both in the body of the contract and in the signature, as an agent, it is virtually certain that he will be held to be not a party. If agency is mentioned in the one place but not in the other, there is a presumption that he is not a contracting party, but the presumption may be rebutted from the circumstances. It is all a matter of words, conduct and circumstances. Where an agent is held liable on a contract he is almost invariably held entitled as well.

199

2. Trade usage or custom may lead to an agent becoming personally liable and entitled. In *Fleet v. Murton* (1871) two brokers in the colonial fruit trade signed this contract: "We have this day sold for your account to our principal, etc. (signed) A and B, Brokers." The principal was not named, but he was clearly disclosed and the brokers clearly intended to contract as agents. The principal refused to accept some of the goods and the third party, the seller, sued the brokers. He won, on the basis of a custom in the fruit trade that a broker was personally liable if the name of his principal was not inserted in the written contract.

3. As has already been stated, where an undisclosed principal comes into the contract the agent is liable and entitled along with the principal.

4. Sometimes a person purports to act for a principal when he is in fact acting for himself. If he purports to act for an unnamed principal, he can enforce the contract for himself. If he purports to act for a named principal, he can only enforce the contract for himself if he notifies the other party that he was really acting for himself, and even then only if the other party would not be prejudiced.

5. Where the principal is non-existent, as in *Kelner v. Baxter* (above), it is easy to infer that the agent intended personal liability. However, the agent is not automatically liable; it will depend upon what the parties intended.

6. Where the agent executes a deed he will be liable on it even when his principal is named. As already stated, an agent cannot execute a deed unless he has been appointed by deed.

There is a different way in which an agent may be made liable. In *Collen v. Wright* (1857), A, describing himself as the agent of P, agreed in writing to lease to X a farm which belonged to P. Both A and X believed that A had P's authority to make the lease. This was not in fact so. X first sued P for specific performance and failed. He then sued A (or rather his executors) for the costs which he had incurred. He won. The court found a separate implied contract whereby A promised X that he had P's authority, in return for X's promise to enter into the lease. So here is a very early example of a "collateral contract". (See Chap. 4.) This particular instance of collateral contract is sometimes called an "implied warranty of authority". This phrase is perhaps somewhat misleading; what is implied is not a warranty in the main contract, but a separate contract altogether.

In two situations legislation has come to the agent's aid. (1) An agent under a power of attorney who acts after it has been revoked (either by actual revocation or by the occurrence of any event, such as the death of the principal, which has the effect of revocation) incurs no liability to the donor or the third party if at the time of acting he did not know of the revocation: Powers of Attorney Act 1971, s.5. (2) A debt incurred after commencement of bankruptcy, which would otherwise be void, is deemed to have been incurred before the bankruptcy by section 284(5) of the Insolvency Act 1986, and accordingly is enforceable.

Payments

Where A has made a contract on behalf of P with X, it may happen that either P or X makes a payment, in discharge of his contractual obligation, to A. Suppose A does not pass on the money, either because he is fraudulent or because he becomes bankrupt. Must the payer pay again?

In a contract of sale, for example, there are two situations to be considered: (1) A, on behalf of P, buys goods from X; P pays A; A does not pay X. (2) A, on behalf of P, sells goods to X; X pays A; A does not pay P. We will consider these in turn.

Agent for purchase

Here P is the purchaser, through the agency of A. X is the seller. P pays the purchase money to A. The money does not reach X. X now claims the purchase price from P.

Where the seller, X, knew that A was acting as an agent, the general rule is that the buyer, P, remains liable to X, and must pay again. But the circumstances may be such that X is estopped from denying that P's payment to A is a good discharge. This will be so if the seller's conduct shows that he looked to the agent alone for payment, thus inducing the principal to settle with the agent. But it takes strong circumstances to raise an estoppel. In *Irvine v. Watson* (1880, C.A.) P employed A, a broker, to buy some oil for him. A bought from X, disclosing the fact of agency but not his principal's name. It was a term of the contract that payment should be made "by cash on or before delivery". In fact X delivered the oil without waiting for payment. P, not aware that X had not been paid, paid A. A became insolvent. X sued P. It was proved in evidence that it was not an invariable custom in the oil trade to insist on prepayment even where the contract stipulated for cash on or before delivery. P argued that he was justified in paying A, because the terms of the contract made it reasonable for him to assume that, since the oil had been delivered, X must have been paid by A. This argument was rejected by the court. The clause about prepayment in the contract was not enough to raise an estoppel, because X was perfectly entitled if he wished to deliver the oil without getting prepayment. This case shows that the general rule—that the buyer must pay again—is not easily displaced. In a case such as this, therefore, P would be wiser not to pay the purchase price to, or through, A, but to pay it direot to X.

The question arises whether the rule applies if the seller thought that the agent was acting for himself. Suppose A buys goods from X apparently on his own account, whereas in fact he has an undisclosed principal, P. P pays the purchase money to A, who does not pay X. X then discovers the existence of P. Can X compel P to pay the purchase price again? In *Heald v. Kenworthy* (1855) it was held that he could. In other words it was held that the general rule applies even though the principal is an undisclosed principal. It seems that only where X has in some way induced P to act to his detriment will X be estopped from suing P.

Agent for sale

Here P is the seller, through the agency of A. X is the buyer. Suppose X pays the purchase money to A, and A does not pay P. Can P compel X to pay again? Where A is known to be an agent the answer turns on whether A is authorised to receive the purchase money. If A is so authorised, the buyer, by paying A, has discharged his contractual duty; if A is not authorised, the buyer must pay again. The general rule is that an agent authorised to sell is not authorised to receive the purchase money. But, of course, in a particular case the agent may have authority to receive the money. If he has been expressly authorised to receive it, the matter is clear. If not, then the buyer will only escape double payment if he can show that the agent had implied authority, or apparent authority, or usual authority to receive the payment.

But the foregoing does not apply where A appears to be selling on his own account. If the buyer, in that situation, pays A, he can rely on that payment if he is sued by P, a formerly undisclosed principal. The question whether or not A has P's authority to receive payment is irrelevant.

A similar distinction between a disclosed agency and an undisclosed agency exists in connection with set-off. Suppose A, an agent for sale, owes a personal debt to the buyer X. The question arises, can X set off his debt against the purchase price? The answer is that if X knows A to be an agent he cannot set off A's debt. On the other hand, if X believed that A was acting on his own account, and then, later, an undisclosed principal is revealed, X can set off what A owes against the purchase money.

In all matters of payment there is a general principle that the intervention of an undisclosed principal, P, should not put the other party, X, in a worse position than he would have been in had A really been (as X thought) acting for himself.

Election

It may happen that both the principal and the agent are liable on a contract. This does not mean that the other party can recover twice over. He has to "elect" whether he will hold the principal liable or the agent, and his election releases the other. What amounts to an election is a question of fact.

If X, the other party to the contract, obtains *judgment* against the principal or the agent, then, though the judgment debt is not paid, X cannot then sue the other. However, in *Clarkson Booker Ltd v. Andjel* (1964, C.A.) X was able to sue A successfully, even though he had earlier issued a writ against P. It was said that such was not a final election for P, because X had also threatened to sue A and had never withdrawn that threat, and because he had not proceeded with his action against P.

HOW AGENCY ENDS

The contract of agency may come to an end in any of the ways in which contracts generally may be discharged. Thus it may end by performance, agreement, frustration or breach. The reader may care to go over this topic again when he has read Part Five of this book.

Modes of Termination

Performance

When both principal and agent have performed their contractual obligations the contract of agency comes to an end. An agency of necessity ends when the circumstances giving rise to the necessity cease.

Notice

If the contract of agency provides that it may be determined by notice being given, then the giving of such notice as provided in the contract will bring the agency to an end. As with other contracts if no period of notice is specified then reasonable notice must be given, and what is reasonable will depend on the facts. An implied agency, no less than an express one, can be determined by notice. Thus, a wife's implied authority to pledge her husband's credit for necessary household expenses can be terminated by the husband's giving her notice to that effect.

Agreement

If principal and agent agree to end their contract, that is effective.

Frustration

It is not practicable to go through all the events which might possibly frustrate a contract of agency, but three events in particular must be mentioned. *Death* of either party puts an end to the agency. *Insanity* of either party puts an end to the agency. The *bankruptcy* of the principal puts an end to the agency. The *bankruptcy* of the agent puts an end to the agency if it makes him unfit to perform his duties.

Breach

As with any other contract, if either party breaches the agency contract, the other party is entitled to treat himself as discharged and to sue for damages for the breach.

Effects on Third Party

When the contract comes to an end the actual authority of the agent terminates. But the ending of the contract does not necessarily terminate the agent's apparent or usual authority. For example, apparent or usual authority does not end by notice given by the principal to the agent; to end it, the principal must give notice to the third party. Whilst a principal's insanity terminates the agent's actual authority, he may still have apparent authority. In *Drew v. Nunn* (1879, C.A.) P, when sane, gave his wife, A, authority to act for him and held her out to X, a tradesman, as having that authority. P then became insane. His wife bought goods on credit from X, who did not know of P's insanity. Later P regained his reason. X successfully sued P for the price of the goods supplied. Although A's actual authority was terminated by P's insanity, her apparent authority continued.

In another case on insanity, *Yonge v. Toynbee* (1910, C.A.), X started an action against P. P instructed A, a solicitor, to defend the action for him. P then became insane. Not knowing of P's insanity, A entered an appearance and delivered a defence. X then learnt of P's insanity, and got the proceedings struck out. He sought an order against A for the costs of his abortive action against P, arguing that A had taken steps in that action without authority. X succeeded because an insane person could only defend proceedings by his guardian *ad litem* and because parties to proceedings are entitled to rely on an implied warrant of authority by a solicitor acting for a party to those proceedings.

Irrevocable Agency

There are two situations in which agency is irrevocable. That means that the purported revocation of the agent's authority is not of any effect, and the authority continues.

Authority coupled with an interest

If the agent's authority is given to him (for consideration or by deed) to secure some interest of his which exists independently of the agency, that authority cannot be revoked by the principal. In *Carmichael's* case (1896, C.A.) A promoted a company, with the idea that the company should buy from him a mine which he owned. P agreed to underwrite 1,000 shares in the company, and he authorised A to apply for the shares on his behalf. This authority was held to be irrevocable, because it was coupled with an interest, namely, the interest that A had in the shares being taken up, since if they were not taken up he would not get the purchase money for the mine.

This rule applies only where the authority is given for the protection of an interest which already exists. It does not apply where the interest arises after the giving of authority.

Irrevocable power of attorney

It is provided by section 4 of the Powers of Attorney Act 1971 that where a power of attorney is expressed to be irrevocable and is given to secure (a) a proprietary interest of the donee of the power, or (b) to secure the performance of an obligation owed to the donee then, so long as the donee has that interest or is owed that obligation, the power shall not be revoked by the donor without the consent of the donee, nor shall it be revoked by the death, incapacity or bankruptcy of the donor, nor, if the donor is a body corporate, by its winding up or dissolution.

Additionally the Enduring Powers of Attorney Act 1985 makes general provision for a power of attorney to be created in a prescribed form so as to constitute an "enduring power" of attorney. When the attorney has reason to believe that the donor is mentally incapable he must give notice to certain relatives and then register the power of attorney with the court. This gives the opportunity for any objections to be raised. Using this procedure the Act provides that the power of attorney can survive any subsequent mental incapacity (but not death or bankruptcy) of the donor.

With effect from January 1, 1994, the E.C. Commercial Agents Directive was implemented in the United Kingdom by Regulations which require manufacturers to provide their commercial agents with written terms of appointment. The Regulations deal with other issues, such as commissions, and introduce the concept of compensation for the agent when the agency is terminated.

PART FIVE

UNTYING THE BOND

CHAPTER SIXTEEN

PERFORMANCE

THE last part of this book is called "Untying the Bond". This will consider the four ways in which a contract may come to an end: performance, agreement, frustration and breach. In the final chapter remedies will be considered.

The most obvious way in which a contract may come to an end is by its being performed. If A and B make a contract under which A is to perform some service and B is to pay him for it, then when A has performed his service and B has paid the money, both parties have discharged their contractual obligations, and the contract is at an end.

The question arises: What amounts to performance?

THE GENERAL RULE

The general rule is that performance must exactly match what the party agreed to do, so that if he does something less than—or different from—what he agreed to do he has not discharged his contractual obligation, and consequently is not entitled to payment. In *The Kathleen* (1874) a ship was abandoned after a collision. It was later saved by third parties, who brought it to an intermediate port. It was held that the owners were not entitled to "freight" (that is the charge for the carriage of goods) even though the contract of carriage exempted the shipowners from liability for loss caused by collisions, and even though the collision was entirely due to the fault of the other ship.

A party who has fallen short of complete performance cannot sue on the contract because his own complete performance is a "condition precedent" to his right to sue. This rule, requiring complete performance, sometimes leads to unjust results. In *Cutter v. Powell* (1795) Cutter agreed to serve as second mate on a ship bound from Jamaica to Liverpool. He was to be paid 30 guineas "provided he proceeds, continues and does his

209

duty . . . from hence to the port of Liverpool''. The ship sailed on August 2. It arrived at Liverpool on October 9. But Cutter had died at sea on September 20. It was held that his widow could not recover anything for the work he had done. The contract was said to be ''entire''; nothing was to be paid unless Cutter had performed his entire duty under the contract. Although this was a hard case, it was not so unjust as at first sight appears. The ordinary rate for such a voyage at the time was about £8, so the contract figure was almost four times the ordinary rate. Lord Kenyon C.J. said it was ''a kind of insurance''. It was a kind of insurance from the point of view of the shipowner; from Cutter's point of view it was a kind of gamble.

If the general rule, that performance to be effective must be complete performance, were maintained in all its rigorous logic, it would frequently lead to injustice. In practice it is subject to four exceptions, which will be looked at in turn. It is also subject to the doctrine of ''frustration'', which will be considered in Chapter 18.

THE EXCEPTIONS

Severable Contracts

Cutter v. Powell (above) is an example of an entire contract. But not all contracts are entire; some are severable. Whether any particular contract is entire or severable depends upon the intention of the parties, which has to be determined by considering the express and implied terms of the contract. The problem is: Does the contract mean that the party in question is not to be entitled to payment unless and until he has completely performed his whole obligation, or does it mean that he can sue for payment when he has performed some part of what he undertook to do? In *Cutter v. Powell* the contract was construed to be of the first kind (entire), as was the contract in *Vlierboom v. Chapman* (1844). In that case a shipowner agreed to carry a cargo of rice from Batavia to Rotterdam. He in fact carried it only to Mauritius. It was held that he was not entitled to any freight. On the other hand, the contract in *Ritchie v. Atkinson* (1808) was held to be severable. A shipowner agreed to carry a cargo of hemp, freight to be £5 a ton. He in fact only took part of the cargo. It was held that he could recover freight proportional to the quantity carried.

210

It is commonly said that a *contract* is entire or severable, but it would be more accurate to speak of a particular obligation within a contract as being entire or severable. Thus the obligation to carry to a particular destination is entire (*Vlierboom's* case); the obligation to carry a particular quantity is severable (*Ritchie's* case).

Prevention of Performance

If a party to a contract performs part of the work that he has undertaken, and is then prevented by the fault of the other party from finishing the work, he can sue. This is so whether the contract (or his obligation) is severable or entire. He can either sue for damages for breach of contract, or he can sue on a *quantum meruit* and so obtain a reasonable remuneration for the work he has done. In *Planché v. Colburn* (1831) the plaintiff agreed to write a book on costume and ancient armour, to be published by the defendants in a series called "The Juvenile Library". He was to be paid £100 on completion of the book. He collected material and wrote part of the book. The defendants then abandoned the series. On a *quantum meruit* claim ("as much as he has deserved") he was awarded £50.

Acceptance of Partial Performance

If one party partially performs his obligation and the other party accepts the work, it may be possible to infer that the parties have agreed to abandon the original contract (whether severable or entire) and to make a new one, under which the party making partial performance is entitled to a reasonable remuneration. In *Christy v. Row* (1808) the plaintiff's ship was carrying the defendant's coal from Shields to Hamburg. The ship was prevented by "restraint of princes" from reaching Hamburg, and the master, *at the request of the consignee*, delivered some of the coal at Gluckstadt, a town on the Elbe below Hamburg. The plaintiff successfully sued for freight.

Such a new promise to pay will be inferred only where the beneficiary has a genuine choice whether to accept or reject the benefit of the work done. In *Sumpter v. Hedges* (1898, C.A.) the plaintiff agreed to build two houses on the defendant's land for £565. He did work to the value of about £333 and then abandoned the contract. The defendant himself completed the buildings. The plaintiff's claim for a *quantum meruit* failed. No new implied promise to pay could arise from the mere fact that the defendant had reoccupied his own land and gone on with the building. He had no choice between accepting or rejecting the white elephant. But the plaintiff was awarded a reasonable sum in respect of the materials which he had left on the site and which the defendant had used in completing the buildings. A promise to pay a reasonable sum for these materials could be inferred from the defendant's choosing to use them.

Substantial Performance

A party who performs his obligation defectively, but substantially, can enforce the contract. In *Boone v. Eyre* (1779) the plaintiff conveyed to the defendant a plantation in the West Indies together with the slaves on it. He sued for the price. The defendant pleaded that the plaintiff was not lawfully possessed of the slaves. Lord Mansfield held that this was no defence. That case is perhaps the origin of the doctrine of substantial performance. It was given a revival in *Dakin v. Lee* (1916, C.A.), which involved a contract for repairs to be done to a house. The work as done did not accord with the contract in certain respects. The Court of Appeal gave judgment for the plaintiff repairer, but with a deduction equal to the cost of putting right the defects. *Dakin v. Lee* was followed in *Hoenig v. Isaacs* (1952, C.A.). The plaintiff agreed to redecorate and furnish the defendant's flat for £750. The defendant complained of faulty design and bad workmanship, but he paid £400. The plaintiff sued for the balance, £350. The court found that there were defects in the furniture, and assessed the cost of putting them right at £55. The defendant argued that, if the plaintiff was entitled to anything at all, it was certainly less than the contract price and should be assessed on a *quantum meruit* basis. The Court of Appeal held that the plaintiff had made substantial performance and that he was entitled to the contract price, less the cost of making good the defects.

Of course there are limits to the doctrine of substantial performance, and these are well illustrated by the case of *Bolton v. Mahadeva* (1972, C.A.). The plaintiff had contracted to instal central heating in the defendant's house for £560. At the trial it was proved that the house was 10 per cent less warm than it should have been and that because of a defective flue there were fumes in the living rooms. It would have cost £174 to put right these defects. The Court of Appeal held that the plaintiff was not able to rely on the doctrine of substantial performance. So the plaintiff got nothing.

The doctrine of substantial performance can be applied to an entire contract, no less than to a severable one. In *Hoenig v. Isaacs* (above) Somervell L.J. said that it could have been applied in *Cutter v. Powell* if the sailor had served all the way to Liverpool but had "failed on some occasion in his duty as mate". This emphasises again that it is not a whole contract which is entire, but an obligation within a contract.

This discussion of the doctrine of substantial performance will no doubt recall to mind the distinction between conditions and warranties, considered in Chapter 4. That distinction does indeed come into the question of defective performance. If the defect in performance amounts only to a breach of warranty, the "defective performer" is a "substantial performer" and he can sue for his money, though he must submit to a deduction equal to the cost of making good the defect; if it amounts to a breach of condition he cannot sue. As Chapter 4 showed, not all contractual terms can be brought within the framework of conditions and warranties: see the *Hong Kong Fir* case (1962, C.A.) and the *Cehave* case (1976, C.A.). With "intermediate" or "innominate" terms, the test is whether B, the other party, has received substantially the whole benefit which it was the intention of the parties that he should obtain under the contract. If yes, then A, the "defective performer", is a "substantial performer" and he can sue for his money; if no, then he cannot sue.

Where a party performs only partially or defectively, although, as we have seen, he may be able to sue on the contract, he is not entirely discharged. If the incompleteness or defectiveness of his performance amounts to a breach of contract, he can be sued for that breach. Thus, in *Ritchie v. Atkinson* (see p. 210, above), a case decided in the context of severable contracts, although Ritchie won his action for proportional freight, he was later held liable in damages for failing to carry the rest of the cargo; see *Atkinson v. Ritchie* (1809).

TENDER OF PERFORMANCE

A tender of performance is an offer of performance. Tender of performance is equivalent to performance itself. The reason for this rule is that since one party often cannot complete performance without the concurrence of the other party, justice demands that if he makes an offer to perform which is rejected by the other party he should be treated as discharged. In *Startup v. Macdonald* (1843) the plaintiff agreed to sell 10 tons of oil to the defendant and to deliver it to him "within the last 14 days of March". The plaintiff tried to deliver the oil at 8.30 p.m. on March 31, a Saturday. The defendant refused to accept it, because of the lateness of the hour. The plaintiff was awarded damages for non-acceptance. This case would probably not be decided in the same way today. Section 29(5) of the Sale of Goods Act 1979 provides: "Demand or tender of delivery may be treated as ineffectual unless made at a reasonable hour; and what is a reasonable hour is a question of fact." It is doubtful whether 8.30 p.m. on a Saturday night is a reasonable hour to start examining and weighing 10 tons of oil. But the principle of *Startup v. Macdonald* is unimpaired; a valid tender of goods discharges the tenderer from further liability and entitles him to damages for breach of contract.

The effect of a tender of money is not quite the same. Tender of a money payment does not discharge the tenderer from liability. He need not make any further tender, but his obligation to pay remains. If he is sued, he pays the money into court, and if the other party goes on with his action he (the other party) will be ordered to pay the costs. For a tender of money to be valid it must be in "legal tender" and it must be of the exact amount due. The debtor is not entitled to ask for change. But, of course, he can always leave the surplus with the creditor.

TIME OF PERFORMANCE

If the contract states a definite time for performance, the question may arise whether the time is "of the essence" of the contract. That is the classic way of putting it. The broad answer is that at common law time is of the essence and in equity it is not. At common law, unless the contract provides otherwise, performance must be completed by the date specified. If it is not completed by that date, the other party can sue for repudiatory breach. But by the Sale of Goods Act 1979, section 10(1), stipulations as to time of *payment* are not of the essence of a contract of sale, "unless a different intention appears from the terms of the contract". Section 10(2) says: "Whether any other stipulation as to time is or is not of the essence of the contract depends on the terms of the contract.'' Courts of equity have always rather leant against time being of the essence. Thus, in contracts for the sale of land, time is not necessarily of the essence, and specific performance may be decreed despite the failure of the plaintiff to keep to the time fixed for completion, if this can be done without injustice to the defendant. But time is of the essence, even in equity, in some situations: (1) if that is expressed in, or can be inferred from, the terms of the contract; (2) if the circumstances are such that it is vital that the agreed date should be kept to, for example where the subject-matter of the contract is something which fluctuates in value, such as a block of highly speculative shares; and (3) where one party has already delayed, and the other party notifies him that unless performance is completed within some reasonable specified time he will treat the contract as broken. In such a case time becomes of the essence by virtue of the notice. In this last case, the party serving the notice may do so immediately the other party fails to carry out his obligation by the stipulated date, even though at that stage time was not of the essence of the contract; it is not necessary to wait until there has been unreasonable delay by the party in breach before serving the notice, though the notice has to give a reasonable period of time in which to perform the obligation: see *Behzadi v. Shaftesbury Hotels Ltd* (1992). See also *Rickards (Charles) Ltd v. Oppenheim* (1950, C.A.).

The rules of common law and equity on this matter were brought together by statute in 1873. The relevant enactment is now section 41 of the Law of Property Act 1925, which provides: ''Stipulations in a contract, as to time or otherwise, which according to rules of equity are not deemed to be or to have become of the essence of the contract, are also construed and have effect at law in accordance with the same rules.''

Until recently many lawyers were under the impression that, in relation to a contractual term where time was not of the essence, failure to perform by the stipulated time was not a breach of contract at all. This was an error, as was made clear by the House of Lords in *Raineri v. Miles, Wiejski (Third Party)* (1981, H.L.). The true position is this: if time is of the essence, late performance is a repudiatory breach; if time is not of the essence, late performance is not a repudiatory breach, but it is a breach, and it entitles the injured party to damages. (See also *Lombard North Central plc v. Butterworth* (1987, C.A.) and *Behzadi v. Shaftesbury Hotels Ltd* (1991).) Section 41 of the Law of Property Act 1925 does not negative the existence of a breach of contract where one has occurred, but in certain circumstances it bars any assertion that the breach has amounted to a repudiation of the contract.

VICARIOUS PERFORMANCE

This arises where A engages B, by contract, to perform some service and then B gets C to perform the service in fact. If this is done with the knowledge and consent of A, no difficulty is likely to arise. But if it is done without A's consent, what then? The answer is that the ''creditor'' (that is the party to whom something, not necessarily money, is due under a contract) cannot object to vicarious performance unless it really matters to him that B should perform the service personally. To take an obvious example, if B's duty under the contract is to pay a sum of money to A, A cannot refuse to accept the money because in fact C, not B, pays it to him. And the same principle has been applied to performances other than the payment of money. In *British Waggon Co. v. Lea* (1880) B contracted to let out railway wagons to A and keep them in repair for seven years. It was held that the contract could be performed by C; it did not matter to A who kept the wagons in repair, so long as the work was properly done.

If the work were not properly done it would be B, not C, who would be liable to A. For this reason it is misleading to speak of vicarious performance as being an ''assignment of liabilities''. The phrase is sometimes used, but it is not really correct. The liability is not transferred. The original ''debtor'' remains liable, for bad work, for example, and the sub-contractor does not become liable on the contract; he may be liable in tort, however, for negligence. In *Stewart v. Reavell's Garage* (1952) the plaintiff took a 1929 Bentley to the defendants' garage to have the brakes relined. With the plaintiff's consent, they arranged for the work to be done by a sub-contractor. The work was done badly, the brakes failed and the car crashed into a tree. The defendants were held liable for the sub-contractor's bad workmanship. Since the plaintiff had agreed, the defendants were obviously entitled to perform vicariously, but that did not lead to any transfer of liability.

Whenever a contracting party performs his obligation vicariously he remains liable to the other party for any bad workmanship or other breach which may occur. This is so, even in a quite ''impersonal'' contract. In a ''personal'' contract a still stricter rule applies; the contractor is not *per-*

mitted to delegate performance at all. This is true of such obviously personal contracts as a contract to paint a portrait, and it is also true of less obvious cases. For instance, in *Edwards v. Newland* (1950, C.A.) the principle was applied to a contract to store goods. It was said that the owner of the goods relies on the skill and integrity of the contractor. In such a case, vicarious performance does not count as performance at all; the debtor is not discharged, and the creditor is not bound to pay for the work that has been done.

CHAPTER SEVENTEEN

AGREEMENT TO DISCHARGE OR VARY A CONTRACT

THE contractual bond is founded on the agreement of the parties. The parties may, by agreement, untie the bond.

In its simplest form, discharge by agreement occurs where A promises to give up *his* rights under the contract in return for a promise by B to give up his rights. In that case the contract is at an end. Or the parties may add to this discharge of the old contract new promises which constitute a new contract. For example, B has agreed to sell to A a television. Before it is delivered, they may agree that B is to sell to A a video recorder, not a television. Where this happens it is usually by means of express agreement, but it can happen by implied agreement. B may agree to sell to A a dozen bottles of red wine. In the event, B delivers a dozen bottles of wine, of which six are red and six are white. A, if he wishes, can accept the dozen bottles delivered. If he does so, the first contract is discharged by agreement and a new contract comes into existence. The first contract is not discharged by performance, because there has not been performance, but it is discharged by implied agreement.

Discharge by agreement may arise out of a term in the contract itself. The most important instance of this is where the contract contains a provision for notice. This is commonly the case in a contract of employment. If the provisions as to notice are complied with, the contract is discharged by agreement. If one or other party purports to end the contract without complying with the provisions as to notice, that is a breach. Breach will be considered in Chapter 19.

Just as the parties may agree to *discharge* a contract, so they may agree to *vary* a contract. Indeed, it is sometimes not easy to say whether they are varying a contract or discharging one contract and making a new one. To substitute a video recorder for a television is undoubtedly to discharge the first contract and make a second. On the other hand, to change the date on which the television is to be delivered is merely to vary the con-

218

tract. But there is a more debatable borderland in between. Although the distinction is often not important, sometimes it is, as will be seen.

Two points arise in connection with discharge and variation which require some discussion. These are formality and consideration.

FORMALITY

As a general proposition, it can be said that contracts can be discharged or varied by an agreement in any form the parties wish—by deed, in writing, by word of mouth, or by conduct. For example, in *Berry v. Berry* (1929) a husband entered into a deed of separation, in which he covenanted to pay his wife £18 a month. Some years later, by a written contract not under seal, he agreed to pay her £9 a month plus (if his earnings were in excess of £350 a year) 30 per cent of the excess. This wife brought an action claiming arrears on the basis that £18 a month was due. It was held that that claim was not open to her; the second agreement had validly replaced the original deed, and the second agreement had been complied with.

It might seem, at first sight, that the discharge or variation of a written contract by word of mouth would conflict with the parol evidence rule. But this is not so. Chapter 4 said that that rule "does not prevent extrinsic evidence being given to prove that the contract does not yet operate or has ceased to operate". So a party can give evidence of an oral agreement to end the contract. The parol evidence rule also does not apply "where the written agreement is not the whole agreement". A party can give evidence to prove that the original written agreement has been varied by a subsequent (as distinct from an antecedent) oral agreement.

Some contracts, however, although they can be discharged by subsequent oral agreement, cannot be varied in that manner. This is particularly true of contracts which were required to be evidenced in writing by the Statute of Frauds, of which one type remains, contracts of guarantee: see also Chapter 7. (The same principle applies to contracts required by other rules of law to be made in a particular manner.) The position can be stated in three rules.

1. If the discharge is total it will be effective even though it is not evidenced in writing.

2. If the discharge is only a partial discharge, so that in effect it is a variation, that discharge must be evidence by writing, and if it is not it is of no effect. In *Goss v. Nugent* (1833) there was a written contract for the sale of land, which, among other terms, bound the vendor to make good title. Later the purchaser agreed orally not to insist on title being made to part of the land. Then the purchaser changed his mind and declined to go on with the contract. The vendor sued. He failed: he was unable to deliver the title that he had agreed to deliver by the original contract; that contract still stood, the oral variation being of no effect. (It should be noted that, at the time when this case was decided, contracts for the sale of an interest in land were required to be *evidenced* in writing. Now, they must be in writing, to comply with the requirements of the Law of Property (Miscellaneous Provisions) Act 1989.)

3. If the oral discharge is a total discharge coupled with the making of a new contract in substitution, it is effective to put an end to the original contract and the new contract is not enforceable.

It is sometimes difficult to decide whether the parties intended variation or whether they intended total discharge plus substitution. If they intended variation then the original contract is enforceable in its unvaried form; if they intended total discharge plus substitution then nothing is enforceable, since the original contract is gone and the new one is not evidenced in writing.

CONSIDERATION

In Cases of Discharge

Just as a contract is formed by agreement plus consideration, so discharge by agreement requires consideration. Where the contract is executory, in the sense that neither party has completely performed his obligation, no difficulty arises. If A promises to give up his rights and B promises to give up *his*, that is a good discharge. Consideration moves from both A and B. But if A has completely performed his obligation under the contract, and he releases B from *his* obligation, there is no consideration moving from B. The consequence is that A could go back on his promise to release B. It is similar to the situation looked at in Chapter 2, under the heading "Part Payment of a Debt", involving *Pinnel's* case and *Foakes v.*

Beer. If the doctrine of promissory estoppel (see pp. 40–42, above) is strong enough to overthrow *Foakes v. Beer*, consideration will not be necessary for discharge by agreement.

The difficulty can be overcome by B giving to A some new consideration in return for A giving up his rights under the contract. What is required is "accord and satisfaction". Accord is agreement and satisfaction is consideration. A has painted B's house, for which service the contractual price is £2,500. B cannot pay this sum. He offers, instead of paying £2,500, to rewire A's house. A agrees. There is accord and satisfaction. It should be noted, however, that the requirement of consideration seems to have been modified by the Court of Appeal's decision in *Williams v. Roffey Bros & Nicholls (Contractors) Ltd* (1990): see Chapter 2.

At one time it was thought that the satisfaction could only become effective when it was executed. But the modern law is that an executory promise may constitute effective satisfaction, if that is what the parties have agreed. In *Elton Cop Dyeing Co. v. Broadbent & Son Ltd* (1919, C.A.) A bought some machinery from B which turned out to be defective, and A claimed damages for breach of warranty. By a compromise agreement, A agreed to withdraw his action and B agreed to make good the machinery, bearing half the cost of so doing. A then sued on the original contract. He failed. B successfully pleaded accord and satisfaction. It was held that the compromise agreement, properly construed, meant that A accepted as satisfaction, discharging his original cause of action, B's *promise* to make good the machinery. If B did not eventually carry out that promise, A could sue him on that.

In Cases of Variation

If a variation is for the benefit of both parties, then it contains within itself its own consideration. Suppose A has agreed to buy from B a car to be delivered and paid for on October 31. It turns out to be convenient to both A and B that delivery should be postponed until November 30, and they agree to that new date. That is an effective variation. Consideration moves from A and from B; A gives up his right to receive delivery on October 31 and B gives up his right to make delivery and take payment on October 31.

If, however, a variation is made for the benefit of only one of the parties, the situation is different. If B (the seller) agrees, for the sole benefit of A (the buyer), that delivery of the car shall be postponed from October 31 to November 30, A has given no consideration. Does this mean, then, that the indulgence granted by B has no effect? If this were so it would lead to some unjust results. B would be able to issue a writ on November 1 for non-acceptance by A, and (even more unjustly) A would be able, if sued by B for non-acceptance on November 30, to plead that he was excused because B was in breach of his contractual duty to deliver on October 31.

Even the common law did not go to this length. The party for whose benefit the indulgence had been granted was not allowed to repudiate it. Thus, in the example, A could not refuse acceptance on November 30 by arguing that B was in breach of his contractual obligation to deliver on October 31. The common law evolved a doctrine of "waiver", under which, in many cases, the party who had granted the indulgence was not allowed to go back on his word. Thus, in the example, B might not be permitted to insist on his contractual right to make delivery and take payment on October 31. The doctrine of "waiver", however, was dependent upon the mysterious distinction between waiver and variation. If the court found that an indulgence was a waiver (or forbearance), it would give effect to it; if it found that an indulgence was a variation it would not. It is not possible to find in the cases a rational line of distinction between the two.

Courts of equity were free to take a more consistent view, and hold that a party who had granted an indulgence to the other was bound by it. This view now prevails in all courts. It is an application of the doctrine of "promissory estoppel", and, since it does not conflict with *Foakes v. Beer*, it has received general acceptance.

In *Alan (W.J.) & Co. v. El Nasr Export & Import Co.* (1972, C.A.) a contract for the sale of coffee provided for the price expressed in Kenyan shillings to be paid by irrevocable letter of credit. The buyers obtained a confirmed letter of credit expressed to be for payment in sterling. The sellers raised no complaint about the terms of the letter of credit, and they drew on the credit in part payment of the contract price. While shipment of the coffee was in progress, sterling was devalued. The sellers claimed such amount in Kenyan shillings as would make up for the devaluation. The Court of Appeal held that the sellers, by their conduct in accepting the letter of credit and/or in drawing on it, had waived the right to be paid in Kenyan currency. In accordance with the principle of *Hughes v. Metropolitan Railway Co.*, the sellers' claim must fail. (See also p. 40, above.)

CHAPTER EIGHTEEN

FRUSTRATION

IN early days the law took the view that contractual obligations were "absolute". As expounded in *Paradine v. Jane* (1647) this meant that if a person undertook by contract to do something he was absolutely bound to do it. If subsequent events made it impossible for him to do it, he was in breach of his contract and was liable in damages to the other party. In 1863, however, in the case of *Taylor v. Caldwell*, a major dent in this rule of absoluteness was made. Caldwell had agreed to give Taylor the use of The Surrey Gardens and Music Hall on four named days for the purpose of holding concerts there. Just before the first of these days the hall was destroyed by fire. Taylor sued for damages for breach of the agreement. The court gave judgment for the defendant. Blackburn J. said: "We think . . . that the Music Hall having ceased to exist, without fault of either party, both parties are excused, the plaintiffs from taking the gardens and paying the money, the defendants from performing their promise to give the use of the Hall and Gardens and other things."

THE EXTENT OF THE DOCTRINE

From this case there developed the doctrine of frustration, under which the parties to a contract are excused further performance of their obligations if some event occurs during the currency of the contract, without the fault of either party, which makes further performance impossible or illegal, or which makes it something radically different from what was originally undertaken. The present extent of the doctrine will be considered under those three heads.

223

Impossible

A contract may become impossible in three ways.

Subject-matter destroyed

This point is well illustrated by *Taylor v. Caldwell* itself. The contract related to "The Surrey Gardens and Music Hall", and though only the music hall was destroyed that was enough to frustrate the contract, because the object of the contract was rendered impossible. So total destruction of the subject-matter is not necessary.

Death

A "personal contract" is ended by frustration if either party dies. The contracts covered by this rule include contracts of employment and apprenticeship and of agency.

Subject-matter unavailable

A contract is frustrated if a thing or person required for its performance ceases, through some extraneous cause, to be available for that purpose. Thus a charterparty may be discharged if the ship is damaged; a contract for the sale of goods may be discharged if the goods are requisitioned; a contract of service may be discharged if one of the parties becomes ill, or is imprisoned. See, for example, *Marshall v. Harland & Wolff Ltd* (1972), *Egg Stores (Stamford Hill) Ltd v. Leibovici* (1977) and *F.C. Shepherd & Co. Ltd v. Jerrom* (1987).

Even temporary unavailability may discharge a contract, if the interruption is such as to make performance after it substantially different from what was originally undertaken. In *Jackson v. Union Marine Insurance Co. Ltd* (1874) a ship was chartered to carry rails from Newport to San Francisco in January. It went aground in Caernarvon Bay on its way to the port of loading, and was not fully repaired until August. It was held that the delay frustrated the contract.

An important factor in deciding whether or not there has been frustration is to consider the ratio of the likely length of the interruption to the contract period as a whole. In *Morgan v. Manser* (1948) a music hall artiste, known professionally as "Cheerful Charlie Chester", was called up for war service in 1940. His 10-year contract with a manager (made in 1938) was held to be frustrated by the call-up, since it was likely that Cheerful Charlie would be in the Army for a very long time.

On the other hand, in *Nordman v. Rayner and Sturgess* (1916) an agent, engaged under a long-term contract, was interned during the First World War. He was from Alsace and was anti-German in his sympathies. It was held that the agency contract was not frustrated, since his internment was not likely to last long. In this type of case, though the trial may be held years later, the court has to consider what the prospects must have looked like at the time the event in question happened.

Illegal

A contract is discharged by frustration if, during the currency of the contract, further performance becomes illegal. A clear example of this principle is that a contract is frustrated if legislation (including delegated legislation) is passed after the contract was made, which renders it illegal. Another example is where the outbreak of war means that further performance of a contract would amount to "trading with the enemy". See *Fibrosa Spolka Akcyjna v. Fairbairn Lawson Combe Barbour Ltd* (1943, H.L.).

As with destruction of the subject-matter, so with illegality, it is sufficient if the "object of the exercise" is defeated; the fact that some minor part of the contract could still be performed does not save it from frustration.

Radically Different

The highwater mark of the doctrine of frustration was reached in a series of cases, usually called "the coronation cases", which arose out of the postponement of the coronation of King Edward VII. These cases establish that a contract may be frustrated, though it does not become impossible or illegal, if it becomes futile. In *Krell v. Henry* (1903, C.A.) Henry hired a room in Pall Mall for the days on which the coronation processions of King Edward VII were due to take place. Both parties understood that the object of the letting was to watch the processions from the windows of the room, but this was not stated in the contract. The King's illness caused the processions to be postponed. Henry could still have come and sat in the room, but it would have been futile. The Court of Appeal held that the contract was frustrated. The doctrine of frustration, it was held, can apply where a "state of things", essential to the contract, "fails to be in existence". This decision has been doubted but never overruled.

In *Davis Contractors Ltd v. Fareham U.D.C.* (1956, H.L.) a building company had agreed to build 78 houses for a local authority in eight months for the sum of £92,425. Owing to shortages of skilled labour and building materials the work took 22 months, and the builders incurred additional expenses of £17,651. The builders claimed that the contract was frustrated. The builders wanted to claim a sum in excess of the contract price, on a *quantum meruit* basis. To be able to do so, they had first to get rid of the contract, because a *quantum meruit* claim is not open so long as the contract stands. Hence their argument for frustration. The House of Lords held that there was no frustration. Lord Radcliffe said: ". . . [I]t is not hardship or inconvenience or material loss itself which calls the principle of frustration into play. There must be as well such a change in the significance of the obligation that that thing undertaken would, if performed, be a different thing from that contracted for." In another passage Lord Radcliffe used the phrase "radically different". This case shows that the principle of *Krell v. Henry* is narrowly confined.

FRUSTRATION IN THEORY AND PRACTICE

In Chapter 10 the similarity between "possibility mistake" and frustration was pointed out. In spite of this similarity, theorising about frustration has tended to proceed quite independently of any discussion about mistake. There are numerous theories as to the basis of frustration, but the broad issue lies between two. One theory is that frustration is based on the supposed *intention* of the parties, in the sense that if the parties, at the time of contracting, had contemplated the catastrophic event that later occurred, they would have said: "If that happens, all will be over between us." Another theory is that frustration is a rule of law, by which the courts *impose* a just solution. There has been a shift over the years: the doctrine came in as an aspect of "the implied term", but it has now become a substantive rule of law.

It really comes down to a question of risk. Is it reasonable to put the risk of some catastrophic event upon either A or B, the parties to the contract? Or should A (and/or B) be excused for not performing?

The important point about frustration is that it excuses the parties. If a ship is delayed, will the court say that the delay is a breach by the shipowner (or, in other circumstances, by the charterer) making him liable in damages? Or will the court say that it is not a breach by either party, but is a frustration, which excuses both parties?

Whatever the theoretical basis of the doctrine, a court faced with the question "Frustration or Not?" has to consider the whole terms of the contract, the whole circumstances surrounding its formation, and the whole circumstances which are alleged to constitute frustration.

There are four points which may arise and which require discussion.

Self-Induced Frustration

The doctrine only applies where the frustrating event comes about without the fault of either party. This is sometimes put by saying that a party cannot rely on self-induced frustration. In *Maritime National Fish Ltd v. Ocean Trawlers Ltd* (1935, P.C.) A chartered to B a trawler, the *St Cuthbert*, which was no good unless fitted with an otter trawl. Both parties knew that it was not lawful to use an otter trawl without a licence. B applied for five licences, but was only granted three. He was asked to name the ships to which the three licences should apply, and he named three ships other than the *St Cuthbert*. A sued for the hire money, and B argued that the charter was frustrated. This argument was rejected by the Privy Council on the ground that "it was the act and election of the [charterers] which prevented the *St Cuthbert* from being licensed for fishing with an otter trawl". See also *J. Lauritzen A.S. v. Wijsmuller BV ("The Super Servant Two")* (1989, C.A.).

The burden of proving that the alleged frustration was self-induced lies on the party who asserts that it was.

Events Provided For

Sometimes a contract lays down what are to be the rights and duties of the parties if some misfortune, such as unavoidable delay, happens. A difficult question may then arise as to whether the provision in the contract covers the event which has in fact happened. If the contractual provision does cover the event, then that provision governs the rights and duties of the parties, and the general law of frustration is excluded. (There is one exception to this founded on public policy; if illegality supervenes, the contract is frustrated whatever the parties may have agreed between themselves.) If the contractual provision does not cover the event, then the law of frustration may apply. The courts tend to construe the contractual provision narrowly, so as to allow the doctrine of frustration to apply.

In *Metropolitan Water Board v. Dick, Kerr & Co.* (1918, H.L.) contractors agreed to construct a reservoir in six years. The contract provided that in the event of delays "howsoever occasioned" the contractors were to have an extension of time. The Minister of Munitions made a wartime order that the contractors were to stop work and sell their plant. Although that event was literally within the delay clause, the contract was held to be frustrated. The delay clause, it was held, did not "cover the case in which the interruption is of such a character and duration that it vitally and fundamentally changes the conditions of the contract. . .".

The contractual provision may be held not to apply, not because it is too narrow in scope, but because it is only designed to protect a party from liability and not to exclude the possibility of frustration. This (rather difficult) point is illustrated by *Jackson v. Union Marine Insurance Co. Ltd* (1874), considered on page 224. The charterparty provided that the ship should proceed with all possible dispatch (dangers and accidents of navigation excepted) to Newport, to load. It went aground before it ever got to Newport, and was not fully repaired for eight months. The charterparty was held to be frustrated. At first sight, one might think that the provision "dangers and accidents of navigation excepted" would mean that the charter was not frustrated, and that the charterer would remain bound by the contract. But the court held that the exception of "dangers and accidents of navigation" only served to save the shipowner from liability for not proceeding "with all possible dispatch". It did not follow from the fact that the shipowner was excused for the delay that the charterer was shut out from relying on the delay as a frustration.

It is common for contracts these days to contain what are called "*force majeure*" clauses, the effect of which is to release both parties from their obligations under the contract on the occurrence of certain stipulated events. For example, in *Channel Island Ferries Ltd v. Sealink U.K. Ltd* (1988), the clause stated: "A Party shall not be liable in the event of non-fulfilment of any obligation arising under this contract by reason of Act of God, disease, strikes, lock-outs, fire, and any accident or incident of any nature beyond the control of the relevant party." Since the courts tend to be slow to invoke the doctrine of frustration, there are considerable advantages in including a *force majeure* clause in a contract. An appropriately drafted clause will enable the parties to agree upon the allocation of risk in specified circumstances.

Events Foreseen

If the event which is alleged to have frustrated the contract was foreseen, or should have been, by one party but not by the other, that party cannot rely on frustration. (Here again illegality is an exception.) In *Walton Harvey Ltd v. Walker & Homfrays Ltd* (1931, C.A.) A granted to B the right to display an advertisement on the outside of A's hotel for seven years. Within the seven years, the local authority compulsorily acquired, and then demolished, the hotel. The contract was held not to be frustrated; A knew, and B did not, that there was a risk of compulsory acquisition. A was held liable in damages.

Where the event was foreseen, or should have been, by both parties the position is not so clear. There are dicta in two cases that in such a situation frustration is possible. The cases are *Tatem v. Gamboa* (1939) and *The Eugenia* (1964, C.A.). But those dicta seem to be inconsistent with the following passage in the speech of Lord Radcliffe in the *Davis Contractors'* case (1956, H.L.):

> "Two things seem to me to prevent the application of the principle of frustration to this case. One is that the cause of the delay was not any new state of things which the parties could not reasonably be thought to have foreseen. On the contrary, the possibility of enough labour and materials not being available was before their eyes and could have been the subject of special contractual stipulation. It was not made so."

Leases

It has been held in many cases that the doctrine of frustration does not apply to a lease. The idea is that a lease is more than a contract in that it creates an interest in land. Whatever happens, the land will always be there, and so the interest in the land will always be there. Thus, where a building was very seriously damaged by a bomb, the tenant remained liable on his covenant to pay rent and on his covenant to repair the property: see *Redmond v. Dainton* (1920).

For many years the point was left open in the House of Lords. In *Cricklewood Property and Investment Trust Ltd v. Leighton's Investment Trust Ltd* (1945, H.L.) there was a building lease for 99 years from May 1936. Before any building had been done, the Second World War broke out and government regulations made it impossible for the lessee to build the shops which they had covenanted to build. The lessors sued for the rent, and the lessees pleaded frustration. The House of Lords unanimously held that the lease was not frustrated. When the restrictions were imposed the lease still had more than 90 years to run, and so the interruption was not likely to last for more than a small proportion of the term. Four of the Law Lords gave their views, *obiter*, on whether frustration could ever apply to a lease. Two said that it could, and two said that it could not. The fifth Law Lord expressed no opinion on the point. Then in 1981 in *National Carriers Ltd v. Panalpina (Northern) Ltd* the House of Lords stated that there was nothing in principle to prevent the ordinary contractual doctrine of frustration from applying to a lease. This decision does show that the courts are prepared to extend the doctrine of frustration in appropriate circumstances.

EFFECTS OF FRUSTRATION

Where frustration occurs, the contract comes to an end at the moment of the frustrating event. Neither party has any choice whether or not to treat the contract as discharged; it is automatically discharged. The rights and liabilities of the parties become crystallised, as it were, at the moment of frustration. In the classic phrase, ''the loss lies where it falls''. That is the common law position. That will be looked at first; the effect of statute will then be considered.

In *Chandler v. Webster* (1904, C.A.) the plaintiff hired a room overlooking the coronation procession route for £141 15s., payable immediately. In fact he paid only £100 at the time, and still owed the balance when the announcement of cancellation was made. He sued to recover back his £100. It was held that his claim failed, and also that he remained liable to pay the balance, £41 15s. The contract was frustrated, but the loss lay where it fell. The plaintiff's claim to recover back the £100 lay in quasi-contract, which would be successful only if there was a total

230

failure of consideration. The Court of Appeal held that, since frustration ends the contract only from the moment of frustration and does not make the contract void *ab initio*, the failure of consideration was not total. As to the £41 15s., the defendant's right to receive that had accrued before the moment of frustration, and remained enforceable.

In *Krell v. Henry* (above, at pp. 225–226), the practical result was different, though stemming from the same basic idea. The contract is that case was in different terms. The agreed price for the room was £75. The hirer paid £25 on June 20, and agreed to pay the balance, £50, on June 24. It was on that very day that the announcement of cancellation was made. The owner of the room sued for the £50. He failed. There is a rule of law that if a debt is due on a named day the debtor has until the last moment of the day in which to pay. Therefore at the moment of frustration the owner did not have an accrued right to the £50. (The hirer put in a counterclaim to recover back his £25, but he withdrew this in the Court of Appeal.)

Forty years later *Chandler v. Webster* was overruled by the case of *Fibrosa Spolka Akcyjna v. Fairbairn Lawson Combe Barbour Ltd* (1943, H.L.). Fairbairn agreed, in July 1939, to make machinery for Fibrosa (a Polish company) for £4,800 of which £1,600 was payable in advance. In fact Fibrosa paid only £1,000. On September 3 war was declared, and on September 23 Gdynia (the place of delivery) was occupied by the Germans. The contract was thus frustrated. Fibrosa sued to recover back the £1,000. They won. The House of Lords held that there had been a total failure of consideration. Lord Simon said that, whereas in the formation of a contract consideration may be a promise, when one is considering "failure of consideration" it is actual performance that one is thinking of as being the consideration. If there is no performance there is a total failure of consideration.

But the law was still far from perfect. The payment could only be recovered back where the failure of consideration was total. In *Whincup v. Hughes* (1871) the plaintiff apprenticed his son to a watchmaker for six years at a premium of £25. After one year the watchmaker died. The plaintiff failed to recover back any part of the premium; the failure of consideration was not total. Also, where a party was allowed to recover back an advance payment this might cause injustice to the other party. In the *Fibrosa* case itself, the English company had gone to considerable expense for which it got nothing.

Then came the Law Reform (Frustrated Contracts) Act 1943, which is only concerned with the effects of frustration; it has nothing to say on the earlier question whether the contract has been frustrated or not. There are four main points in the Act.

1. The Act extends the decision in the *Fibrosa* case by providing that money paid before the frustrating event ("the time of discharge") can be recovered back, even though the failure of consideration is only partial.

2. Money due (payable), but not in fact paid, before the frustrating event, ceases to be payable.

3. A party who has incurred expenses may be awarded his *expenses*, up to the limit of the sums paid or payable to him before the frustrating event. Notice that if nothing was paid or payable before the frustrating event, he will not be able to get any expenses at all.

4. A party who has gained a *valuable benefit* under the contract before the frustrating event may be required to pay a just sum for it. This is so whether or not anything was paid or payable before the frustrating event.

There are three contracts to which the Act is expressed *not* to apply. These are: (1) any charterparty (except a time charter or a charter by way of demise) and any non-charter contract for the carriage of goods by sea; (2) a contract of insurance; and (3) certain contracts for the sale of goods. The provision concerning sales of goods is couched in rather obscure language, but it seems that the contracts which are excluded are contracts for the sale of *specific* goods which are frustrated by the *perishing* of the goods. If the goods are not specific or if frustration occurs by some cause other than the perishing of the goods, the Act *does* apply. Why this distinction should be made is not clear.

The purpose of the 1943 Act is to escape from the arbitrary common law rules that "the loss lies where it falls" and to *apportion* the loss, in a fair way, between the parties. To this end, the court is given a wide discretion as to how much to award for expenses or for a valuable benefit.

It is useful to reconsider in the light of the 1943 Act some of the cases considered in this chapter, such as *Chandler v. Webster*, the counterclaim in *Krell v. Henry*, the *Fibrosa* case, and *Whincup v. Hughes*, and see how they would have been decided if the Act had been in operation at the time.

A case not so far considered is *Appleby v. Myers* (1867). The plaintiff agreed to erect some machinery in the defendant's factory and then to keep it in running order for two years. The price was to be £459. When the erecting of the machinery was nearly complete, an accidental fire destroyed the factory and all that it contained. The plaintiff sued for £419 in respect of work done and materials supplied. He failed: the contract was frustrated and no money was due at the moment of frustration. The question arises whether Appleby should have been any better off if his case had arisen after the passing of the 1943 Act. Appleby would not get any expenses under the Act, because nothing was paid or payable before the moment of frustration. Did Myers "obtain a valuable benefit"? The Act refers to the obtaining of a valuable benefit "before the time of discharge". There was some nearly completed machinery in Myer's factory before the time of discharge, so in a sense he did obtain a valuable benefit, unless one takes the view that incomplete machinery is not a benefit. But viewing the events as a whole, in the long run Myers did not obtain any benefit, so probably Appleby would get nothing. This conclusion is supported by section 1(3) of the Act. The court is required to award for "valuable benefit" such sum as it considers just, having regard to all the circumstances, including "the effect, in relation to the said benefit, of the circumstances giving rise to the frustration". In *Appleby v. Myers* the circumstance giving rise to the frustration was the fire, and the effect of that on the benefit (if any) constituted by the partially installed machinery was to destroy it.

CHAPTER NINETEEN

BREACH

A breach of contract occurs where a party fails to perform, or shows an intention not to perform, one or more of the obligations laid upon him by the contract.

FORMS OF BREACH

Where a party fails to perform one of his obligations, that may be called *actual* breach; where he shows an intention not to perform, that may be called *anticipatory* breach.

Actual breach may take one of three forms. Non-performance is one form of breach. If A, a shipowner, charters his ship to B, undertaking to have the ship at Liverpool for loading by a certain date and then never takes his ship to Liverpool, that is a breach of contract by non-performance. Another form of actual breach is defective performance. If A attempts to get his ship to Liverpool, but arrives late, that is a breach of contract by defective performance. A third form of actual breach is the non-truth of a statement which is a term of the contract. If it is written into the contract that the ship is suitable for carrying cars, and in fact it is not, that is a breach of contract.

Anticipatory breach means a breach which occurs before the date of performance laid down in the contract. There are two forms of it: explicit repudiation and implicit repudiation. If A, in June, contracts to charter his ship to B from August 1, and then in July A notifies B that he has no intention of putting the ship at B's disposal, that is explicit repudiation. If C contracts, in September, to charter his ship to D from November 1, and then in October C sells the ship ("free from any charter arrangements") to E, that is implicit repudiation.

234

EFFECTS OF BREACH

Any breach of contract entitles the innocent party to sue for damages. In some circumstances, but not all, a breach gives the innocent party the additional right to treat himself as discharged (or excused) from further performance of the contract (which includes the right to refuse to accept any attempted further performance by the party at fault). This right has often been described as "the right to treat the contract as discharged" and sometimes (though less commonly) as "the right to rescind the contract". It should have been clear since 1942, when the case of *Heyman v. Darwins Ltd* was decided by the House of Lords (see below), that these expressions are incorrect. But in fact it has taken two further decisions of the House of Lords finally to eliminate them. The first in time was *Johnson v. Agnew* (1980, H.L.). Lord Wilberforce said:

"In the case of an accepted repudiatory breach the contract has come into existence but has been put an end to or discharged. Whatever contrary indications may be disinterred from old authorities, it is now quite clear, under the general law of contract, that acceptance of a repudiatory breach does not bring about 'rescission *ab initio*'. I need only quote one passage to establish these propositions. In *Heyman v. Darwins Ltd* Lord Porter said: 'To say that the contract is rescinded or has come to an end or has ceased to exist may in individual cases convey the truth with sufficient accuracy, but the fuller expression that the injured party is thereby absolved from future performance of his obligations under the contract is a more exact description of the position. Strictly speaking, to say that, upon acceptance of the renunciation of a contract, the contract is rescinded is incorrect. In such a case the injured party may accept the renunciation as a breach going to the root of the whole of the consideration. By that acceptance he is discharged from further performance and may bring an action for damages, but the contract itself is not rescinded.' "

Then in *Photo Productions Ltd v. Securicor Transport Ltd* (1980, H.L.) Lord Wilberforce cited the same passage from *Heyman v. Darwins Ltd* to make the point that it is incorrect to "pass . . . from saying that a party, victim of a breach of contract, is entitled to refuse further performance, to saying that he may treat the contract as at an end. . .". It may be understandable shorthand to say that the contract is ended or discharged, but it is not correct; the victim is discharged but the contract itself is not discharged.

Some breaches of contract merely entitle the innocent party to sue for damages; that is so, for example, in the case of breach of warranty. Some breaches (which may be described as repudiatory breaches) entitle the innocent party, in addition to suing for damages, to treat himself as excused from further performance. This is the case with breach of condition and also with "fundamental breach" in the sense of a breach which has the effect of depriving the innocent party of substantially the whole benefit that it was intended that he should get from the contract. (See in Chapter 4 above, under the heading "Conditions and Warranties".) So in all cases the test is whether the breach is of vital, as distinct from minor, importance.

A point which needs emphasis is that even where the breach is such as to give the injured party the right to treat himself as discharged, he need not treat himself as discharged. He has a choice (or election). The choice can be described as a choice either to accept or not to accept the wrongdoer's conduct as being a repudiation of the contract. More shortly, one can say that the injured party has a choice whether or not to accept the repudiation. There is nothing automatic about it. If the injured party decides to affirm the contract and to continue his obligations, he may still sue the wrongdoer for damages for any loss he has suffered as a result of the breach. But, as Lord Simon L.C. said in *Heyman v. Darwins Ltd*, above, the innocent party must act in such a way "as to make plain that, in view of the wrongful action of the party who has repudiated, he claims to treat the contract as at an end".

Anticipatory Breach

Some special features of anticipatory breach need to be pointed out.

It used to be thought that anticipatory breach always entitles the innocent party to treat the contract as discharged, (or, to put it in modern terms, to treat himself as discharged) and that the test of "vital or minor importance" does not arise. But, since *Decro-Wall v. Practitioners in Marketing Ltd* (1971, C.A.) this is no longer so; in cases of anticipatory breach the same test applies as in cases of actual breach. Thus, the innocent party must act so as to make plain that he claims to treat the contract as at an end. There is no reason why the acceptance of an anticipatory repudiation should not take the form of words or conduct which make it

236

plain that the innocent party is responding to the repudiation by treating the contract as at an end. Thus, a failure to perform contractual obligations is capable of amounting to an acceptance of an anticipatory repudiation of a contract: see *Vitol SA v. Norelf Ltd, The Santa Clara* (1993).

Where one party commits an act of repudiatory anticipatory breach, the other party, the innocent party, can sue at once, and need not wait for the contract date of performance to come round. If he does sue at once, he can win even though at the time of action his right is contingent. In *Frost v. Knight* (1872) Mr Knight promised Miss Frost that when his father died he would marry her. While his father was still alive, Mr Knight broke off the engagement. Miss Frost sued him. She won, even though it was not certain that the contingency on which Mr Knight's promise was founded would ever be fulfilled. After all, Mr Knight or Miss Frost might have died before Mr Knight senior. A promise to marry is no longer enforceable at law, but that does not invalidate the principle of *Frost v. Knight*. That principle is, however, very much qualified by *The Mihalis Angelos* (1971, C.A.) which shows that if the rights lost to the plaintiff by reason of the anticipatory breach are certain to be rendered valueless, the plaintiff is entitled at most to nominal damages. A charterparty contained an expected readiness to load clause (clause 1): "expected ready to load Haiphong under this charter about 1st July 1965." By clause 11 it was provided: "Should the vessel not be ready to load . . . on or before the 20th July 65 charterers have the option of cancelling this contract." By July 17 it had become clear that the vessel would not be ready to load by July 20. On July 17 the charterers cancelled the charter. The Court of Appeal held that they were entitled to "terminate the charter" forthwith (see p. 63, above). The Court of Appeal further held that even if the charterers had not been so entitled under clause 1, so that the purported cancellation was a wrongful repudiation, the owners would have been awarded only nominal damages because the charterers would on July 21 have become entitled to cancel under clause 11 and would undoubtedly have done so.

The innocent party, faced with anticipatory breach, need not sue at once. He may go on treating the contract as still alive, hoping that the other party will change his mind. If he takes this course, however, he is taking a risk, because events may happen to destroy his right of action. In *Avery v. Bowden* (1855) Bowden chartered Avery's ship, *The Lebanon*, and agreed to load it with a cargo at Odessa within 45 days. During this period Bowden repeatedly advised Avery to sail his ship away, as it would be impossible to provide him with a cargo. Avery, however, refused to accept this advice, and kept his ship at Odessa, hoping that Bowden would after all fulfil his obligation to load a cargo. Before the 45 days were up, the Crimean War broke out. That frustrated the contract, since Odessa became an enemy port. Assuming that Bowden's repeated statements amounted to a breach, Avery could have accepted the breach and sued at once. By choosing to keep the contract alive, he lost for ever his right to sue, because the contract became frustrated before the loading days had expired. See also *Fercometal Sarl v. Mediterranean Shipping Co. S.A. (The Simona)* (1988, H.L.), in which the House of Lords emphasised that if an innocent party elects to affirm a contract he is not absolved from further performance of his own obligations under the contract. They also pointed out that if a repudiation by anticipatory breach is followed by affirmation of the contract, the repudiating party can escape liability if the affirming party is subsequently in breach of the contract.

Where a party, faced with anticipatory breach, chooses to keep the contract alive, all he usually does is to wait, as the shipowner did in *Avery v. Bowden*. Avery could not go on with his own contractual duty to receive cargo into the ship, because that required Bowden's co-operation. But occasionally circumstances arise in which the innocent party can go on with his contractual duties without the other party's co-operation. This was so in *White and Carter (Councils) Ltd v. McGregor* (1962, H.L.). The plaintiffs were advertising agents who supplied local authorities with litter bins on which they attached plates carrying advertisements. The defendant engaged the plaintiffs to advertise his garage in this way for three years. Later the same day the defendant cancelled his order. The plaintiffs refused to accept his repudiation. Although they knew that the defendant did not wish it, they prepared advertisement plates, attached them to litter bins, and displayed them. The plaintiffs sued for the full contract price for the three-year period. The House of Lords, by a majority of three to two, upheld their claim. This is a rather startling result, but it is a logical conclusion from the principle that a party has an election whether to accept a repudiation or not. Lord Reid qualified his decision (that the plaintiff should have the agreed sum) by saying that if a plaintiff had ''no substantial or legitimate interest'' in completing performance, he could only claim damages. This qualification was applied in *Clea Shipping Corporation v. Bulk Oil International* (1984). The charterers of a ship (*The Alaskan Trader*) told the owners that they had no further use for it, but the owners kept the ship at readiness, fully crewed. The court held that the owners were not entitled to hire money under the contract, but only to damages for the charterers' breach.

CHAPTER TWENTY

REMEDIES

SEVEN remedies will be discussed in this last chapter of the book. Rectification will not be considered again, as it was mentioned in Chapters 4 and 10; nor will the special code of adjustment remedies laid down by the Law Reform (Frustrated Contracts) Act 1943, which were looked at in Chapter 18, be considered further.

RESCISSION

Rescission was considered at some length in Chapter 8 in connection with misrepresentation, and was touched on in connection with duress and undue influence in Chapter 9, and in connection with mistake in Chapter 10. Chapter 19 (on breach) made it clear that it is incorrect to use the word rescission in reference to acceptance of a repudiatory breach of contract. Rescission (*e.g.* for misrepresentation) is rescission *ab initio*. That means that the contract is treated as though it had never existed. Acceptance by the innocent party of a repudiatory breach of contract by the wrong-doing party does not have that effect. The contract is recognised as having existed and, indeed, as still being in existence. It seems to follow from this distinction that, whereas the right to rescind for misrepresentation is lost if the injured party cannot provide restitution of what he has received under the contract, no such principle should apply to acceptance of repudiatory breach. There is at least one case to the contrary—*Thorpe v. Fasey* (1949)—but that case must be regarded as impliedly overruled by *Johnson v. Agnew* (1980, H.L.). It can be said with confidence that inability to make restoration does not debar the innocent party from accepting repudiatory breach.

A related, but separate, question arises: If the innocent party *is able* to make restoration, will the court require him to do so? The answer seems to be Yes. The clearest illustration of the point is that where a buyer of goods rightfully rejects the goods for breach of a condition as to quality, the ownership of the goods vests (or re-vests) in the seller: see *per* Bankes L.J. in *Hardy v. Hillerns & Fowler* (1923, C.A.). (Of course, the buyer may have a right to damages.) The principle is the same where it is money, as distinct from other property, that the innocent party has received under the contract. Thus, a seller of goods who accepts the buyer's default must return any part of the purchase price that has been prepaid. (But, of course, the seller may have a right to damages.) There is one qualification to this principle, namely that where the buyer makes a prepayment, not simply as a "part payment" of the total price, but as a "deposit" (that is, an "earnest" of the buyer's intention to perform the contract), the seller who accepts the buyer's default may keep the deposit. There is a rather uncertain equity jurisdiction to give relief against forfeiture of a deposit; it is not settled whether it enables the court to give relief wherever it would be "unconscionable" for the seller to keep the money, or whether it is limited to cases of fraud.

DAMAGES

Damages can be sued for by the party injured by breach, whether or not the breach is repudiatory. It is outside the scope of this book to deal with the differences between damages in contract and damages in tort. There are indications in some recent cases that the law may be beginning to move towards the assimilation of damages in contract and damages in tort. In a claim for damages based on a breach of contractual obligation, contributory negligence is not a defence: see *Barclays Bank plc v. Fairclough Building Ltd* (1995).

General Principle

The object of awarding damages for breach of contract is to put the injured party, so far as money can do it, in the same position as if the contract had been performed: see *Robinson v. Harman* (1848). In upholding this principle, the Court of Appeal has stressed that the object is to compensate the injured party for his loss not to transfer to him, if he has suffered no loss, the benefit which the wrongdoer has gained by his breach of contract: see *Surrey County Council v. Bredero Homes Ltd* (1993). The injured party is not to be put in the same position as if the contract had never been made, but in the same position as if the contract had been performed. That is the key to the fact that damages often yields a higher sum than an indemnity in connection with misrepresentation.

The injured party can never obtain more in damages than the loss which he has suffered. Therefore if he has suffered no loss, he may win his action (because breach of contract is actionable *per se*) but he will get only nominal damages and may not get his costs.

Remoteness of Damage

The injured party may sometimes get less than the loss which he has suffered. There is a general principle of exclusion called the principle of "remoteness of damage". The idea is that it is not just or practicable to award damages for every consequence, however unusual, which may flow from a breach of contract. When a court is awarding damages, two questions face it: (1) what consequences should be compensated for? and (2) how should the damages be quantified?

The dividing line between damage which should be compensated for and damage which is too remote to be compensated for was laid down in *Hadley v. Baxendale* (1854). The plaintiffs, mill-owners at Gloucester, engaged the defendant carrier to take a broken mill shaft to Greenwich as a pattern for a new one. The defendant promised to deliver it at Greenwich the next day. Owing to his neglect, the mill shaft was delayed in transit. The plaintiffs claimed damages for loss of profit arising from the fact that the mill was stopped for longer that it need have been, which in turn arose from the delay in transit. All that the carrier knew was "that the article to be carried was the broken shaft of a mill and that the plaintiffs were the millers of that mill". In delivering the judgment of the court, Alderson B. said:

> "Where two parties have made a contract which one of them has broken, the damages which the other party ought to receive in respect of such breach of contract should be such as may fairly and reasonably be considered either arising naturally, *i.e.* according to the usual course of things, from such breach of contract itself, or such as may reasonably be supposed to have been in the contemplation of both

parties, at the time they made the contract, as the probable result of the breach of it.''

This statement has come to be known as ''the rule in *Hadley v. Baxendale*''.

Applying that principle to the facts of the case, the court held that the carrier was not liable for loss of profit. The loss did not arise ''according to the usual course of things''; ''in the great multitude of cases'' the absence of a shaft would not cause a stoppage at the mill, because, for example, the mill-owner might have another shaft in reserve. And the special circumstances that the mill could not restart until the shaft came back was not known to the defendant and so could not ''reasonably be supposed to have been in the contemplation of both parties''.

The rule in *Hadley v. Baxendale* has been considered in many cases since 1854, and has been approved in the House of Lords, in *Koufos v. C. Czarnikow Ltd (The Heron II)* (1969). The defendant shipowner agreed to carry a cargo of sugar belonging to the plaintiffs from Constanza to Basrah. He knew that there was a sugar market at Basrah and that the plaintiffs were sugar merchants, but he did not know that they intended to sell the cargo immediately on its arrival. Because of a breach of contract by the defendants, the sugar reached Basrah nine days later than it should have done. The plaintiffs sold the sugar (3,000 tons) at £31 2s. 9d. per ton. If there had been no delay they could have sold it at £32 10s. per ton. They claimed something over £4,000 as loss of profit. The House of Lords unanimously upheld the plaintiff's claim, on the footing that the loss should be regarded as arising in the usual course of things and so as being within the contemplation of the parties.

Whereas the Court of Exchequer in *Hadley v. Baxendale* gave only one judgment, the House of Lords in *The Heron II* gave five, and it is not easy to bring together all that was said. The present state of the law may be put in this way: the rule in *Hadley v. Baxendale* stands; it is not two rules, but one rule with (possibly) two branches, dealing with usual and non-usual consequences respectively; usual consequences are *presumed* to be in the contemplation of both parties; non-usual consequences may be held to have been in the contemplation of both parties if the evidence shows that a reasonable man, knowing what the defendant knew or ought to have known of the special circumstances, would have thought them liable to result; and a consequence may be liable to result though it is considerably less than a fifty-fifty chance.

The working of the rule in *Hadley v. Baxendale* may be illustrated by two cases. In *Diamond v. Campbell-Jones* (1961) the defendants contracted to sell some premises in Mayfair to the plaintiff for £6,000. The defendants wrongfully repudiated the contract. They knew that the plaintiff was a dealer in real estate, but they did not know that he intended to convert the premises himself. The defendants were held liable for loss of the profit which the plaintiff would have made by resale, but not for loss of the much larger profit which he might have made by converting the premises. On the other hand, in *Cottrill v. Steyning and Littlehampton Building Society* (1966) the vendor of land knew that the purchaser intended to develop it himself. On breach of the contract to sell, the vendor was held liable in damages for the loss of the profit which the purchaser would have made by developing the property.

Quantification

After deciding which consequences should be compensated for, the court then has to consider how to quantify the loss, how to translate the loss into a money sum.

The market value

This rule, which applies particularly to the sale of goods, is that if there is a market for the goods, then prima facie the loss is quantified by reference to the market. If a seller fails to deliver the goods, the buyer can go into the market and buy similar goods at the market price. His loss (if any) will be the amount by which the market price, at the time the goods ought to have been delivered, exceeds the contract price. Conversely, if a buyer refuses to take delivery, the seller can go into the market and sell the goods at the prevailing price. He will recover in damages the amount by which the market price, at the time the goods ought to have been accepted, is below the contract price. In *Shearson Lehman Hutton Inc. v. Maclaine Watson & Co. Ltd* (1990) Webster J. said in respect of a buyer's breach a market would exist where either, if the seller actually offers the goods for sale, there is one actual buyer on that day at a fair price or, if there is no actual offer for sale, there are sufficient traders potentially in touch with each other to evidence a market in which the actual or notional seller could if he wished sell the goods. The market price of the goods is then either the "fair price" obtained by the actual sale or, in the absence of an actual sale, a fair price for the total quantity of goods sold on the market on the relevant day, or such price as might be negotiated "within a few days with persons who were members of the market on that day and who could not be taken into account as potential buyers on the day in question only because of difficulties of communication". These principles also apply in the case of a seller's breach. This definition of "market" is limited.

Where there is no market the loss must be calculated in some other way. If it is the seller who defaults, and the buyer has contracted to resell the goods, it is generally accepted that the resale price may be taken as representing the value of the goods, and the damages will be the difference between the sale and resale prices. For this purpose, it does not matter that the seller had no notice of the resale contract.

Where there is no market and it is the buyer who defaults (by refusing to accept delivery), the extent of the damages will depend on the supply position. In *W.L. Thompson Ltd v. Robinson Gunmakers Ltd* (1955) the defendants bought a Vanguard car from the plaintiffs, and then refused to accept it. The plaintiff's profit would have been £61. The defendants argued that the plaintiffs could have sold the car to another customer, or (as they in fact did) returned it to their supplier. The court rejected this argument, because it was proved that the supply of Vanguards exceeded the demand. The plaintiffs had therefore sold one Vanguard less than they otherwise would, so that their loss was the whole loss of the bargain. In *Charter v. Sullivan* (1957, C.A.) the defendant bought a Hillman Minx car from the plaintiff and then refused to accept it. The plaintiff's profit would have been £97 15s., but he was awarded only nominal damages. It was proved that he could sell as many Minx cars as he could get from the makers, so that he could resell *this* car without loss. Both these cases were decided at a time when cars could be sold only at fixed list prices, so that in that sense there was no market. A market involves freedom for prices to fluctuate in response to the pressures of supply and demand.

Speculative damages

In some cases the quantification of damages is extremely difficult, and may involve the court in speculating on what might have happened if there had been no breach of contract. But in a proper case the court will not be deterred, by the difficulty or by the need to speculate, from making an award of damages. In *Chaplin v. Hicks* (1911, C.A.) the defendant, an actor and theatrical manager, agreed with the plaintiff that if she would attend an interview with 49 other actresses she would have a chance of being selected as one of 12 to whom he would give employment. The defendant broke his contract by failing to give the plaintiff a reasonable opportunity to attend the interview. When sued, he argued that the plaintiff should have only nominal damages, since she would have had only a one in four chance of being selected. At the trial the jury awarded the plaintiff £100 damages. The Court of Appeal held that the award should stand. Of course, in 1911, damages of £100 was far more than nominal.

But though the court will speculate if that is unavoidable, it will not speculate where the plaintiff could have produced evidence of his actual loss and has not done so. In *Clark v. Kirby-Smith* (1964) a solicitor negligently failed to acquire for his clients a new tenancy of business premises, and they sued him for damages for loss of the new tenancy. It was held that as no evidence of the value of the new tenancy had been given, though it could have been, they should have only nominal damages of £2.

Taxation

In some cases the incidence of taxation has to be taken into account in quantifying the damages. In *British Transport Commission v. Gourley* (1956, H.L.) the plaintiff was injured in a railway accident and he sued in negligence, claiming damages for, against other things, loss of earnings. It was estimated that if the plaintiff had not been injured his earnings over the rest of his working life would have come to £37,000. But the defendants argued that since the plaintiff's earnings would have been taxed, the damages should be reduced to take account of this factor. It was estimated that Gourley's earnings *after tax* would have been only £6,000. So the issue was whether his damages should be £37,000 or £6,000. The House of Lords decided for £6,000.

Gourley's case was brought in tort, but the same principle applies in contract. The reasoning of the principle is that the plaintiff ought not to make a profit out of the tort or breach of contract. In the case of an ordinary individual, damages for loss of earnings are not themselves taxable, whereas the earnings which the damages represent would have been taxable had they come to him as earnings. The principle of *Gourley's* case only applies where both these factors are present—non-taxable damages representing taxable earnings. Thus, since a trader is taxed on damages which come to him for breach of a trading contract, no deduction is made by the court from his damages. Where damages represent some non-taxable item those damages are not reduced by the court.

One aspect of this matter is affected by statute. Section 148 of the Income and Corporation Taxes Act 1988 brings within the tax net "golden handshakes", and imposes tax on damages for wrongful dismissal in so far as they exceed £30,000. If a plaintiff proves a gross loss of income by reason of wrongful dismissal of more than £30,000, the court will apply the *Gourley* principle to the (tax-free) sum of £30,000, but not to the balance, because that will in due course be taxed in the plaintiff's hands. A quite different way of dealing with the problem was adopted in *Shove v. Downs Surgical plc* (1984). The judge first considered what was the amount of the plaintiff's *net* loss from his wrongful dismissal, and concluded that it was £60,000. He then considered, on the basis of evidence and argument, what sum would, *after tax*, leave £60,000 in the plaintiff's hands. On this basis he awarded the plaintiff £83,000.

Mitigation

Where a breach has occurred the injured party, if he accepts the breach as discharging the contract, must take all reasonable steps to mitigate the loss occasioned by the breach. So, a buyer, faced with the seller's refusal to deliver the goods due on March 15, must go into the market at once to buy replacement goods. If he waits unreasonably until, say, April 15, and the market price has risen, he will not receive in damages the difference between the contract price and the April 15 price, but only between the contract price and the March 15 price. Similarly, an employee wrongfully dismissed must mitigate his loss by accepting a reasonable offer of other employment.

Reasonableness is at the heart of this principle. The injured party is not required to act with lightning speed, or to accept any old offer of other employment that comes along, or to embark on some difficult course. For example, in *Pilkington v. Wood* (1953) the plaintiff instructed the defendant, a solicitor, to act for him in the purchase of a house. The defendant negligently advised the plaintiff that the title to the house was good. This breach of contract led to all sorts of unfortunate results, and the case is interesting on remoteness of damage. But we are concerned with it in reference to mitigation. The defendant argued that the plaintiff should have mitigated his loss by taking legal proceedings against the vendor for having conveyed a defective title. The judge rejected this argument, holding that the duty to mitigate does not oblige the plaintiff to "embark on a complicated and difficult piece of litigation against a third party".

The burden lies on the defendant to prove, if he can, that an opportunity of mitigation has been neglected.

Agreed Damages

Sometimes the parties to a contract provide, in the contract itself, that a specified sum is to be payable in the event of breach. Such clauses are called "agreed damages clauses" or "liquidated damages clauses".

This kind of clause is a perfectly permissible, because the quantification of damages in court can be a difficult, long and expensive process. So, in a building contract it is frequently provided that if the builder is late in completing he will pay damages of £x per day. A demurrage clause, common in charterparties, is of this nature. Where there is an agreed damages clause in the contract, the plaintiff can recover the specified sum although his actual loss may be less. If his actual loss is more than the specified sum he can still only recover the specified sum.

But a clause of this kind may be challenged on the ground that it is a "penalty", a threat held over the head of a party, to try to force him to perform the contract. If the court holds that the clause is a penalty clause it is disregarded, and the plaintiff cannot recover more than his actual loss. If the actual loss turns out to be more than the sum mentioned in the penalty clause (an unlikely but possible event), the plaintiff is permitted to ignore the clause and recover damages in full: see *Wall v. Rederiaktiebolaget Luggude* (1915). There is a Canadian case to the contrary, *Elsley v. Collins Insurance Agencies Ltd* (1978), and the point may one day have to be reconsidered in England.

In deciding whether a clause is or is not a penalty, the following rules have been evolved.

1. The fact that the payment is described in the contract as a "penalty" or as "liquidated damages" (or any similar phrase) is relevant but not decisive.

2. It will be held to be a penalty if the sum stipulated for is extravagantly greater than the damage which could conceivably follow from breach.

3. It will be held to be a penalty if the breach consisted only in not paying a sum of money, and the sum stipulated is greater than the sum which ought to have been paid.

4. There is a presumption (but no more) that it is a penalty when "a single lump sum is made payable ... on the occurrence of one or more or all of several events, some of which may occasion serious, and others but trifling, damage".

5. "It is no obstacle to the sum stipulated being a genuine pre-estimate of damage, that the consequences of the breach are such as to make precise pre-estimation almost an impossibility. On the contrary, that is just the situation when it is probable that pre-estimated damage was the true bargain between the parties."

These rules are set out in *Dunlop Pneumatic Tyre Co. Ltd v. New Garage and Motor Co. Ltd* (1915, H.L.).

ACTION FOR AN AGREED SUM

There is a distinction between an action for damages and an action for an agreed sum. In the old terminology an action for an agreed sum is an action in debt. An action for an agreed sum is exemplified by an action to recover the contract price of goods sold and by an action to recover the contract remuneration for work done.

In an action for an agreed sum questions of remoteness and quantification do not arise. And, as the law stands at present, the question of mitigation does not arise either. In *White and Carter (Councils) Ltd v. McGregor* (1962, H.L.) which was looked at in Chapter 19, the defendant argued that the plaintiffs ought to have mitigated their loss by reletting the advertising space. The majority of the House of Lords held that no question of mitigation arose because there had been no operative breach (as the plaintiffs had not accepted the defendant's "anticipatory breach"); mitigation means mitigation of damages, and it was not damages that was being sued for.

SPECIFIC PERFORMANCE

Specific performance is an order issued by the court to a defendant to perform a promise that he has made. Where a plaintiff claims specific performance (or an injunction) the court has power to award damages either instead of, or as well as, ordering specific performance (or an injunction). In English contract law damages is by far the most usual remedy, and specific performance is comparatively rare.

As was pointed out in the Introduction to this book, to say that a contract is "an agreement enforceable at law" does not mean that every contract can be made the subject of specific performance. In lawyer's language damages is as much "enforcement" as is an order for specific performance.

There are a number of principles which limit the scope of specific performance.

Not Where Damages Adequate

If the court takes the view that damages will adequately compensate the plaintiff, it will not order specific performance. Thus specific performance is very rarely ordered of a contract for sale of goods. There is no absolute bar against it, and, indeed, it is expressly provided for in section 52 of the Sale of Goods Act 1979. But in practice it is very rarely granted. In *Cohen v. Roche* (1927) the court refused to grant specific performance to a buyer of a set of Hepplewhite chairs.

There is no bar against granting a decree of specific performance of an obligation to pay money. If damages would not be an adequate remedy, the decree will be made. This was done in *Beswick v. Beswick* (1968, H.L.) which was considered in Chapter 13 at pp. 178–179.

The law takes the view that a buyer of a particular piece of land, including the most ordinary suburban house, is not adequately compensated by damages if the vendor breaks his contract. So he can obtain specific performance. The vendor can also obtain specific performance, on the principle that as it could be ordered against him it is just to allow it to him.

The Court's Discretion

Specific performance is an equitable remedy and, along with other equitable remedies, it is discretionary. It is not obtainable, as damages is, as of right. An instance of this difference is to be found in Chapter 10, in connection with mistake. In *Wood v. Scarth* (1855 and 1858) the plaintiff first sued for specific performance and failed and then sued for damages on the same facts and won.

The court's discretion is not an arbitrary discretion. It is exercised in accordance with settled principles. It may be summarised by saying that the court will only grant specific performance where to do so would be just and equitable.

Some Contracts Not Specifically Enforceable

There are some contracts of which specific performance will not be granted.

Personal service contracts

Specific performance will not be ordered of a contract of personal service. It is considered as undue interference with a man's personal liberty that he should be compelled to serve an employer if he does not wish to do so. Similarly an employer cannot be compelled to continue to employ a person whom he does not wish to have as an employee. This rule only applies where the contract involves services of a personal nature. The mere fact that work of some kind is involved in a contract is not a bar to specific performance.

Contracts which require constant supervision

Specific performance will not be ordered of a contract of such a nature that constant supervision by the court would be required. In *Ryan v. Mutual Tontine Association* (1893, C.A.) the lease of a service flat required that the lessors should provide a porter who would be "constantly in attendance". A lessee who applied for specific performance of that obligation failed.

Contracts which lack mutuality

Specific performance will not generally be ordered in favour of a party unless the court could order it, if the facts so required, against him. So an infant cannot get specific performance, because specific performance cannot be ordered against him. There are many exceptions to this rule. For example, a party who has not signed a memorandum of a contract for the sale of land can get specific performance against the party who has signed. Possibly the explanation of this is that by bringing proceedings the plaintiff introduces a kind of mutuality, in that once he has invoked the jurisdiction of the court the court is enabled to hold him, as well as the defendant, to the agreement.

INJUNCTION

An injunction is a decree by the court ordering a person to do or not to do a certain act. In the law of contract it can be used to restrain a party from committing a breach of contract. It will not be granted if its effect would be to compel the defendant to do something which he could not have been ordered to do by a decree of specific performance. In a case concerning The Troggs pop group, *Page One Records Ltd v. Britton* (1968), the plaintiffs moved for an interlocutory injunction to restrain The Troggs from engaging as their manager anyone other than the first plaintiff. The injunction was refused, on the ground that to grant it would in effect compel The Troggs to continue to employ the first plaintiff. Despite this principle, the Court of Appeal (Stamp L.J. dissenting) in *Hill v. C.A. Parsons & Co. Ltd* (1972, C.A.) granted an interlocutory injunction to the plaintiff, restraining his employer from treating the employment as at an end. It was emphasised that the circumstances were very exceptional.

An injunction may be granted, restraining the breach of a negative undertaking in a personal service contract, if its effect is merely to encourage, and not compel, the defendant to perform a positive service. In *Warner Brothers Pictures Inc. v. Nelson* (1937) a film actress, professionally known as Bette Davis, agreed to act for the plaintiffs for a fixed period, during which she undertook not to act for any third party, nor to engage in any other occupation, without the plaintiffs' written consent. The court granted an injunction, but only to the extent of restraining her from acting for third parties. This would not compel her to act for the plaintiffs, because she could earn a living by doing other work.

QUANTUM MERUIT

This form of remedy has been mentioned on several occasions in this book.

A party can claim on a *quantum meruit* ("as much as he has deserved") where the contract makes no express provision for remuneration. Thus, if a contract for the sale of goods does not fix the price, the buyer must pay a reasonable price. This is stated in section 8(2) of the Sale of Goods Act 1979, but that is merely declaratory of the common law.

Where there is an express contractual provision for remuneration, the general principle is that a plaintiff cannot succeed on a *quantum meruit* unless he can show that the contract was really void or that it has been discharged in some way. See the discussion of this point in reference to *Davis Contractors Ltd v. Fareham U.D.C.* (1956, H.L.) at p. 226 in Chapter 18.

There are exceptions, however. For example, where one party prevents the innocent party from completing his performance, the innocent party can sue on a *quantum meruit*; see page 211, above. Also, a party may sue on a *quantum meruit* where he partially performs his contractual obligation and the other party voluntarily accepts that partial performance; see pp. 211—212, above.

CLAIMS IN QUASI-CONTRACT

It is outside the scope of this book to discuss the whole wide field of quasi-contract. But two forms of quasi-contract must be mentioned because they provide remedies to a person in a contractual situation.

(1) Money paid under a contract which is void can generally be recovered back; see, for example, *Strickland v. Turner* (1852) at p. 123, above.

(2) Money paid under a contract where there is a total failure of consideration can be recovered back. An example is *Rowland v. Divall* (1923, C.A.). Rowland, who was a car dealer, bought an "Albert" car from Divall for £334. He repainted the car and sold it to Colonel Railsdon for £400. Later the car was seized by the police as (unknown to Rowland, Divall and Railsdon) it was stolen property. Rowland repaid the £400 to Railsdon, and brought an action in quasi-contract to recover back his payment to Divall of £334, on the ground that there had been a total failure of consideration. Rowland succeeded. The Court of Appeal held that he had not "received any portion of what he agreed to buy ... He did not get what he paid for—namely a car to which he would have title".

EXTINCTION OF REMEDIES

A right of action for breach of contract may become extinguished by effluxion of time. The Limitation Act 1980 provides that an action founded on a "simple contract" (that is, a contract not under seal), or an action for an account, cannot be brought after the expiration of six years from the date on which the cause of action accrued. An action on a "specialty" (that is, a contract under seal) cannot be brought after the expiration of 12 years. Where damages are claimed for personal injuries the period is, in general, three years.

Where there is fraud or mistake the period of limitation does not begin to run until the plaintiff has discovered the fraud or mistake or could with reasonable diligence had discovered it.

In the case of a minor, or other person under a disability, time does not begin to run until the disability is removed; for example, until the minor comes of age.

If the person liable makes a written acknowledgment of the debt or makes any payment in respect of it, time begins to run again.

The statutory provisions do not apply to claims for specific performance or an injunction or other equitable relief. But this does not set equity so far apart from the common law as at first sight appears. Where a court is exercising an equity jurisdiction it will apply the statutory rules "by analogy" or it will apply the equitable doctrine of "laches". Laches may, for example, defeat a claim founded on undue influence, as was seen in Chapter 9.

These rules, both statutory and equitable, for the extinction of remedies are founded on a principle of policy in the law that it is in the general interest that there should be "an end to litigation".

INDEX

INDEX